D1685999

THE INTERNATIONALIZATION PROCESS

THE ROBERT GORDON UNIVERSITY
KEPPLESTONE LIBRARY

THE ROBERT GORDON UNIVERSITY

0004386436   ABERDEEN

WITHDRAWN FROM
THE ROBERT GORDON UNIVERSITY
LIBRARIES

The **European Science Foundation** is an association of its 56 member research councils, academies and institutions devoted to basic scientific research in 20 countries. The ESF assists its member organizations in two main ways: by bringing scientists together in its scientific programmes, networks and European research conferences, to work on topics of common concern; and through the joint study of issues of strategic importance in European science policy.

The scientific work sponsored by ESF includes basic research in the natural and technical sciences, the medical and biosciences, the humanities and social sciences.

The ESF maintains close relations with other scientific institutions within and outside Europe. By its activities, ESF adds value by co-operation and co-ordination across national frontiers, offers expert scientific advice on strategic issues, and provides the European forum for fundamental science.

This volume arises from the work of the ESF Scientific Programme on Regional and Urban Restructuring in Europe (RURE).

Further information on ESF activities can be obtained from:

European Science Foundation
1, quai Lezay-Marnésia
F-67080 Strasbourg Cedex
France

Tel. (+33) 88 76 71 00
Fax (+33) 88 37 05 32

THE INTERNATIONALIZATION PROCESS:

EUROPEAN FIRMS IN GLOBAL COMPETITION

Edited by
Jan-Evert Nilsson, Peter Dicken
and Jamie Peck

P·C·P
Paul Chapman
Publishing Ltd

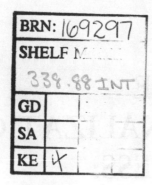

BRN: 169297
SHELF N...
338.88 INT
GD
SA
KE ⅄

Copyright © 1996, The European Science Foundation

All rights reserved

Paul Chapman Publishing Ltd
144 Liverpool Road
London
N1 1LA

Apart from any fair dealing for the purposes of research or private study, or
criticism or review, as permitted under the Copyright, Designs and Patents
Act, 1988, this publication may be reproduced, stored or transmitted, in any
form or by any means, only with the prior permission in writing of the
publishers, or in the case of reprographic reproduction, in accordance with
the terms of licences issued by the Copyright Licensing Agency. Inquiries
concerning reproduction outside those terms should be sent to the
publishers at the abovementioned address.

British Library Cataloguing in Publication Data

Nilsson, Jan-Evert
  Internationalization Process: European
  Firms in Global Competition
  I. Title
  338.88094

  ISBN 1–85396–319–4

Typeset by Dorwyn Ltd, Rowlands Castle, Hants
Printed and bound by The Baskerville Press, Salisbury, Wiltshire

A B C D E F G H   9 8 7 6

Contents

Preface   vii

Notes on contributors   ix

1 Introduction: the internationalization process   1
   Jan-Evert Nilsson

2 Alcatel: a European champion for a globalizing market   13
   David Charles

3 Gildemeister and Maho: protecting the home base   38
   Heike Bertram and Eike W. Schamp

4 SmithKline Beecham: global push and repositioning   61
   Jeremy R. Howells

5 Arthur Andersen: from national accountancy to international   74
   management consultancy firm
   Frank Moulaert

6 Thomson Consumer Electronics: from national champion to   90
   global contender
   Julien Savary

7 Tootal: internationalization, corporate restructuring and   109
   'hollowing out'
   Jamie Peck and Peter Dicken

8   MoDo, SCA and STORA: from national pulp producers to   130
    European forestry companies
    Jan-Evert Nilsson

9   British Steel: the limits to internationalization   146
    Ray Hudson

10 Conclusion   161
    Jan-Evert Nilsson

References and bibliography   165

Index   174

Preface

This book has its origins in a four-year research programme carried out under the aegis of the European Science Foundation. The programme itself was concerned with the topic of Regional and Urban Restructuring in Europe (RURE) and was based upon the observation that the regional and urban structure of Europe is undergoing profound change as a result of both long-term and short-term processes of transformation. The RURE programme involved almost a hundred participants from some twenty European countries. Its agenda was extremely wide ranging but a central thread running through the entire programme was that the primary processes restructuring the European system are the far-reaching transformations in the production system. Within the production system itself, it is clear that the business firm – particularly the international or transnational firm – is a primary agent of change. Most significantly, it is the transnational corporation – an institution with the capability of co-ordinating production and distribution across national boundaries from one centre of strategic decision-making – which exerts the greatest influence on shaping and reshaping urban, regional and national economies.

In the particular work reported in this volume, the focus was explicitly on the internationalization processes of firms set within the context of their different geographies and histories and within different sectors of the economy. Over a span of several meetings of the participants, a particular way of approaching this problem was evolved and case-study firms were selected according to specific criteria. The eight case-study firms were chosen very carefully in terms of an agreed conceptual framework which was based upon the two primary dimensions of the nature of the firm's product or service (whether unique or standardized) and the nature of the production process involved (flexible production or mass production). The aim, in each case, was to explore the major driving forces in the firm's internationalization process from a historical perspective, demonstrating, in particular, some of the ways in which the firm's changing functional and geographical division of labour is the outcome of complex forces operating within and beyond the confines of Europe.

The editors would like to acknowledge the help and support of the following: Professor Arie Shachar of the Hebrew University of Jerusalem and Professor Sture Oberg of Uppsala University who were the Codirectors of the RURE programme; Dr Anders Malmberg, Uppsala University, who was the Programme Co-ordinator; Dr John Smith of the European Science Foundation and all the colleagues who participated in the programme.

Jan-Evert Nilsson,
Peter Dicken and
Jamie Peck
Stockholm and Manchester

Notes on contributors

Heike Bertram is an assistant in the Institute of Economic and Social Geography at the Johann Wolfgang Goethe University, Frankfurt/Main, Germany.

David Charles is Senior Research Associate at the Centre for Urban and Regional Development Studies, University of Newcastle, England.

Peter Dicken is Professor of Geography at the University of Manchester, England.

Jeremy R. Howells is Senior Research Associate at the Judge Institute of Management Studies/ESRC Centre for Business Research, University of Cambridge, England.

Ray Hudson is Professor of Geography at the University of Durham, England.

Frank Moulaert is Professor of Economics and Sociology at the University de Lille I, France.

Jan-Evert Nilsson is Director of NORDPLAN, Stockholm.

Jamie Peck is Reader in Geography at the University of Manchester, England.

Julien Savary is Lecturer in Economics at the University of Social Sciences, Toulouse I, France.

Eike W. Schamp is Professor of Economic Geography at the Johann Wolfgang Goethe University, Frankfurt/Main, Germany.

1

Introduction:
the internationalization process

Jan-Evert Nilsson

Introduction

The fact that more and more firms now operate internationally and, in some cases, globally, has become widely accepted. It can be argued, moreover, that the transnational corporation is the most important single force creating global shifts in manufacturing and service activities (Dicken, 1992). In almost all major economies throughout the world, the significance of domestic and/or foreign-based transnational corporations is increasing. Such corporations, directly and indirectly, account for more than three-quarters of world trade in goods and services. The increasing internationalization of production is occurring as industrialized economies converge in terms of their industrial structure and as newly industrializing economies emerge as new global centres of production.

Attempts to theorize such developments are legion. Indeed – and perhaps not surprisingly – there is no universally agreed theory of international production. Some twenty years ago, John Dunning (1977) first introduced his self-styled 'eclectic' theory as a heroic attempt to synthesize the partial explanations derived from theories of industrial organization, international trade and location. To some, Dunning's eclectic theory has been accepted as the most useful theoretical framework; to others, however, it is regarded as being little more than a list of factors involved in the internationalization process. Meanwhile, individual theories of internationalization derived from specific conceptual and ideological perspectives continue to coexist. Ietto-Gillies (1992), for example, provides a concise summary of alternative theoretical approaches. Within the business and management literature, of course, the emphasis tends to be on *how* business firms *should* internationalize rather than on *why* they do so. Much of the attention in that literature is on the strategies and structures of international firms and on possible future development trajectories (see, for example, Bartlett and Ghoshal, 1989; Ghoshal and Nohria, 1993).

The theories tell us that it is economically rational to go abroad, and to do that by foreign direct investment and other modalities including strategic alliances and various out-sourcing arrangements. They tell us that, in general, internationalization is a profitable strategy for a growing firm. They also underline that the speed and the pattern of internationalization reflects the history of the actual firm. Internationalization is considered to be a sequential learning process based on an explicit strategy. The theories give no more than a general explanation of why firms go international. They also show that internationalization may be a sequential process, even if the speed and pattern may vary between firms. However, the theories are of little help when trying to understand the internationalization process in a *single* firm. Whilst each of these alternative theoretical approaches enriches our understanding of the highly complex phenomenon of the internationalization of production they are, by definition, attempts at generalization. At the same time, we need to increase our knowledge and understanding of *how* business firms *actually internationalize*. The purpose of this volume, therefore, is to explore the actual processes and trajectories of internationalization within a carefully selected set of firms. A particular focus within each of the case studies is the evolving *spatial division of labour* as each of the firms has internationalized.

A conceptual framework for the analysis of the internationalization of firms

The most appropriate approach to the study of the transnationalization process is through the deployment of a conceptual model which makes it possible to identify relevant categories of transnational corporations. We can assume that a firm's strategic situation is determined primarily by the nature of the product and by the nature of its production and distribution processes (Nilsson, 1986). Organizational and geographical structures, functional and spatial divisions of labour and modes of competition all vary along with the strategic context in which firms operate.

Such a conceptual model can be visualized as a matrix, where the nature of the product is represented on the vertical axis and the nature of the production process is represented on the horizontal axis. In Table 1.1. the product axis can be divided into standard products and unique products (Johansson and Westin, 1987). Standard products are based on generally available technology and are, in most cases, easy to replicate. Identical products are delivered by a large number of producers. The large number of competitors reduces the margins. The producers have to compete on price in auction-like

Table 1.1   Characteristics of different types of products

Aspect	Standard products	Unique products
Competition	Price competition	Dynamic monopoly
Market	Auction market	Network relations
Margins	Low	High
R & D	Process innovations	Product innovations
Value added	High	Low

Table 1.2 Characteristics of different types of production processes

Aspect	Mass production	Flexible production
Adjustment cost Productivity Labour	High Capital intensity Unskilled	Low Organization Skilled

markets. Investments in R & D are small and primarily focused on cost-reducing improvements in the production and delivery process.

Unique products, on the other hand, are in many cases protected by patents and make use of technology which is not widely available. In the case of services, technological uniqueness often depends on the methodology of service provision. These products are difficult to replicate, and the number of competitors in these market segments is small. The competitive strength of producers of unique products is based on the characteristics of their products. Investment in R & D is large and primarily focused on product and methodology development. An ongoing flow of innovations is necessary in order for firms to retain a leading competitive position. In Table 1.2, two types of production processes are identified – standardized mass production or flexible batch production (cf. Piore and Sabel, 1984). A flexible production process is characterized by low adjustment costs. It is possible to adjust production according to short-term changes in the pattern of demand.

In mass production, on the other hand, it is only possible to manufacture a particular type of good or provide highly standardized services. Adjustment costs are high because it implies investments in new equipment. The level of productivity in mass production depends on capital intensity and scale of markets. Modern, highly automated plants show higher productivity than older labour-intensive plants. For firms based on mass production, the level of investment is the key to productivity increases. The situation is quite different in firms with flexible production. In such firms the level of productivity in flexible production depends on the way production is *organized*. The success of the Japanese engineering industry, for example, is considered to be based on a superior organization of manufacturing (Schonberger, 1982).

The conceptual model presented here divides production into four generic categories: resource-intensive production, labour-intensive production, custom-based production and R & D-based production. These are illustrated in Table 1.3. *Resource-intensive production* is characterized by the fact that various producers offer identical products. The production process lacks the flexibility which would make it possible to use the production equipment for other kinds of production. Typical producers in this group are process industries that refine raw materials – production of chemical raw materials, iron and steel, pulp and paper, aluminium and ferroalloys. In these cases the production process can be used only in the production of one distinct standard product.

The standardized nature of the products means that individual producers can only influence prices at the margin. Thus, the competitive strength of a

Table 1.3   Generic types of production

Production processes Products	Flexible production	Mass production
Unique	Custom-based production	R & D-based production
Standard	Labour-intensive production	Resource-intensive production

company is determined by its production costs. Three factors have a strong influence on competitive strength. The first is the cost of raw materials, support services and other input factors. In many cases, production is based on proximity to cost-competitive raw materials or input factors. The Scandinavian pulp and paper industry, for example, is based on access to virgin fibres. The Norwegian aluminium industry is based on cheap energy. The second factor is the age of the factory. The nature of the production process leads to a strong correlation between capital vintage and the level of productivity. A high investment rate is a prerequisite. It normally necessitates the gradual enlargement of the capacity of the factory in order to maintain its technological advantage. Finally, the exchange rates play an important role in competitive strength as the price of the product in most cases are set in US dollars.

Labour-intensive production companies produce standard goods using flexible production processes. Craft production is the extreme example of flexible production. It has long been used by firms operating in markets too narrow and variable to repay the specialized use of resources of mass production. Production of standardized goods for which the demand was too unstable to make the use of dedicated equipment profitable should be assigned to this group. As firms have faced the need to redesign products and methods to address rising costs and growing competition, they have introduced new ways to reduce the cost of flexibility in production. Three main types of product can be identified as belonging to labour-intensive production. One group consists of capital goods based on proven technology, e.g. hydropower generators, electrical motors and ships. The second group is consumer goods, e.g. shoes, clothing, bicycles and furniture. These consumer goods must be produced in a flexible way to allow the production of a multitude of different models and to keep up with changing fashions. The third group is service industries, such as mass tourism and chains of fast-food restaurants. McDonald's depends on a combination of cheap labour and the availability of quality foodstuff at low prices.

In *custom-based production* firms produce unique products in a flexible production process. A unique product is one that is only offered by one or a very small number of producers. The product differs from other available products in that it is tailor made to customer requirements. The product or service is offered to a limited number of clients. The ability of a company to apply new technology and methods for systems developed to produce customized solutions is the most important competitive variable in this type of production. In order to succeed, firms in this category must have a qualified marketing organization that meets customer needs and effectively guides production accordingly. For companies engaged in custom-based production, specialization and flexibility are two key factors. Specialization is a necessary condition to make it possible to develop a tailor-made solution to the customer's problem. Technical and organizational flexibility are necessary in order to make production of customized goods profitable as, for obvious reasons, they must be produced in short runs and sometimes even as unique products. A profitable customized product is one whose value to the customer is greater than the production cost. Customized production creates opportunities for large profit margins as the price is determined primarily by the benefits to the customer, rather than by the producer's costs.

It is primarily capital goods and customized business services bought by professional buyers that belong to this category or products. Computer systems, telecommunication systems, flexible manufacturing systems, machine tools, strategic management consulting and business systems integration are examples of custom-based products. Such capital goods and customized business services are distinguished by their use of new technology and advanced methods of analysis or system development. This means that technical standards have not yet been set and that a large number of technological and methodological alternatives are still open. When the production volume increases, a standardization of the technical solutions will normally occur. At that point in the process certain basic concepts will be granted and standards for customization are established. As the technology and methodology matures, the possibilities of customizing will gradually be reduced. The products become less unique and production methods more standardized. Production tailored to fulfil the special needs of individual customers is seldom confronted with sudden changes in the competitive situation. The fact that this kind of production often requires a close co-operation between producer and customer, which normally must be established over a long period of time, makes the producer–buyer relation relatively stable. Changes in the economic situation of the customer, however, will be reflected in demand and thereby affect the volume of production.

R & D-intensive production has similar features to both custom-based and resource-intensive production. It resembles custom-based production in that the products are differentiated and involve ongoing technological and methodological innovation. In this case, however, the innovation rarely involves any close contact with the customer. Instead, the innovation starts with a conscious R & D effort within a particular field. A strong tie between production and R & D is necessary if the innovations are to be put into production quickly. In some cases, R & D efforts take place internally within a company; in other cases there is a co-operation with other companies or external research institutes. Medicines and aeroplanes are typical examples of R & D-intensive products. These products are based on larger R & D investments made over a long period of time. Thus large and sustained R & D investments have to precede profits.

The ability to develop and produce technologically superior products is the single most important variable in the achievement of sustainable competitiveness in this kind of production. In order to succeed it is necessary to have an R & D organization that can import new technical opportunities and translate them into products for which there is a demand. Access to specialized expertise is one key concept here. By developing a technologically superior product, the price can be based on the value of the product to the customer instead of relative production costs. This creates opportunities for large profit margins which, in turn, will encourage competitors to develop similar competing products. Hence, the monopoly of the innovative producer will always only be temporary. The timespan of a situation characterized by monopoly is a major determinant of profit rates. When other companies succeed in producing attractive copies of the product, the product will change from being a high-margin unique product to a low-margin standardized product. In order to maintain a dynamic monopoly, therefore, continuous innovations are required. Through development of new, technologically superior products the company can remain ahead of the competition. The ongoing standardization process places a high priority for innovator firms to produce and sell in as large a volume as possible during the period when the product is unique. In order to achieve this, mass production is required and, hence, an efficient and standardized production process must be established.

The internationalization process

The driving forces behind the internationalization process and the pattern of internationalization vary between these four different types of production. Certain *resource-intensive companies* have long-established traditions as transnationals. The chemical and oil industries, for example, contain many old-established transnational corporations. The basic driving force behind the internationalization process in these firms has in most cases been access to natural resources. Oil companies are forced to establish crude-oil production in countries with petroleum resources. The situation is identical for mining and, at least partly, for the pulp industry. In this way, the hunt for natural resources induced resource-based companies to internationalize at an early stage of their development. Subsequently, the internationalization process was pushed further by growing economies of scale. In most cases the organization of resource-intensive transnational companies has been basically hierarchical. In many cases a centralized organization has been preferred because production is typically concentrated in one or a few standard products. The complexity of the organization, therefore, is low.

This picture changes when firms start to integrate vertically. Through integration, the resource-intensive firm in many cases adds labour-intensive products to its production. Pulp and paper companies add production of corrugated cardboard, aluminium producers start manufacturing profiles and vessels, steel companies integrate the production of metal goods and so on. In such cases the increased integration is followed by changes in the organization. The complexity of the organization increases and the need to decentralize increases. Akzo, a Dutch chemicals firm, provides an example. In Akzo the organizational structure of the basic chemicals division is far less complex than the structure of the other divisions, which consist of a variety of products and market segments (de Smidt *et al.*, 1991).

Increased vertical integration also influences the pattern of internationalization. The internationalization process will not any longer solely be directed by access to natural resources but by access to large markets. During the last decade the internationalization of resource-intensive production in most cases has been based on acquisitions and joint ventures. The chemical industry and the pulp and paper industry show many examples of this. In 1988 Akzo acquired Diamond Chrystal Salt Cy. The acquisition created an opportunity for Akzo to bid for market leadership. In the same year, the US firm Peenwalt broadened the scope of its EC activities as it made acquisitions in Italy, Denmark and Germany. These acquisitions contributed towards the diversification of both the product mix and market scope (de Smidt *et al.*, 1991).

However, with growing internationalization the complexity of the firm's organization increases and further decentralization appears to be necessary. Slowly the internationalization process affects the whole range of corporate activities. The extent to which the location of research laboratories and divisional head offices are affected depends on the pattern of internationalization. Where the process is based on acquisitions and joint ventures, these activities may also become internationalized, depending on the number and quality of labs in the merged firms. Otherwise laboratories and divisional head offices will continue to be highly concentrated in the home country (de Smidt and Meijerink, 1990).

The reduction of trade barriers since the Second World War, lower transportation costs and the development of information technology have transformed the conditions for competitiveness of *labour-intensive production* and opened the door to transnational firms. The reduction of trade barriers opened new possibilities for firms to compete in foreign markets. European corporations were also confronted with stronger foreign competition in their home markets. Euroopean production of clothes, furniture, toys, food, tools, domestic appliances and so on were previously primarily nationally orientated. However, during the last fifty years this production has gradually become internationalized.

Reduced transportation costs and new information technology have made it possible to use cheap labour in less developed countries. The relocation of labour-intensive production from industrialized nations to developing countries during the 1960s and 1970s illustrates this. The relocation of labour-intensive production has been an important force behind the shift in the global economy (Dicken, 1992). For Thomson Consumer Electronics, a subsidiary of the large French electronics firm Thomson, production in low-cost countries, mostly in east Asia, is a central aspect of their international strategy. The firm manages more than 12 plants in Singapore, Thailand, Malaysia, Taiwan, China and Mexico. All small-screen TVs, audio products and many VCRs are produced in these low-cost countries (Savary, in this volume). The same pattern can be seen in software production and data processing.

Another driving force has been the emergence of global brands. The ambition to develop well-known brand names is part of a strategy to create differentiation among standard products. To a large degree the differences are based on the images which the brand names represent – in the clothing industry, for example, brand names like Levi, Gant, Lacoste and Benetton. Initially, global brands increased the distance between the customer and the producer. It became more difficult to adjust production to local changes in fashion trends. Global brands were primarily a way of making profit from economies of scale. The value of flexibility in the production process was reduced. However, during the last decade the situation, from this point of view, has changed. Progress in information technology has created new possibilities to take advantage of flexibility in the production process. New opportunities to establish a close and ongoing interchange with suppliers and distribution channels have been created. Firms may restructure or integrate their activities with suppliers, modify the strategies of channels, and recombine or integrate activities with buyers.

The Italian clothing company Benetton is a good example. Production takes place through a network of owned and independent manufacturing facilities, which are connected closely to franchised retailers using state-of-the-art information systems. Throughout the production process, Benetton redesigns and recombines activities to minimize inventory, ensure rapid delivery and allow rapid responsiveness to local fashion trends. The firm makes efforts to take advantage of the flexibility in the production process. Garments are first manufactured and only later dyed, after colour preferences based on information from retailers in many countries are better established. The importance of geographical distance is reduced by the use of information technology. Instead, time distance in the internal information network becomes of critical importance.

Custom-based production is based on the presence of sophisticated and demanding buyers. A firm may gain initial competitive advantages if domestic buyers are more sophisticated or demanding than buyers in other countries. Sophisticated buyers, in this sense, represent an opportunity. Physical and cultural proximity between producers and buyers may help the firm to perceive new needs and develop new products. A stable network between the producer and the buyer is established. Studies of the Swedish investment goods industry show many examples of successful networks of this type (see Håkansson, 1987). Other illustrations can be found in the user groups of systems houses like the Cap Group or Cap Gemini. The internationalization process in firms with custom-based production is normally controlled by the desire to establish closer relations with sophisticated and demanding foreign buyers. Firms here are seeking to enlarge their international network and transform it into a transnational network (Johansson and Mattson, 1988). The leading Swedish producer of industrial robots, Asea, which later merged with the Swiss Brown Boveri to create ABB, is an example. During the 1970s and 1980s the firm built production or assembly facilities in the USA, Japan, France and Spain. The facilities in the USA and Japan were located close to the automotive industry, which was considered to be an especially demanding customer. Asea's success in the robot market reflected early home-market penetration and the presence in Sweden of important robot-using industries. In the 1970s Sweden had, together with Japan, the most robot-intensive economy in the world. Asea provided a broad range of robots to the automotive and auto-related industries. Volvo and Saab were two demanding domestic customers. Similar stories can be told about other Swedish producers of investment goods and US audit and management consulting firms which are developing networks of accounting and consulting offices in Europe.

One aspect of the internationalization process concerning custom-based production is particularly worthy of note. The desire to get in touch with sophisticated foreign buyers means that internationalization in this case is used partly as a means to sustain and strengthen the firm's technological and/or organizational leadership. In order to keep a leading position, corporations have constantly to improve and upgrade their products. Becoming international early can lead to learning advantages which help sustain the firm's innovative position. In this type of production, internationalization is more of a central part of the firm's R & D strategy than a way to exploit economies of scale. This has implications for the organizational structure. Transnational firms engaged in custom-based production are forced to have a more decentralized organization than firms engaged in labour-intensive and resource-intensive production. In order to learn from sophisticated foreign buyers the units abroad must have R & D capabilities. Transnationalization, therefore, tends to be followed by decentralization in R & D activity. Transnational Swedish firms like Alfa Laval, Atlas Copco and Sandvik have a fairly large number of overseas centres, which are responsible for management, production and research. These companies are organized like networks (Forsgren, 1989). The structure is the same in management consulting firms such as Arthur Andersen (see Moulaert, in this volume) and system houses like Cap Gemeni (Moulaert and Tödtling, 1995).

International competition in custom-based production takes a form that can be termed multidomestic. Competition in each nation or region is essentially independent. The firm is present in many nations, but competition takes place on a country-by-country basis. The gradual growth of firms to transnational multicentre networks exerts a strong influence on management. The parent company no longer plays the same leading role as important knowledge of production and markets is now to be found in overseas subsidiaries. These subsidiaries acquire a strategic role in the business conducted by the company in their respective markets. In an organization where different centres are responsible for several functions, they will also have certain power to influence other centres. The old centre loses part of its strategic domination of overseas subsidiaries, but each subsidiary, for its part, has no strategic influence over the group outside its own operations. The result will be that the strategic behaviour of these firms will evolve from actions by different actors in the network (Forsgren, 1990). Top management is one actor, but not the only one, in this process. In a firm consisting of many large, fully fledged centres in several countries, implementation of a strategy is partly beyond the control of the top management at the headquarters. The internationalization process represents the combined effect of many centres' actions. The relations between different business units in such a transnational company may grow weaker, making it more relevant to talk about a network of firms rather than a single company (Ghoshal and Bartlett, 1990). Such multinational firms are transformed to transnational multicentre networks.

Two factors play an important role in the internationalization process of *R & D-based production*. First, companies go international because it is necessary to achieve a production volume large enough to cover the R & D investments. The timespan during which these corporations can generate cash flow from their unique products is restricted. In the pharmaceutical industry, where new drugs are protected by patents, products may have a strong market position for a maximum of 10–15 years. In the electronics industry, which normally does not use patent protection, the timespan is much shorter because of rapid technical development. This is also the case for business integration consultants, whose integrated organization of systems development is renewed every half a decade. The restricted timespan for paying off the R & D investments makes it necessary for corporations engaged in R & D-based production to have access to efficient global distribution channels. As speed is a critical element in the global strategies of leading R & D-based firms, alliances may be formed to enable simultaneous market penetration (Ohmae, 1985).

Secondly, such companies increasingly internationalize their R & D activities through strategic alliances (Contractor and Lorange, 1987). One basic reason for this is that the speed of technological development increases the uncertainty and cost of advanced R & D. In many cases, today, not even leading companies accept the full risk of premium R & D projects. Instead they rely on strategic partnerships with competitors. The Siemens–Philips megabit-chips project is one European example of such a strategic alliance. This is a strictly R & D-based partnership. The partnership alternative is not chosen because of the technical risks in the project. Shortening product life cycles reduces the repayment periods and leads to an increase in commercial risks. In the telecommunications industry the economic lifetime of the old electromechanical equipment was 25 years. Today, digital equipment is supposed to pay off in 8–12 years (de Smidt, 1990).

There are a number of studies showing a sharp rise in the number of technical alliances in the semi-conductor and biotechnology industries (OECD, 1986), as well as in the automobile industry. However, many companies prefer to strengthen their technological capabilities by either developing these internally or taking over appropriate companies. Co-operation is sought primarily as an alternative when necessary to overcome shortcomings in corporate capabilities, or if the costs and uncertainty of particular technological developments are considered to be too high. Strategic alliances seem to manifest themselves in different formal arrangements depending on the character of the technology. Preliminary analyses show that different patterns emerge for technologies at distinct stages of development. Thus the pattern of co-operation in biotechnoloy is less transparent than co-operation in the semi-conductor industry (Hagedoorn, 1990).

The message of this chapter is that change in the organization of transnational companies must be related to the type of production. The driving forces behind the internationalization process vary between different types of production. The changes which can be observed, therefore, partly reflect the distinctiveness of the development patterns of different types of production. In Europe the importance of custom-based production and R & D-based production has increased since the middle of the 1970s. Rapid technological development has contributed to the opening up of new markets for such production. In the same period most resource-intensive and labour-intensive production activities have experienced mature markets and international overcapacity. The pattern of internationalization in custom-based and R & D-based production therefore has dominated the view of organizational changes in transnational corporations. Hence the growing importance of concepts such as international networks.

An overview of the case studies

The case studies which form the core of this book follow the logic outlined in this chapter. The case-study firms were chosen to exemplify some of the diversity of experience within each of the four categories discussed in the preceding section. They also provide a means of operationalizing and interrogating the conceptual framework outlined here. Table 1.4 identifies the companies and locates them within the analytical matrix.

SmithKline Beecham, ranked third in global pharmaceutical sales revenues, is a typical research-intensive corporation which allocates large resources to

Table 1.4 The case study firms

Production processes Products	Flexible Production	Mass Production
Unique products	Alcatel Gildemeister and Maho	SmithKline Beecham
	Arthur Andersen	
Standard products	Thomson Consumer Electronics Tootal	British Steel SCA, STORA and MoDo

develop new products, which can be patented and sold globally. The long-term success of a firm like SmithKline Beecham is based on its ability continually to introduce unique drugs on the market.

Two German machine tool firms and a French producer of telecommunication equipment are chosen to represent custom-based production. Gildemeister and Maho are both typical of the emergence of the German machine tool industry sector in which craft production of customized machines dominates. Alcatel is the second largest telecoms equipment supplier in the world, and with a strong presence in a number of important European markets.

The consumer electronics industry has emerged as a fast growing, at least until recently, global industry, with world products and intense price competition. The French Thomson Consumer Electronics sells and manufactures significant quantities in all the three major regions of the world economy. The other case-study of labour-intensive production is Tootal, one of the world's longest-established textiles companies. Tootal was in some sense already a multinational in the nineteenth century, which reflects that the textile industry probably has the longest history as a global industry.

Steel industry and pulp and paper industry are two examples of resource-intensive production. British Steel Corporation emerged as a result of nationalization in the 1960s, encompassing the largest British bulk steel producers. The aim was to modernize the British steel industry in order to enhance the efficiency of production. SCA, Stora and MoDo are the three largest Swedish forest companies, which started their internationalization process in the 1960s. The speed of the process accelerated in the 1980s when non-European corporations started to acquire pulp and paper producers on the European continent.

Arthur Andersen is a well-known American accounting, financial audit and tax firm which also includes a large management and information technology consulting business, with activities in more than 70 countries. Andersen's trademark is their integrated and codified consulting methodology which is used worldwide and makes it possible to combine the generality of methodology with the specificity of markets.

2

Alcatel: a European champion for a globalizing market

David Charles

Introduction

The transnational character of the telecommunications equipment industry has been transformed during the 1980s. As an example of state dominance in purchasing and regulation, the market for telecommunications products was less international than many other aspects of the electronics sector in the 1970s. Subsequently the combination of technological development, market demand for service growth and liberalization, and the strategic concerns of particular governments to ensure a significant presence in the nascent global market have led to the emergence of a set of global firms absorbing, or forging alliances with, many of the existing national players.

The telecommunications industry has a particular place in the history of the electronics industry: it is one of the oldest elements with its origins in the electrical industries of the late nineteenth century. Indeed, whilst the other industries of that time have largely remained as heavy electromechanical activities, telecommunications is unique in making the transition to a purely electronic and digital technology. As such the transition between different forms and periods of industrial organization, whether considered in terms of labour process, inter-regional spatial organization or globalization, has led to different outcomes and observed processes of change than in most of the other electronics activities.

Much of the literature on the geography of transnationals, and on new forms of industrial organization, has focused on the electronics industry. Similarly in analyses of territorial production clusters, such as in Storper and Walker's (1989) work on geographic industrialization, the electronics industry occupies a key position. Yet these studies tend to focus more on the semi-conductor, computer or defence electronics industries, whilst telecommunications continues to be a more traditional sector dominated by huge firms with production facilities in older industrial regions. Thus although the telecommunications production sector is perhaps less illustrative of the brave new worlds of post-Fordism, there is a valuable case to be made for analysis of the sector as an example of state-regulated Fordism curently being reshaped by the twin processes of flexible production technology introduction and market liberalization. Somewhat paradoxically, these forces have led not to disintegration and the erosion of oligopoly, but to the reverse and to the extension of certain dominant national firms into the global market.

This chapter reviews the growth of one such national firm which, by acquisition, has become the largest in the world. The history, strategy and organizational form of the internationalization process are examined to explain the nature of the evolving spatial form of the firm. First, however, some context is required to outline the pressures for change, and the competitive environment within which such global restructuring has become possible.

The telecommunications industry: globalization trends and pressures

The telecommunications industry is typically considered as consisting of two main elements: the provision of services and the supply of equipment. Alcatel, the subject of this chapter, is involved only in the equipment supply industry, although the development, and particularly the opening up to international competition of national equipment markets, depends fundamentally on the dynamics of the service sector. Such trends are, however, well reviewed elsewhere, and will not be repeated here other than in summary form.

Within the equipment sector there are a number of established product market definitions. Whilst useful for the statistical analysis of the product markets, these definitions are also often used by the firms in the industry to divisionalize their organization. The main division of equipment is between public infrastructure and private or customer premises equipment. Additionally the public infrastructure is increasingly split between different carrier technologies through the growth of mobile communications.

At the heart of the public networks are the central office switches (essentially large computers for assigning calls to the correct destination and carrying out necessary management and billing tasks), and the transmission technology which carries the signal between switches and between the terminal and the switch. Transmission is not, however, simply cable and optical fibre, but encompasses sophisticated technologies for boosting signals, converting between different carrier technologies and multiplexing many calls down the same trunk line. Public networks are usually based on fixed wire technology, although with some radio trunk-line capacity in the form of microwave or satellite. Mobile technology in the form of cellular telephony or the new PCN, or plain old radio, may be essentially identical to the fixed network between switches (or even use the same network), but instead of a fixed local loop has a network of radio transceivers linking to portable handsets and terminals.

In the private equipment sector, also known as subscriber equipment or customer premises equipment, all the equipment is installed on the customer's premises, and in liberalized markets is capable of being bought by the customer. For a larger user this can include small networks consisting of private switches (PABX) with local transmission equipment, which can then be used for linking together different sites using leased point-to-point lines from the public networks. Finally there are the terminals at the end of the line, whether in the form of telephone handsets, facsimiles, data terminals or pagers. Increasingly a proportion of terminals are designed for use with mobile telecommunications networks, and the new CT2 standard permits use both for fixed and mobile networks through the ability of handsets to interface with private-base stations attached to the fixed network, or public-base stations attached to specific radio-based networks.

Alcatel is a full-range equipment supplier covering all forms of network and terminal equipment, with the exception of some data terminals and facsimile. The origins of the company as a national equipment supplier led to the inclusion of a full competence to supply all the requirements of the French PTO, which the company has strengthened through acquisition, as will be explained later. Although there are some particular strengths in terms of global market share, it must be recognized that as the world's largest supplier Alcatel would be expected to be dominant across a number of product markets. What is more interesting are the weaknesses – for what they illustrate about the general nature of the telecommunications industry. Thus Alcatel's main weakness is in new forms of terminal, especially fax, where despite being the only European firm manufacturing standard fax machines in the mid-1980s, Alcatel was forced to withdraw from the market because of the superior competitiveness of the Japanese, who now have a monopoly of fax terminal supply. Other niches where Alcatel, as with other major communications firms, is weak, are in the data terminals and networks that are connected up to telecommunications networks. These products are more typically the preserve of computer manufacturers, and specialized data-networking firms. The only telecommunications suppliers to cross the boundaries into the computing industry successfully are the major Japanese firms (NEC, Fujitsu and Hitachi), although both AT&T and Siemens have computing subsidiaries, but with a limited degree of integration.

The distinction between products and services is being blurred somewhat, notably by the increased importance of software in the functionality of telecommunications networks. As such, network software might be considered as an element of the service offering, or might be supplied to the service operator by an erstwhile equipment supplier either embedded in a system or as a separate item. Also, freestanding software companies may provide distinct network management software and consultancy to the PTO in competition with equipment suppliers or the PTO's own internal software expertise.

Such changes in the relationship between the equipment and service industry reflect the radical change of technology underpinning telecommunications from an electromechanical system that aimed physically to connect subscribers by signals crudely converted from sound to electrical waves, to an electronic digital system that takes a variety of inputs, converts them to digital codes and conducts a variety of manipulation and transmission activities to send them to their recipient. As such, for example, the exchange may not take place in real time, but involve recording, and non-voice messages may be transferred into other formats for the recipient. These changes have had profound effects on the type of equipment provided, on production processes, on corporate organization and on the nature of markets.

A key development associated with technological change, and in part both influenced by and influencing it, has been the liberalization of the state-regulated service sector in many countries, starting with the US market, followed by the UK and then other EC markets, and spreading into other countries around the developed and developing world (Hills, 1988).

Liberalization has involved several main processes:

- The prime change has been the erosion of the monopoly of PTOs through the establishment of alternative services by new operators (such as cellular networks) and the entry of competitors in the main voice-telephony market in some countries. New PTOs are less likely to imitate the procurement policy of the incumbents, and their cost competition places pressures on existing PTOs to seek price cuts from suppliers.
- Associated with the erosion of service monopoly has been the elimination of PTO monopoly rights over the rental or sale of subscriber equipment, such that equipment manufacturers and other suppliers may now sell customer premises equipment direct to the consumer. So, for example, in the case of telephone handsets, rather than the PTO buying high-quality handsets at high prices from domestic suppliers to rent to subscribers, high-street electrical shops can sell cheap far-eastern imports for less than the cost of one year's rental.
- There has been a process of harmonization of technical standards to reduce non-tariff barriers to trade.
- In order to reinforce the opening up of national markets in the EC, legislation has been passed opening up equipment procurement to international tender such that PTOs cannot restrict their purchasing to domestic firms without good reason.
- In some countries there has been the privatization of both PTOs and equipment suppliers, with consequent changes in corporate culture away from following state policies towards more commercial objectives.
- As a consequence of the liberalization of service provision, and to reduce the potential abuse of monopoly positions, EC and other state governments have enforced the separation of service provision and service regulation. Formerly when PTOs were arms of state policy they were also responsible for regulatory concerns, such as standards and equipment approval, a position which is unacceptable for a private or competitive company.
- As an element of this last development there has been the removal of type approval responsibility from network operators of all kinds. Previously, network operators could restrict the access of a product on to the market by claiming technical incompatibility or slowing the process of giving

permission for connection to their network. Under new regulatory frame-works type approval is given by an independent organization on strictly technical criteria and with the minimum of delay, thus allowing non-domestic competitors equal access to a market. Indeed, further moves to mutual-type approval will permit firms to undergo type approval in one market, which will then be acceptable in other markets (OECD, 1992).

The cumulative effect of these processes has been to open up national markets to external equipment providers, to reduce geographical market entry barriers and to reduce public control over the ownership of specific telecommunications suppliers. Consequently during the 1980s, the level of trade in telecommunications products grew at a faster rate than that of other manufactured products (OECD, 1991; CEC, 1992). In general the EU countries have seen a declining balance of trade in telecommunications products, although it is still positive on account of the exports of France and Germany. Other EU countries have seen increasing trade deficits, although in many cases with other EU countries. But in the UK, with the most liberal market, the flood of imports from southeast Asia and North America has resulted in an escalating non-EU trade deficit.

However, although this process has led to new emerging competition within specific national markets, overall concentration in the industry on a global basis has increased, as the economies of scale and scope of operating in the telecommunications sector have increased in importance, particularly owing to high R & D and software costs (Charles, Monk and Sciberras, 1989). In part this has also been intensified by the erosion of protection in specific markets, and the emergence of price competition that has left many smaller suppliers exposed to the cost implications of small-volume production.

Table 2.1a   The ten largest global telecommunications equipment suppliers, 1984

Company	Base	Sales (£m)
1. AT&T	USA	7,590
2. ITT	USA	3,500
3. Siemens	Germany	2,530
4. Northern Telecom	Canada	2,460
5. Ericsson	Sweden	2,380
6. NEC	Japan	2,010
7. Alcatel-Thomson	France	1,935
8. GTE	USA	1,710
9. Philips	The Netherlands	893
10. GEC	UK	746

Source: Monopolies and Mergers Commission, 1986.

Table 2.1b   The ten largest global telecommunications equipment suppliers, 1990

Company	Base	Sales (US$m)
1. AT&T	USA	12,201
2. Alcatel	France	11,986
3. Siemens	Germany	8,603
4. Ericsson	Sweden	7,478
5. NEC	Japan	7,361
6. Northern Telecom	Canada	6,769
7. Motorola	USA	3,560
8. GTE	USA	3,390
9. Bosch	Germany	3,280
10. Fujitsu	Japan	3,128

Source: IDATE, 1991.

It is against this background of the growing importance of economies of scale, and of the opening up of national markets to more open competition, including price competition, that the telecommunications equipment industry has seen considerable international restructuring, and a consolidation of capacity into a smaller number of dominant firms (Amin, Charles and Howells, 1992). Thus there has been a shift from a fragmented series of national oligopolies to a smaller number of global players competing across a wide range of more open national markets.

This has had a notable effect on the ranking of the largest firms (Tables 2.1a and b). In 1984, AT&T was in clear first place based on its captive market in the USA, and was over twice the size of any of a second tier of firms that were mainly dominant in national markets but with some limited degree of internationalization. AT&T itself was, until 1980, forbidden to compete overseas as a result of a market agreement with ITT (AT&T had a captive market in its state-regulated service operations in the USA, and in return for being allowed to retain this, they had to forswear using this huge advantage to compete in ITT's non-US markets). Outside the top eight firms in 1984 there was then a large number of smaller national firms, such as GEC, which still aimed to offer a full range of independently designed products covering switches, transmission and terminals.

Since then, many of the larger firms have been actively involved in acquisition and in forming alliances with the smaller national firms, boosting their scale so that there are now five firms that are more than half as big as the leading firm. The 1990 data show that AT&T was still narrowly larger than the Alcatel group, although the acquisition of Telettra by Alcatel in 1991 overturned this position. A key factor in the growth of certain of the firms has been the emergence of new technologies since 1984, notably fax and cellular technologies, which have predominantly benefited the Japanese (e.g. NEC and Fujitsu) and the US company Motorola (the most successful cellular supplier), which has entered the leading group at rank seven. Some companies have withdrawn from the market, notably Philips, which has pulled out of infrastructure supply, selling its capacity to AT&T although retaining a strong market position in cellular. GTE also, despite retaining a position in the top ten, has withdrawn from production in Europe, selling its PABX business to Siemens. Another strong new entrant is Bosch which has entered via three main routes: growth in cellular telephony related to its core automotive electronics business, acquisition of business systems capacity in the form of Telenorma and Jeumont Schnieder, and acquisition of infrastructure capacity in ANT. Meanwhile nationally based firms such as GEC/Plessey, STC, Matra, Telettra, Italtel, etc., have all moved into the sphere of influence of (if not bought outright by) one of the leading firms.

In addition to promoting market access, returns to scale and globalization, liberalization has also affected the nature of corporate structures in the industry. In the past the close relationship between national PTOs and their suppliers encouraged an engineering approach to market relations. The equipment suppliers' engineers would discuss requirements with the customers and supply dedicated products, often on cost-plus contacts, and in many cases with the active involvement of the PTOs in the design. Corporate organization focused on discrete products as black boxes, with little need to consider the system as a whole, or to engage in marketing activities. Liberalization, coupled with increased system complexity, has changed this. Now PTOs are seeking to buy equipment off the shelf, with the supplier taking the responsibility for integration into the existing network. Liberalization of customer premises markets has opened up the exposure of equipment suppliers to direct relationships with the users rather than via the PTO, and in the case of products such as telephones this has involved addressing mass consumer markets through the retail chains, and a shift to consumer electronics patterns of product redesign and marketing.

As a consequence the firms have been undertaking three kinds of restructuring: in geographical patterns of production, product divisional structures and functional groups within divisions. Taking the geographical structure first, the need to achieve economies of scale, combined with the increased permeability of markets and globalization, has allowed firms to concentrate certain forms of production in particular countries rather than to replicate all products in each market. Formerly PTOs could insist on local production, implying that an international supplier of telephones had to operate with a number of suboptimally sized plants: now these can be rationalized. Secondly, in addressing systemic markets, the firms are rethinking some divisional structures to combine products that are sold as a package rather than those with a similar technology. Thus a cellular telecommunications division might sell switching systems and transmission equipment to PTOs as well as handsets to the end customer, perhaps sourcing some of the products from the switching division, but drawing on a wider expertise of cellular systems than would a switching-products division. Finally, within individual divisions there is a far greater market awareness and marketing leadership than in the past, and new spatial outcomes in the establishment of more significant offices of marketing and systems solutions staff close to the customer rather than close to manufacturing. In some cases specialized marketing staff will be assigned to customers to give a strategic overview of that customer's full needs, rather than seeing requirements from the perspective of each product division.

Overall, then, it can be seen that technological, market and regulatory developments have led to considerable rationalization and concentration in the telecommunications industry. Within this Alcatel has been the most dramatic case of international growth, mainly through a process of acquisition. The next section outlines this process.

History of Alcatel

Alcatel originates from three main source companies, united by merger over the course of the early 1980s. Throughout, the company has emerged from the tension between a state policy to develop a strong national telecommunications and electronics industry, and the ambitions and objectives of the management of Alcatel. Thus it is important to recognize the role of state policy in the creation of Alcatel, but also to see that in certain ways the direction of the company can be regarded as a failure of policy (Cawson *et al.*, 1990; Sally, 1993).

The origins of Alcatel as a national champion in telecommunications lie in the 1960s when the Direction Générale de Télécommunications (DGT), the French telecommunications operating agency, favoured the CIT Alcatel subsidiary of CGE as the domestic supplier of digital switching. Until that time the French market had been largely subservient to international firms such as Ericsson and ITT, but the DGT used the modernization of the network as a means of displacing non-French firms and building up the technological competence of Alcatel. Associated with this was a close relationship between the engineers in the public CNET research laboratories and the engineers in Alcatel, made closer by the insistence that Alcatel opened a new laboratory at Lannion near to the CNET laboratory that was supporting digital-switching research.

However, in 1974 the DGT was given a wider role in championing industrial restructuring in the electronics sector and, after criticism of the cosy relationship between CNET and Alcatel, was keen to introduce more domestic competition. At this point Thomson, which had long harboured ambitions to get into telecommunications, was brought into the market through the actions of the DGT forcing the sale to Thomson of ITT and Ericsson subsidiaries, although one small subsidiary, CGCT, was left in ITT hands.

In 1981 all three main telecommunications suppliers, CGE, Thomson and CGCT, were nationalized as a consequence of the new industrial policy of the incoming socialist administration. In this new industrial policy, there was a changed role for the DGT: rather than being a sponsor of the industry through procurement, and therefore exerting considerable control and influence, the DGT was to be the source of investment and operating subsidies to the nationalized electronics firms. Thus the DGT and the Ministry of Industry were to lose power over the firms as a result of taking ownership, as henceforth the state would be responsible for covering losses, such as might be a result of tight margins on sales to the DGT. The Industry Minister was keen for the firms to avoid large losses which would reflect badly on government policy. The firms also controlled the flow of reporting information and therefore were able to outmanoeuvre the government.

It was the result of this paradoxical acquisition of power, despite state ownership, that CGE and Thomson were able to restructure both their companies and the French telecommunications industry. CGE had identified that their Alcatel subsidiary needed to grow in order to be internationally competitive, and that this could only be achieved through acquisition, both in France and overseas. Alcatel was at that time profitable but there was a future threat from larger suppliers such as Siemens and AT&T. Thomson, in contrast, was in serious trouble, losing money from telecommunications and other markets. Thomson was having to supply switches designed by ITT and Ericsson under licence, and had additionally acquired plans for a digital exchange from ITT, which were rapidly developed as the MT20 exchange. The cost of this commitment was excessive for the relatively small scale of the company and hence Thomson had decided that the rational solution was to exit from telecommunications and consolidate in consumer goods, components and defence. In negotiation, CGE and Thomson therefore arranged an asset swap whereby CGE acquired all the telecommunications activities in exchange for some consumer, components and military electronics which Thomson absorbed. Having made the deal without government knowledge, the firms then sold the idea to key government figures, thereby circumventing the inevitable criticism from the DGT which wished to preserve competitive tendering. As further evidence of the political skill of the companies, the French government was also persuaded to inject cash into Thomson to offset its telecommunications losses so that the new merged company would not be saddled with debt, and furthermore the DGT was to accept higher prices paid for equipment. There was also a significant rationalization of the merged group, with the loss of 7,000 jobs, 5,000 from former Thomson plants, and the development of the Thomson MT switch, was run down and discontinued (Sally, 1993).

The merger gave CGE 85% of the French central-office switching market, and a substantial share of other product markets. Overall the company moved into fourth place globally in switching-equipment sales. However, Alcatel was also observed to have weaknesses both in a lack of scale and in an orientation towards a French market, but also in that it had inherited two switches, one of which was outdated. The company was therefore looking to a new international alliance to improve its access to other markets, and was in negotiation with AT&T, among others. However, it was ITT that was to prove receptive to advances.

ITT was a more significant company than Alcatel in terms of its European telecommunications production activities. One of the early global firms, ITT was a classically decentralized conglomerate with only financial controls from the centre. Each nationally based telecommunications company was responsible for its own product range and it was only in the later days of ITT that attempts were being made to co-ordinate product policy, notably through the System 12 exchange.

It was the System 12 exchange that showed up the fundamental weakness of ITT despite its being the second-biggest telecommunications supplier in the world. Central-office switches are at the core of any global telecommunications firm, yet they are the most costly products to develop, estimated R & D costs for a typical digital exchange being of the order of US$1 billion. ITT was faced with the prospects of having to develop a switch for a number of discrete national markets, with expected high sales, but without a core market prepared to underwrite development costs. The biggest single market to which ITT had access was the German market via SEL, and it was SEL which led on the development of System 12. However, in Germany there was no state subsidy for the development of switching products, unlike in France, Italy and the UK. German manufacturers were expected to claw back the costs of R & D from higher prices. However, ITT could not count on German sales offsetting all the costs of System 12, as SEL's position in the German market was secondary to Siemens with its own switch, the EWSD. ITT also had only a slim chance to gain access to the North American market. Canada was essentially closed, but in the USA, AT&T had just been subject to anti-trust legislation leading to the breakup of the Bell system, and ITT therefore had an opportunity to sell switches to the new Regional Bell Operating Companies, so long as they could beat other potential suppliers, and especially Northern Telecom of Canada. Thus ITT needed to develop quickly a switch that could be introduced into a number of markets with different technical requirements, had to bring together development engineers from subsidiaries that had rarely collaborated in the past and, at the same time, carry the burden of development costs against competitors that were able to offset those costs against state subsidies or guaranteed sales in vertically integrated affiliates. To make matters worse, the company's engineers decided to adopt a novel parallel processing system for the exchange which was to lead to technical difficulties and delayed project completion.

Consequently, in 1986 ITT was noted to be in some difficulties, principally involving the late delivery of the System 12 switch, and increasing R & D costs, forcing the company to withdraw from the US switch market owing to inadequate resources to adapt the switch to US needs. Throughout 1985, ITT had been resisting corporate raiders looking to break up the conglomerate, which was faced with cash-flow problems in its insurance operations as well as in telecommunications. From ITT's perspective the sale of a controlling stake in the telecommunications group to the French group for US$1.8 billion turned a highly geared, low-profit, capital-intensive asset into cash, slashing the overall capital gearing for the group (*The Financial Times*, 1986). As such the telecommunications sale was only one of several disposals by ITT, which included Abbey Life, Eason Oil and a majority stake in STC of the UK. STC was a broadly based telecommunications company, which had been able to carve out a strong market position in the UK, operated independently of the rest of ITT telecommunications and, as such, had been progressively floated on the London Stock Exchange. At the time of the merger, ITT retained only a 24% stake in STC, which was a US$2 billion turnover company, having itself acquired the UK computer champion ICL, and built up a diverse components business. Hence there was little likelihood of STC being built into the Alcatel deal, although strategically the separation of STC from the rest of the ITT telecommunications group left Alcatel without a strong position in the UK market. The other major EU market where ITT had unloaded its subsidiary was France, where the state had nationalized the local company. Small parts of this had found their way into Alcatel via CGE and Thomson, although the remaining nationalized CGCT was later to go to Matra.

Under the terms of the merger a new holding company, Alcatel NV, registered in The Netherlands, was established to control the telecommunications activities of CGE (the French parent of CIT Alcatel) and those of ITT. ITT retained a share of 30% in the new Alcatel group, although receiving payment from CGE for the difference in value between this and the ITT subsidiaries which made up well over half of the merged group. CGE retained most of the remaining equity in the group, although there were also minority shareholders in the form of Société Générale de Belgique and the Spanish PTO, Telefónica.

As the merger presented quite severe financial hurdles to Alcatel, there was an initial attempt to bring other EU companies into the joint venture to underpin the capital outflow to ITT, and to offset some of the future R & D costs in developing new-generation products. However, Alcatel had little success in this, and was unable to strike any major deals with other of the major EU firms despite press speculation at the time (Dodsworth, 1987). The main alliances that did emerge were as a result of existing joint-venture partners of ITT as in Spain, for example, where Telefónica was an important element of state industrial policy and already had a minority stake in ITT's local production companies (Lera, 1987).

Since the ITT merger, Alcatel has made further acquisitions to build market share in specific product and geographical markets, with a particular interest in cable, transmission and satellite equipment. These will be outlined in more detail in later sections. Also, Alcatel-Alsthom, the parent company (formerly CGE), has strengthened its hold over Alcatel through the buying out of all partners in the holding company, including ITT, although some external equity remains in selected national subsidiaries. Thus the strategy has also become more focused on the ambitions of the French parent.

Strategic context to internationalization

With the formation of Alcatel from the 1986 merger, the new company was established as the second-largest telecommunications equipment supplier in the world, and with a strong presence in a number of important European markets. From such a position the only viable strategy for the firm was to strengthen and expand its international position, especially as its domestic markets in Europe would be exposed to increasing pressure from other EU, US and potentially Japanese competition.

A further and perhaps more implicit strategic objective was to overtake AT&T as the global leader. As such, then, a French-based company would have triumphed over the strength of US rivalry, and provided a foundation for a permanent position in the vanguard of the telecommunications industry. The French government has tacitly backed this strategy in telecommunications as in other industries by allowing and supporting firms with a state shareholding to engage in overseas acquisition, combined with a restriction on foreign ownership of the leading French technology-based firms.

Internationalization in the telecommunications sector also cannot be separated from product strategy, especially as the scale requirements of investment in specific product areas is greater than in most national markets. However, this varies between products, and some products such as switching have far wider implications for internationalization than others such as telephone handsets. Technological strength is especially important in telecommunications, and hence Alcatel is a heavy invester in R & D (11.9% of sales in 1991) and looking to offset this high cost by the achievement of critical mass in the most R & D expensive product areas (e.g. transmission, where they were weak). Alcatel are also having to adopt a strategy of product convergence post-merger as they cannot simply write off acquired products owing to their role in the networks of important PTO customers. So if the acquisition of, for example, Telettra in Italy brought with it a specific transmission product installed in the Italian market, Alcatel must continue to support that product and provide further deliveries if it wishes to keep its market share. A national PTO will generally wish to limit the range of equipment installed within any one technology generation, and by withdrawing a product mid-life an acquirer would risk alienating the customer and losing both the current market as well as preferential access to the next generation of that product. This limits the scope for product rationalization.

A key issue is the origin of the company in European markets – hence the need for a local policy to sell to PTOs. Other EU-based firms have a larger focus on their home markets with exports to Third World countries and some other EU sales, often via acquisition of local partners. By contrast, US/Japanese firms can enter via either acquisition or greenfield sites by targeting the liberalized sections of the market. The non-liberalized markets are, however, virtually impossible to enter without acquisition, owing to the established relationships between the PTOs and national suppliers.

Within this context, then, Alcatel has pursued a twin policy of acquisition and divestment, outlined in the next two sections. Of these the most important is the process of acquisition whereby the company has sought to develop particular product markets through the purchase of smaller competitors and asset swaps. As a consequence of some of these acquisitions, and arising from the earlier ITT merger, Alcatel has also been focusing more explicitly on telecommunications products, and divesting itself of other activities that no longer fit with that strategy.

Patterns of acquisition

Although the main acquisition was of ITT, Alcatel has continued to make acquisitions of both small and large firms in assembling a strategic position in a number of telecommunications product sectors. As few of these acquisitions have cut across major markets, they are best examined within the context of the product areas so that the strategy for internationalization and market share can be seen. It is important to recognize that the scope for acquisition does vary between product sectors. In switching equipment, there are now very few suppliers independent of Alcatel's main competitors, and in most EU markets Alcatel has a market share that would prohibit any further acquisition of switching-product capacity. Hence greater attention has been focused on products where niche suppliers exist, where national market share is lower or where other large firms have businesses that are smaller than the minimum efficient scale. Thus particular targets have been in cables, transmission, satellites and the distribution of private systems.

Cables

In the cables sector Alcatel has focused its strategy on its core French subsidiary, Câbles de Lyon (CDL), and is using this company as a management and ownership vehicle for all its cable interests, renamed as Alcatel Câble since 1991. Alcatel has now established itself as the world's largest supplier of power and telecommunications cable with an integrated capability from metallurgy and optical fibre production through to installation and servicing.

On merging with ITT, the Alcatel group controlled cable interests in France (CDL from CGE), and in the former ITT companies (e.g. in SEL). Over the first two to three years of the joint company, Alcatel exchanged the ownership of many of these cables businesses from national subsidiaries to CDL, in order to strengthen central control. So, CDL's German subsidiary Kabelmetal Electro exchanged its transmission equipment business for the cable business of SEL. Convertible bonds were issued by CDL to raise capital for this restructuring, and to allow further acquisitions.

New acquisitions were sought both in Europe and in North America to reinforce the international scale of the company, including Câbleries de Dour of Belgium, Erkablo of Turkey, Canada Wire and Cable, Irish Cable, Orbitec in France, Holet in The Netherlands and Italco in Italy. In Germany, Alcatel

Câble has been particularly active in building a dominant market share. Starting from a base with Kabellmetal Electro and former SEL businesses, Alcatel acquired in 1991 Vacha Kabel in the eastern Lander, Lacroix and Kress in Lower Saxony and Ehrlers in Hamburg. In 1992 Alcatel agreed to buy AEG's cable business, one of a number of disposals by AEG's parent, Daimler Benz (which also sold its terminal equipment business to Matra). AEG's cable business represents a major acquisition of capacity involving 5,000 employees in three major factories, and sales of 836 million ecu in 1990.

Most recently, Alcatel has bought the former STC submarine cables business from Northern Telecom. Northern Telecom had bought the ITT stake in STC, and after STC sold its ICL subsidiary to ICL's long-time collaborative partner Fujitsu, Northern Telecom acquired the remaining shares in STC and absorbed it fully into its own operations. Specific subsidiaries that did not fit with Northern Telecom's strategies were sold off, including in 1993 the submarine cables business, regarded as a world leader. The reason for the sale of the business is unclear at the present, although Northern Telecom has been producing poor financial results and STC was a more costly acquisition than planned owing to losses and restructuring costs. However, for Alcatel the purchase consolidated the company's primacy in the cable business, and provided a beach-head into the UK.

Transmission

Transmission equipment has been a sector within telecommunications that has not attracted the same degree of interest by academics and financial commentators, but with the consolidation of the switch market and the leap in technologies to digital switching, transmission will be the next product area to see transformation and strategic realignment. A key element in this is the emergence of new technologies to improve the carrying capacity of existing networks, especially as new terminal equipment and switching present the opportunities for sophisticated services such as videoconferencing, which require greater bandwidth.

Alcatel has sought to strengthen its market position in transmission, especially in those countries where the switching market is not so interesting in the medium term. Some PTOs have already invested heavily in digital switching such that Alcatel is either marginalized or has limited market growth. However, in all markets new opportunities can be realized in transmission. Two key acquisitions were Telettra from Fiat and Rockwell's Network Transmission Systems Division. The Rockwell acquisition gave Alcatel a 15% market share in the US transmission market, a second-place ranking, and it provides a strong platform for a more wide-ranging approach to this important market where Alcatel had previously been quite a weak player.

Satellites

Although a relatively small and specialized element of the telecommunications industry, the satellite sector is both profitable and an activity where a company can demonstrate technological sophistication. France, in particular, has viewed an independent European space industry as both technologically desirable and a symbol of political pride. Alcatel, as a reflection of the technological and business ambitions of the French state, has also taken on the role of technological champion in new forms of business, including satellite.

In the domestic arena, Alcatel has gained a dominant position through the formation of an alliance with Aerospatiale (the French aerospace champion) and Alenia (an Italian state-owned company combining airframes and electronics activities). This consortium followed the example of a number of European aerospace businesses in recent years and took a 49% stake in Space Systems Loral of the USA, consolidating the position of Alcatel as coordinating the largest group of satellite system companies in the world.

Subscriber equipment distribution

The acquisition activity described above has largely been concentrated in the public sector market, or at least the PTOs. In the private or subscriber equipment market, Alcatel has been pursuing a sales-led strategy rather than a general expansion of the production base. As with a number of longer-established manufacturers, the company has substantial capacity in private systems and has been cutting some of this capacity rather than seeking to expand it.

However, the importance of local production that is evident still in the public telecommunications market is not replicated in the private systems market, and here the key to higher sales, and to market penetration, is in distribution. Economies of scale in production become more critical in such low-margin, high-volume activities than in the public markets, and the customer is only concerned about good customer support, low prices and features rather than local production and arcane technical standards. Consequently, Alcatel has concentrated on the acquisition of small national distribution companies as a means of improving the sales of its existing private-systems production activities which are themselves concentrated in the core French and former ITT companies.

Overall it can be seen that Alcatel has continued to use acquisition as the prime basis for growth in international markets since the ITT merger. However, this growth has been differentiated by market sector within telecommunications. Certain activities, such as switching and customer premises equipment, have been given a low priority for new productive investment as a result of existing high capacity, and perhaps the possibility of competition policy intervention. In contrast, the company has actively sought to gain market share in transmission and cable, although the organization of these activities is markedly different. Cable is within a unitary product division, whereas transmission is still largely based in the national subsidiaries. In the case of customer premises equipment, Alcatel has followed a different strategy for growth, concentrating on building distribution networks to maximize the existing production capacity, and this reflects the different nature of that most liberalized element of the telecommunications industry.

Table 2.2   Alcatel's divestments

Year	Company	Base
1987	SESA Générale des Services Informatiques Austral Standard Cable	France France Australia
1988	SEL Consumer Products Christian Rovsing Courier and Qume	Germany Denmark USA
1989	CGA-HBS Computer Technik Muller CRAME	France Germany Spain
1990	Cilas Cortelco	France USA
1991	TTN	Italy
1992	Mailroom activities	France, UK, The Netherlands

Source: Alcatel annual reports.

Divestment

Whilst as the telecommunication subsidiary of CGE (now called Alcatel-Alsthom) Alcatel has concentrated on acquiring firms in the telecommunications sector only, acquisitions are rarely pure. In general the parent group, Alcatel-Alsthom, has been the main point of negotiation for wider industrial restructuring (such as the deal with Fiat involving telecommunications, batteries and railway equipment), but even where Alcatel has been presented with telecommunications acquisitions, some of these have included non-telecommunications activities that did not fit with the telecommunications-focus strategy. As Table 2.2 shows, Alcatel has been actively divesting itself of non-core activities in recent years. The telecommunications focus has been made quite explicit and, although the French business in particular encompasses internalized component manufacturing, the wider corporate focus does not include electronic components or other non-telecommunications electronic capital goods. Thus the professional electronics and other category has declined as a proportion of group sales from the time of the merger, from 21.4% of sales in 1987 to 9.3% in 1991.

One product area which ITT Europe had developed was consumer goods, and both the Norwegian and German ITT companies had significant consumer electronics businesses at the time of the merger. Alcatel STK in Norway sold its consumer products activities to a Swedish group and, in the case of SEL, there was a TV business which was sold on to Nokia in 1988 (Fuchs and Schamp, 1990). Also, SEL later sold another subsidiary, Computer Technik Muller, a data products company.

In Spain there was considerable rationalization as the ITT subsidiary had numerous electronics interests, within two groups: ITT Standard Electra and a subsidiary, Marconi España. ITT Standard Electrica was primarily a telecommunications subsidiary, and was retained after significant job reductions. Marconi España was considered by Alcatel to be too diverse for a relatively small firm, overstaffed and with little technological independence. The company was split into several parts for disposal: activities in motor components, consumer products and signals were hived off first, then in 1987 the telephone equipment element of Marconi España was sold to a joint-venture between AT&T-Philips and Amper (an affiliate of Telefónica manufacturing subscriber equipment and PBX). APT Amper took 450 out of 1,270 remaining staff, with sales estimated at 4 billion pesetas. The remaining 850 employees were to be reduced by half following a rescue plan by the Spanish firm Gestiber, but a foreign buyer was being sought for half of the defence business. Amper and Inistel (INI owned) would retain 5% stakes in the defence business.

More recently, Alcatel decided to withdraw from mailroom activities (e.g. franking machines, etc.), which was perhaps a final relic of the post-telecommunications integration, after a period of attempted investment in this sector. One such acquisition, for example, had been Roneo. These small activities based in France (Clichy, Conflans, Bagneux, Le Lude), the UK (Romford), the USA (Hayward, Calif.) and The Netherlands (Drachten) were sold to Adrex, an investment company. This business, with sales of 290 million ecu in 1991, employed 3,600. This followed on the earlier sale of Alcatel's CGA-HBS postal automation and fare-collection activities to Cegelec, another CGE company outside the Alcatel group. In professional electronics, Alcatel Cilas (a specialized laser products unit) was restructured in 1989, and management responsibility and majority ownership were transferred to Aerospatiale in 1990.

Each of the cases outlined above constitute non-core businesses, sold because they did not fit with the current corporate strategy for focusing on the telecommunications sector, and because of their lack of scale and ability to fund investment internally. In the telecommunications sector there has been much less activity, even in terms of plant closures. In general there has been some elimination of small plants in the larger countries, such as France, with a focusing of production in larger units. Only in fascimile machines has there been a withdrawal from a strategic product sector because of competitive pressures. Here Alcatel, as the only EU-based manufacturer of fax machines, eventually recognized the difficulty of long-term competition with the Japanese, and the particularity of the technology that led to fax being more associated with office equipment, such as photocopiers and scanners, than with other telecommunications products.

Organizational structure

Beginning with an inherited organizational structure of national subsidiaries, each offering a range of product lines in parallel and, in some cases, in competition with each other, Alcatel's management has needed to eliminate duplication and standardize product lines. At first the complementarity between the

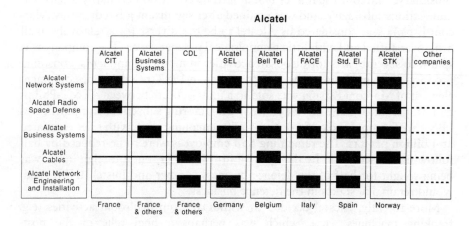

Figure 2.1   Alcatel – matrix structure

ITT companies and the French Alcatel Thomson was not too problematic owing to the absence of ITT in France and the low level of internationalization of Alcatel, but the need for rationalization has increased as further acquisitions built on existing positions in countries where ITT had a significant presence, notably in the case of Telettra in Italy and Spain.

The company has therefore gradually adopted a matrix structure, retaining a strong national organization within the former ITT companies, but adding a new horizontal product-group management with responsibility for the co-ordination of product policy and production. This was begun in the areas of cables and business systems, with Network Systems Group and Radio-communications, Space and Defence following in 1990 (see Figure 2.1).

The need for matrix management for products within the ITT group had become clear prior to the merger, as was evinced with the problems over the System 12 exchange. Within the French Alcatel businesses, there was already some central product direction, although this had been directed to solving the problems of product convergence after the previous merger between Alcatel and Thomson. The general problem with matrix management is the potential conflict of interests between the horizontal and vertical dimensions, product and geographical management in this case. To an extent the position adopted by Alcatel is reminiscent of the old Philips structure of national subsidiaries which controlled both production and market activities, with a weaker pro-duct group structure that tried to co-ordinate product policy and restructuring of the production. In the case of Philips, the problems of subordinating the national interests to the greater needs of the group as a whole led the firm to 'rotate the matrix' and transfer most powers to the product divisions rather than the national organizations. Alcatel has adopted a more mixed position to date, for pragmatic reasons perhaps, and it is as yet unclear whether the full shift to product divisions will be achieved in the near future.

The product group where most restructuring has taken place, such that national organizations have lost control, has been in the cables area, a special case perhaps owing to its distinct product technologies and to the origins of the current Alcatel Chief Executive in CDL. Even before the merger with ITT, CDL was a distinct element within CGE, and it was only after the merger that the cables business was brought into Alcatel, in order to forge links with ITT cables businesses. Subsequently, the cables operations have been split off from several of the ITT national subsidiaries and brought under the direct management control of Alcatel Câble, as it is now known.

Elsewhere in the group, the French public and business systems subsidiaries have been grouped under separate divisions of Alcatel France, and each has acquired some international presence. So Alcatel CIT (public switching) has an Irish subsidiary, and Alcatel Business Systems (France) has sales subsidiaries in the UK and Sweden. ABS also has a 47% stake in the Italian business systems manufacturer, Alcatel Dial Face. As several of the former ITT national companies now have established distinct business systems subsidiaries, and given the increasing competitive pressure in the business systems market from North American and Japanese firms, it is therefore a distinct possibility that further restructuring will lead to all these activities being centralized under one business systems group. Such moves are less likely in the public-switching and transmission market owing to the continuance of national procurement policies and variations in standards over the medium term, but in private systems the liberalization of the market increasingly removes the need for local supply or management control, removing any inhibitions on strategies to maximize the benefits of scale economies.

Spatial organization

The location of production within Alcatel is strongly orientated to markets owing to the historic link between the equipment supply industry and the PTO customers. Domestic sourcing policies ensured that in the companies that have been merged into Alcatel little production was shifted away from the market to low-cost production areas, although there was some development of factories in the peripheral regions of the larger countries.

Data released by Alcatel allows sales by destination and sales by origin for large Alcatel markets and other market regions, and the balance of trade, to be compared (Table 2.3). The dominance of France within the group remains clear in that, despite various acquisitions elsewhere, the French production base remained at around one-third of total output in 1991, although down as a proportion of total output from around 40% in 1987. Similarly, the second-strongest production centre, SEL in Germany, also slipped slightly from 23% of output in 1987 to 21% in 1991, although bolstered by minor acquisitions. The major growth, however, took place in Spain and Italy, both of which doubled in size as a proportion of group output. It is clear that, having gained a dominant position in the French market and an established secondary position

Table 2.3 Alcatel's geographical structure of sales in 1987 and 1991

Million ecu	1987			1991		
	Sales by destination	Sales by source	Balance	Sales by destination	Sales by source	Balance
France	3,475	4,456	+981	3,842	5,113	+1,271
Germany	2,383	2,590	+207	3,028	3,308	+280
Italy	737	673	−64	1,756	1,697	−59
Spain	635	598	−37	1,589	1,591	+2
Belguim	358	544	+186	533	823	+290
Other Europe	1,399	1,316	−83	1,806	1,407	−399
USA/Canada	805	742	−63	947	916	−31
Other world	1,405	278	−1,127	2,244	890	−1,354
Total	11,198	11,198		15,745	15,745	

Source: Alcatel.

in Germany (behind Siemens), Alcatel is now strengthening its position in the other two large markets on mainland Europe. Elsewhere in Europe sales by destination grew more rapidly than sales by output, contributing to the strong positive trade balance from the French, German and Belgian subsidiaries. Whilst there may be individual variations within this, there is the suggestion that in the smaller EU markets Alcatel is limiting the growth of new capacity, and concentrating on the minimum local production to satisfy local procurement policies. The one large European market where Alcatel has only a minimal presence is the UK, where the ITT subsidiary STC was split off from the rest of the company and floated independently, although now it has been acquired and integrated into Northern Telecom. Alcatel has been unable or unwilling to enter the UK market via acquisition and, despite the open nature of the UK market, has only really been able to sell business systems, although the recent purchase of STC Submarine Cables may change this. Outside Europe, Alcatel has struggled in North America until its recent acquisition of Rockwell's transmission business, but has seen quite dramatic sales and production growth elsewhere with new production facilities in India, China and Taiwan, and significant orders in Latin America as well.

At the individual national subsidiary level, there are a variety of spatial production structures depending on the history of the particular firms that have been merged into the group. France, as the core of the company, and the largest national production base, has the most complex spatial production system. Examination of the location of production sites and major offices reveals a series of spatially differentiated organizations within the one firm. One major element is the CIT Alcatel business, which is responsible for the public systems activities of Alcatel France. CIT Alcatel has a historical focus on

Paris, where much of the administration and R & D remains, even though decentralized to the suburbs. However, much of the production for CIT Alcatel has been decanted out from the Ile-de-France to the north and west, to Brittany and Normandy, under the direction of the French state. Some R & D has also been relocated to Brittany. Associated with this product division is also some component production, which is slightly more widely distributed, including some activities in Grenoble. By comparison, the French operations of Alcatel Business Systems are based mainly in the north east of France, in the region of Strasbourg. These plants originated in the main from Thomson rather than CGE Alcatel. Some more specialized activities have been located in regions where particular expertise is concentrated, especially in the case of the satellite business, which is based in the aerospace centre of Toulouse. As noted earlier, there has been some rationalization of this production system, which is probably more complex and distributed than many of Alcatel's competitors, but as yet the regional balance of the company has been retained.

By comparison, in the case of SEL in Germany, rationalization including the sale of TV plants led to the withdrawal from the Ruhr area, and the refocusing and reconcentration of the firm in Baden Württemberg and Bavaria, plus a plant in Berlin. In particular, the corporate core in Stuttgart provides a base for half of the remaining staff (Fuchs and Schamp, 1990). However, acquisitions and the reunification of Germany have added additional sites to this, as SEL has absorbed a former joint venture between the Alcatel parent and the East German government.

Taking a wider corporate perspective, it is clear that the company has retained a range of functions in most of its main markets, even though most production is based in the larger countries. An example of this is in R & D, where Alcatel inherited a widely decentralized network of R & D sites from ITT, as from other subsequent acquisitions (see Figure 2.2). Decentralized R & D is becoming an increasingly necessary feature of the global telecommunications equipment firms as local market access is dependent on the ability of the firm to integrate global products with national telecommunications networks. Inevitably this requires a considerable local software capability. However, beyond this several of the firms are now undertaking significant strategic research and product development in their international divisions. Northern Telecom, for example, has maintained the STC research centre in Essex as a subsidiary of their Bell Northern Research arm, and Ericsson has a long history of product development overseas.

The distinctiveness of Alcatel's non-French research capability, however, is its sheer scale and complexity. Table 2.4 shows the R & D spend of the major subsidiaries, including both the French-based product groups and the main non-French national subsidiaries. Whilst it is clear that the French groups are undertaking a considerable proportion of the total group R & D activity, several of the other northern European subsidiaries are spending equivalent sums proportionately (as in Norway, Switzerland or Denmark) and, in the case of SEL (Germany) or Bell (Belgium), the R & D spend is very large in absolute

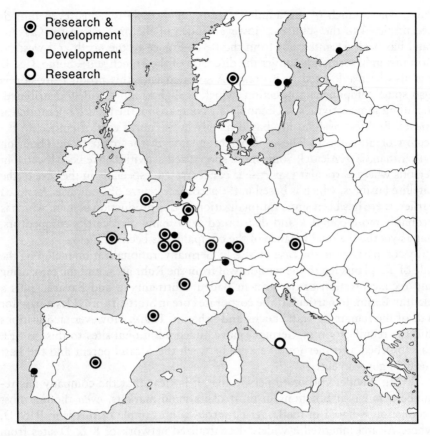

Figure 2.2   Alcatel – R & D sites

terms. Outside Europe, R & D spending levels tend to be lower, although it is interesting to note that Taiwanese spending in 1990 was higher than the USA both absolutely and proportionately, although this was before consolidation of the Rockwell acquisition.

Conclusion

Alcatel must be recognized as a successful example of a European transnational using acquisition as a means to expand both inside the EU and beyond to become the biggest global firm in its sector. However, such growth would not have been possible without the opportunism needed to acquire the ITT businesses which were already the second-largest firm at the time of merger. Subsequent growth has been evolutionary rather than transformative, although still based mainly on acquisition.

None the less, the establishment of such a strong position in the telecommunications markets has not been without problems, and there are a

Table 2.4   R & D expenditure for Alcatel national subsidiaries

Subsidiary and country	Sales (million ecu)	R & D (million ecu)	R & D as a share of sales (%)
Alcatel Australia	295.1	18.8	6.37
Alcatel Austria	173.4	24.9	14.36
Alcatel Bell (Belguim)	793.4	163.6	20.62
Alcatel Business Systems (France)	1272.0	170.4	13.40
Alcatel Business Systems (UK)	178.9	3.5	1.96
Alcatel Cable (various)	3,594.4	45.7	1.27
Alcatel CIT (France)	1,709.0	339.5	19.87
Alcatel Espace (France)	256.9	31.9	12.42
Alcatel Face (Italy)	968.0	73.0	7.54
Alcatel Indetel (Mexico)	188.0	5.4	2.87
Alcatel ISR (France)	42.1	1.1	2.61
Alcatel Kirk (Denmark)	61.5	7.5	12.20
Alcatel Nederland	107.8	3.3	3.06
Alcatel N. America	109.4	6.8	6.22
Alcatel Portugal	125.3	3.0	2.39
Alcatel Radiotelephone (France)	187.0	40.6	21.71
Alcatel SEL (Germany)	1,902.3	305.3	16.05
Alcatel Standard Electrica (Spain)	1,301.6	113.3	8.70
Alcatel STK (Norway)	370.1	68.9	18.62
Alcatel STR (Switzerland)	310.1	53.2	17.16
Alcatel Suomi (Finland)	15.5	2.1	13.55
Alcatel Taisel (Taiwan)	187.3	12.8	6.84
Alcatel Telspace (France)	305.2	69.2	22.67

Source: Alcatel.

number of questions the company still needs to address. As yet, true globalization is still a long way off, as the company has been unable effectively to penetrate the restricted markets of Japan and Canada, the home markets of some of the major competitors (Northern Telecom, NEC, Fujitsu). It is unclear how Alcatel will be able to enter these markets without further acquisition, but in both cases the opportunities are rather limited. The persistence of barriers to entry in these markets, real or perceived, will cause Alcatel to continue to apply pressure to the EU in negotiating within the GATT. Two other important markets where Alcatel has access but has only a very small market share are the USA and the UK. The USA has seen something of a stop-go strategy, but with the Rockwell production base a more persistent attack on this market is likely in future, whilst in the UK the combination of a lack of local production and an extremely vigorous competitive environment seems to have exposed Alcatel's weakness as being over-reliant on close procurement links with PTOs, and unwilling to attack a liberalized market from scratch.

Underpinning some of the problems of expansion and arising from its history of acquisition and merger, Alcatel still retains a legacy of disparate product lines, although considerable effort is being made to achieve standardization and convergence. Thus even if the requirement of certain PTOs for local assembly prevents the company from realizing possible scale economies in production, the firm is also handicapped by the need to retain separate R & D support for multiple products. In addition to these cost penalties and market access difficulties, Alcatel must also face increased competition in its home markets as a consequence of EU liberalization. If market share in those regions is eroded and the company is unable to gain access to other new markets, then further restructuring may be necessary both to reduce costs and potentially to reduce capacity, especially given the general rise in productivities in the industry as a consequence of technical change.

Spatial restructuring in the telecommunications industry must be set, however, in the context of the particularities of public procurement, and the importance placed in some countries on a local manufacturing presence. Thus at present the cost penalties introduced by multiple production sites are not so high as to negate the value of market access. So long as PTO procurement remains a tacit element of national industry policy, then the threat to Alcatel will be limited, but if the EU manages to impose competition in the telecommunications services market, thereby forcing PTOs, to shed their public policy obligations, further rationalization will undoubtedly be necessary.

A further question is the development of the east European market, which is set to expand dramatically in the next decade. Because of its acquisition strategy, and hence spare capacity, Alcatel has been seeking exports into the east rather than needing to build new production capacity. Existing production capacity in Europe is already adequate for Alcatel significantly to increase its exports. By comparison, other non-EU firms are aggressively moving into east Europe, both providing new production plants and acquiring existing firms. Some of these firms, such as AT&T, are able to present east European governments with a package of more than simply equipment production, and can also operate and advise on service provision, and assist in financing with government-supported loans. Another advantage of non-EU firms is that they can offer credibly to east European governments that they will export product into the EU in order to build market share. Currently such firms have little European manufacturing capacity and still import from North America. EU firms (like Alcatel) by contrast have excess capacity in Europe and cannot be expected to develop east European production bases for anything more than the local market, while simultaneously struggling with the political consequences of rationalization in EU markets.

These challenges remain for Alcatel in spite of its having captured the number-one slot in the industry. As yet the liberalization of the telecommunications industry is in its early stages, and major new battles for market share are commencing each year. Whilst there is a stability to the old markets of the EU, North America and Japan, which will not see rapid change, new markets are growing quickly within a varied mix of liberalization states. It will be the manner in which firms address these new internationalization challenges that will dictate whether the existing ranking of firms will persist.

3

Gildemeister and Maho: protecting the home base

Heike Bertram and Eike W. Schamp

Introduction

If internationalization means more than just exports, the German machine-tool sector seems to remain highly domestic. It also retains strong 'craft' industry characteristics (Piore and Sabel, 1984). Machine tools are frequently customized, made to special order or in small batches only. Clients are from many industrial sectors: historically, machine-tool production emerged mainly from the needs of the mechanical engineering industry which is one of its main clients even today, among the newer sectors, such as car manufacturing, electronic and air and spacecraft industries. The technical and economic lifetime of machine tools is long and may cover several decades. Nevertheless, recent technological leaps in such areas as microelectronics, new materials and new tools (such as the laser) happened in the machine-tool sector. Thus it is an old – but still high-tech – industry.

German machine-tool firms themselves are also often very old, having survived a fair number of economic crises, either by merger or by innovations which proved to be technical revolutions. But most firms have remained small and orientated towards a craft-type of production. Despite the age of the sector and its considerable exports – Germany has been the unchallenged largest exporter of machine tools in this century, after all – firms only rarely internationalized. Taking two larger firms as an example, this chapter will examine the hesitant process towards internationalization in the German machine-tool sector. Although global competition has been increasing for some decades, mainly from large Japanese firms, and the German machine-tool sector has repeatedly faced crises, only the recent and most severe crisis at the beginning of the 1990s seemed to push these firms to new efforts in internationalization strategies (Bertram, 1993).

Recently, Penrose's (1980) contribution to the theory of the firm has been rediscovered within evolutionary economics (Foss, 1993). The approach used in this chapter draws upon both theoretical strands in explaining the driving forces governing the history of the firm. According to Penrose, the driving force to growth is, first, the strategic will of the firm – either family owned or governed by management. Apart from their own efforts to gain survival and growth ('survival of the fittest'), firms are, secondly, and according to evolutionary theory, exposed to changes in their economic environment which they are not able to foresee or to govern in advance. Firms must adjust either to opportunities or to challenges often stemming from processes in related sectors. Gowdy (1992) has suggested the term 'exaptation' to describe both the exogenous push and the endogenous response of the firm. Firms which are able and willing to use such a momentum need resources which have not, or have not fully, been used until now. Their capability to adapt to the new situation is based on spare resources or redundancies (Grabher, 1994) with regard to current production, which is, after all, completely contrary to the currently fashionable concept of 'lean production'. Thirdly, firms are confronted with macroeconomic shocks or discontinuities which affect the total national economy at the same time, such as oil crises, wars, stock market shocks or sudden major exchange-rate changes (Gowdy, 1992).

Gildemeister and Maho had run into all kinds of such changes during their lifetimes. They not only survived them but also continued to grow. If we want to understand the growth and internationalization of an individual enterprise, we have to bear in mind that events are the result of an interactive process among, first, expectations and goals of the management, secondly, resources available to the firm, thirdly, different kinds of investment decisions and, fourthly, the time factor or the ever-changing environment. It continuously renders invalid past experiences and decisions based on them which forces the firm to learn permanently. The implementation of investment decisions, for instance, needs time, which means that investments may become obsolete when finished; this, in turn, may even endanger the survival of the whole firm.

From these very brief remarks it should be clear that a long-term examination of an individual enterprise may not aim at comparing the real evolution of the firm with an imagined rational one. Rather, we will try to understand the growth of the firm as a dialectic process of goals of the entrepreneur or manager, his or her will and available resources corresponding to the requirements of the environment. The history of the firm, then, is a sequential process which is determined sometimes by the will of the entrepreneur, sometimes by exaptation and sometimes by different shocks.

The long phase of slow growth

In recent decades, a few 'large' firms have emerged among the small and medium-sized enterprises in the German machine-tool sector. In contrast to the large number of small firms, they did not choose a market niche strategy for special-purpose machines but produced universal machine tools. In this latter market area of universal machine tools, they always faced global competition. Among those 'large' firms a continuous competition about growth took place, in recent decades, although they remained small in comparison to American or Japanese competitors which are two or three times larger. In what follows we

want to present the experiences of one firm from each of the two most important market segments in Germany, specifically those concerned with the production of metal-cutting machine tools. The two cases represent different
strategies, the one of a management and the other of a family enterprise
(Penrose, 1980), and different growth trajectories determined by the contrast
of decision-making of the Gildemeister management and of a technically orientated owner-entrepreneur in Maho. Gildemeister AG was a leading producer
of lathes – besides Traub AG – and, recently, celebrated its 120 years of
existence. Maho AG produced drilling and milling machine tools – besides
Deckel AG – and, at 70 years of age, really was a 'young' enterprise. At the end
of the 1980s, however, it surpassed Gildemeister AG in taking the first position
by turnover among the German machine-tool firms.

Both firms are typical of the emergence of the German machine-tool sector
in which craft production of customized machine tools and, hence, technical
competence, mattered first (Kocka, 1975, p. 48). F. Gildemeister, a mechanical
engineer, founded a repair shop in 1864 in Bielefeld, then a fast-growing centre
of textile and sewing machinery industries. He quickly changed into a
machine-tool firm which grew considerably over the next decades. At the end
of the century, Gildemeister was transformed into a joint-stock company
whose majority still remained the family's property. For nearly 50 years (from
1906 to 1955), the firm was successfully managed by the famous Wilhelm
Berg, a mechanical engineer and later president of the German employer's
association (Keil, 1972; Spur, 1991).

Maho also started from a craft base, but during the economic crisis after the
First World War. At the end of 1920, five craftsmen founded a limited-liability
company for the production of drawing instruments. Two years later, one of
the founders, Michael Babel, took charge of the management and enlarged the
variety of products. With the industrialization for rearmament during the
1930s, the firm grew considerably. Even after the Second World War the firm
continued to produce instruments, but with problems owing to the economic
crisis in the early postwar years which was characterized by the dismantling of
production capacities, a high inflation rate and low industrial production. This
period seemed to end with the economic and monetary reforms of 1948. In the
same year, Michael Babel decided to add machine tools for the firm's own use
– principally drilling and milling machines – to the production of instruments,
as he faced a lack of special machines for instruments production. Although
industrial production in Germany had reached only 65% of that of 1936 by
the end of 1948 (Abelshauser, 1983, p. 64), Babel, like others, obviously
placed his hopes on the changing monetary conditions and expected additional
growth. It was, however, only the unexpected shock of the Korean war which
triggered an export boom for capital goods in West Germany, as this country
was virtually the only larger one in the western world with unused capacities
(*ibid.*, p. 68). This was mainly to the benefit of the machine-tool industry. As
a result, the company became so successful that Babel gave up instrument
production and shifted fully to the machine-tool sector (Maho, 1970). In

retrospect, this proved to be the key decision for the survival of the firm, as drawing instruments today have mainly been replaced by computers.

The 1950s and 1960s were the decades of rising prosperity and increasing reindustrialization in West Germany, and have been labelled the phase of reconstruction (Abelshauser, 1983). Exports grew considerably. Neither of the two enterprises was confined to the domestic market but it remained their important home base. During this 'golden age' of industrial growth both firms continuously invested parts of their profits and modernized. They grew up to be middle-sized producers in a vertically integrated production system and, step by step, developed into more or less local multiplant firms.

When Wilhelm Berg died in 1955, his son-in-law, Grautoff, took over the management of Gildemeister, and started to prepare the firm for future expansion, mainly by continuous rejuvenation of its products. Major steps to growth occurred during the early 1960s when, in 1964, a joint venture with the American company de Vlieg was created in order to produce tools in the neighbouring municipality of Sennestadt, and Gildemeister bought an area for future expansion. In the same year, Michael Babel (Maho) acquired a small factory in Vils, Austria, just a few kilometres beyond the border and from his main factory. Principally, however, both firms grew *in situ* at their traditional locations, mainly owing to the importance of their domestic market. They had become, at the end of the 1960s, medium-sized machine-tool firms, compared to their German competitors. In 1969, Gildemeister had an annual turnover of DM55 million; in the year of Michael Babel's death, in 1970, Maho had reached the middle size of 630 employees and a turnover of DM35 million.

The arduous rise to a domestic large-scale enterprise

The reconstruction phase of the West German economy after the Second World War ended with the first slight recession in 1966–7. By 1968, however, the German economy once more grew considerably and, within it, the German machine-tool sector. In this situation of unbroken expectations into further growth, both firms changed their strategy. The major shareholder of Gildemeister, Grautoff, planned the building up of a large machine-tool combine. He persuaded the public bank, Westdeutsche Landesbank (WestLB), to act as a partner, which took a capital share of slightly more than 25% as a result of an increase of nominal capital. WestLB tried to escape from the simple role of a clearing bank of savings associations and to copy the large private banks then entering the business of company finance. At Maho, Werner Babel, Michael's son who took over the firm after his father's death, planned a push in further growth, despite the enterprise's restricted financial resources.

The growth of the enterprises between upturn and crisis
Gildemeister AG attempted to grow both by horizontal takeovers and investment in vertical integration, supported by WestLB, which enabled the quick acquisition of firms. In 1967, a joint venture was established in one of the

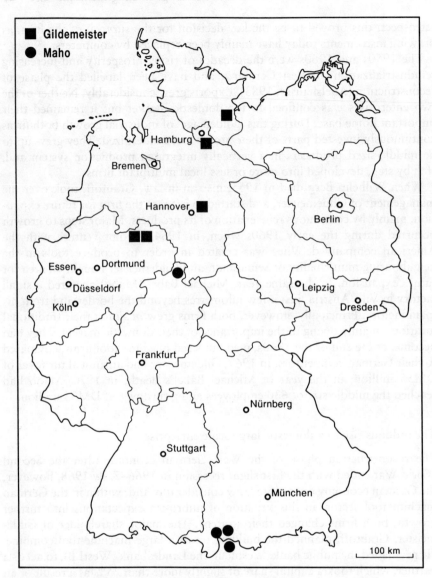

Gildemeister
Maho

Hamburg
Bremen
Hannover
Berlin
Essen Dortmund
Düsseldorf Leipzig
Köln Dresden
Frankfurt
Nürnberg
Stuttgart
München

100 km

Figure 3.1   Spatial pattern of Gildemeister and Maho plants, 1972

major export markets, Italy, but the main focus of the enterprise remained its
growth in West Germany. In the same year, Gildemeister founded a tempering
company in the neighbouring municipality of Sennestadt; one year later, Gildemeister and WestLB acquired 26% each of the traditional machine-tool firm,
Heidenreich & Harbeck (H&H). This was a producer of standardized lathes
with a plant at Hamburg and a foundry at Mölln. In 1972, the Max Müller
Maschinenfabrik in Langenhagen near Hannover was acquired (see Figure
3.1). Parallel to this, capacities were enlarged, particularly in the hope of

opening up eastern European markets. Within one year, from 1969 to 1970, turnover increased by 30% to DM72 million, and orders from the USSR of a further DM80 million came in. In 1972, turnover had already grown to DM205 million, and the volume of orders was DM214 million, among them DM150 million from the USSR.

Gildemeister had grown up to become principally an exporting firm (73% of annual turnover in 1973), but mainly owing to exports in west European and socialist 'markets'. The family enterprise, Maho, on the contrary, was only able to grow more slowly. First, a new plant for parts production (spindles and gear parts) was opened in the neighbourhood (Wertach) in 1970, and in 1972 Maho acquired the small machine-tool firm Thiel Brothers GmbH in Emstal near Kassel (Northern Hesse state) (see Figure 3.1). The shock of the first oil crisis mainly hit Gildemeister AG rather than Maho. At first, exports to the major markets in west Europe (France, Italy, the UK) and the USA broke down, mainly affecting exports of standardized lathes which were produced in the subsidiary, H&H. This caused high losses and a dramatic fall in the company's nominal capital. In close succession, an increase in nominal capital repeatedly proved to be necessary, DM5 million (since 1964) to DM20 million in 1974. This, however, was insufficient with respect to the financial liquidity required for the excessively fast growth of the firm. In consequence, the firm stopped its dividend and the major shareholder, Grautoff, lost a part of his capital and his post as chairman of the executive board. WestLB became the major shareholder and appointed a new chairman of the executive board who, for the first time in the firm's history, came from the outside, namely, from Ford Germany.

Financially, the firm was seriously hit, and, during the following years, was only able to invest defensively. It could, however, use the possibilities offered by the new state policy of city redevelopment and sell its traditional site near the main railway station in Bielefeld for the sum of DM77 million, including relocation and interruption costs. This enabled the firm to establish a greenfield plant in Sennestadt for total costs of DM45 million. Furthermore, the firm stayed with its philosophy to grow by external mergers and by diversification into different markets. In 1975, Knoll was acquired, a firm for deep drilling techniques at Laichingen, south Germany. A further profitable activity was identified in the planning of complete machinery equipment, particularly for state planning countries. So the firm founded Gildemeister Projekte GmbH in 1976 which soon received an order of DM200 million from Iran. Although the markets for machine tools recovered at the end of the 1970s, and the upswing was reinforced by the technical change towards numerically controlled (NC) technology, production of standard lathes in Hamburg still remained in crisis. Consequently, employment in H&H was reduced from 1,000 to 420 by the end of 1977 (Käckenhoff, 1978). In the middle of an upswing of the market for machine tools, Gildemeister was forced to cope with another financial crisis. The Hamburg plant of H&H was partly sold to the Japanese firm Makino Machines, which continued to produce machining centres, a

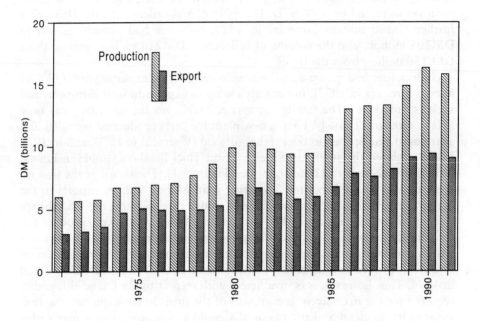

Figure 3.2   The growth of production and exports in the German machine-
tool sector, 1971–92 (*Source*: VDMA, different issues)

product never made by Gildemeister. Although different decisions had been
taken, the crisis was exacerbated in 1981 and 1982 when a general down-
swing in the market occurred (see Figures 3.2 and 3.3). The firm's functional
organization was changed into a divisional one, which was combined with a
spatial division of labour between different plants; the variety of products was
reduced; production of customized machine tools was totally given up; and the
share of bought parts increased (Süddeutsche Zeitung 4.6.82). In total, employment fell from a peak of 4,500 in 1974–5 to 2,500 in 1983 (Fleming,
1983).

While Gildemeister AG still survived, going from crisis to crisis – or as
Fleming (*ibid.*) put it, it was a 'long struggle to survive' – Maho grew at a slow
pace. This firm, too, tried hard to export to east Europe and, in 1975, received
a first large order from the USSR. In total, however, exports seemed to be more
differentiated between countries. Sales were particularly strengthened in the
domestic market, exclusively distributed by the independent machine-tool
merchant house Hahn & Kolb from Stuttgart. Domestic market shares of
Maho for universal drilling and milling machines came up to 25% in 1970 but
increased to 40% within one decade. This growth to DM200 million turnover
in 1980–1 was exclusively achieved by *in situ* capacity expansion at the four
given locations. This strategy proved to be very successful as the firm earned a
remarkable 10% return on turnover in 1980–1.

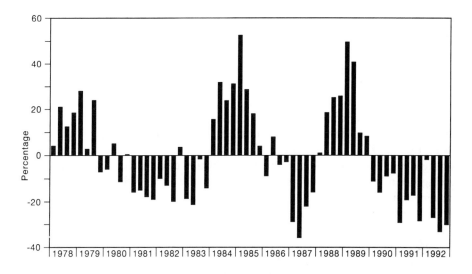

Figure 3.3   Annual changes in incoming orders in the West German machine-tool sector, 1978–92 (*Source*: VDMA)

New technological trajectories

It was not by pure chance that both firms first tried to promote exports to east Europe during the 1970s in order to sell traditional products more intensively. In western markets competition from the emerging large Japanese enterprises became harder and harder. These not only produced standard machine tools more cheaply than the USA and West Germany but also innovated very early into NC machine tools which had been invented in the USA. Price and innovative competition reinforced each other, particularly in the domestic market in West Germany. Japanese firms' share of the German market for machine tools increased from 21.9% in 1970 to 31.5% in 1980 (Maurice and Sorge, 1990, p. 19). Clearly, incremental technological change was no longer possible; a radical change in technologies, via the innovation of microelectronics during the 1970s and 1980s and of new materials and tools such as the laser during the 1980s, was necessary (Häusler, 1992).

In this technological competition, which was exacerbated by the diffusion of computer numerical control (CNC) machine tools at the end of the 1970s, both firms made a relatively early adjustment in their production programme to the new techniques compared to domestic competitors (though not to international ones). Gildemeister AG claims to be the first supplier of standardized NC machine tools on the domestic market. As early as 1965 the firm presented its first NC lathe, and in 1967 another smaller one was produced. It seems that the firm owed this to a young technician who later became one of the most famous technical professors in production control in Germany because he had already earlier prepared for the jump into the technique of NC control. This was Günter Spur who, after having finished his studies in mechanical engineering in Braunschweig, came to Gildemeister at the end of the 1950s to design milling machines – a production which the firm gave up in 1964. After a few years Spur returned to university to finish his PhD and then came back to Gildemeister in 1963 as the head of the design department. During these years he acquainted the firm with NC technology, which laid the ground for future technological innovations. Two years later, Spur was awarded a chair at the technical university of Berlin, where he achieved his fundamental success in the development of machine controls, flexible manufacturing systems and robots (Randow, 1992). Gildemeister, like many other machine-tool firms, has strengthened its ties with technical universities during recent decades, thus giving rise to a network of research contacts of which the later Spur Institute became only one element.

This, however, did not radically change the firm's competitive situation. Only microelectronics really revolutionized techniques: in 1976, Gildemeister AG produced the first universal CNC lathe. The NEF[1] lathe, which was originally designed for easy operation in Third World countries where a skilled worker could be replaced by a less skilled one, had been combined with a computer control. Compared to traditional ones, CNC machines generally have the advantage of a diagnostic system which is able to show defects in the machine. Additionally, as a result of the modular design of such machines, modules may be replaced in case of disruptions. Consequently, repairs at the workplace, which normally interrupt production, are no longer necessary. Attention has frequently been drawn to the technical revolution produced by the innovation of numerical control into machine-tool production. While previously technical know-how was localized in mechanics and hydraulics, the requirements for know-how were now shifted towards microelectronics. Furthermore, the machine tool had to be redesigned in total as modern computer-controlled machines need fewer and simpler mechanical parts (Babel, 1986). In the production of CNC machine tools, then, costs are shifted from mechanical parts production to the assembly of the control device and the development of software. That makes the machine-tool firm increasingly dependent on technical developments in combined sectors: first, from hardware-producing electronics, and, secondly, from software production.

One of the main problems in the early production of the CNC machine tools was the lack of computer controls. Gildemeister AG therefore suggested that Siemens AG, the leading German electrical company, should start computer control production. Siemens refused, and Gildemeister started to develop these controls on its own (Fleming, 1983). During this learning phase, most Gildemeister products were not regarded as best practice until some years later. In 1982, the firm founded a subsidiary, Gildemeister Automation, in Hannover to produce computer controls and the required software, thus becoming able to deliver machine tools, control, training and services combined. As a result, the firm considered itself to be the leading European CNC machine-tool company.

Werner Babel may be called a technical entrepreneur whose roots were in the craft tradition. This is underlined by his different technical publications (Babel, 1986; 1989). His response to the crisis of the early 1970s was more technical than that of Gildemeister. First, he tried to 'upgrade' production into customized machine tools instead of the hitherto made standardized products. The series producer did not have any experience in this field, however. Furthermore, the long-term contacts to clients which are so necessary in this particular business did not exist as he had only distributed via Hahn & Kolb. Having suffered some losses from this new direction Babel took the opportunity of a large order from the USSR for 150 standardized machine tools, to withdraw from it and return to standardized products. Almost at the same time as his main competitor, Deckel AG, which mainly produced low-value small machine tools, from 1976 onwards he concentrated instead (as one of the early adopters in the German machine-tool sector) on NC technology and modular design (*Wirtschaftswoche* 1 February 1986), but chose the high-value large machine-tool sector. During the following economic upswing, this decision proved to be so successful that capacities were hardly sufficient at the end of the 1970s, and Babel began to reflect on further expansion.

On the way to internationalization in Europe

Academics generally try to systematize their understanding of the growth of an internationalizing firm with descriptive models which identify clearly and unambiguously different stages of the firm's growth. The stage of export growth is, first, followed by the establishment of foreign sales agencies, then by the creation or takeover of production plants and, finally, by the establishment of a system of international linkages between the different firm's plants. Models of this kind have been developed, for instance, by Taylor and Thrift (1982) or Dicken (1992). In reality, however, different stages overlap, which means that the first steps towards internationalization could be done at a time when the firm is mainly growing to become a large domestic company.

In this section we will focus on four different aspects of the steps towards internationalizing both firms. Two factors relate to the firm's internal resources, enabling them to match up with global competition, i.e. the technological trajectories chosen and the acquired financial resources, respectively. Access to global markets via the extension of an international distribution network is a third factor and, finally, the organization of the spatial division of labour among different plants and subsidiaries clearly points to the philosophy of the firm, whether it strives to develop an international production network or remains bound to domestic production whilst increasing exports.

The technological trajectory
Both firms faced their major technical breakthroughs in microelectronics during the 1980s. Both were very intensive in R & D expenditures (4–6% of annual turnover). Gildemeister succeeded in developing a completely new

computer control produced in the newly founded Gildemeister Automation GmbH, which was responsible for development, production and sales of mechanical as well as electronic controls. This was the basis of a technological leap between 1983 and 1985 which enabled the firm during the new upswing in world markets to make profits and, finally, to distribute dividends in 1989, for the first time in 15 years. Rising profits were further used at the end of the 1980s for investments in rather expensive research lines, such as controls of production systems.

Maho not only continued its technological strategy of computerizing products during the 1980s but also tried to use best-practice technologies in production. This is by no means common in the machine-tool sector (Bertram and Schamp, 1991). Maho used computer-assisted design (CAD) very early, and tried to extend this into computer integrated development. In 1984, a new plant in Pfronten, with best-practice technology, started production. As the plant reached full capacity one year later, just at the beginning of a new upswing in markets, Maho was able to increase profits (see Figure 3.3). This certainly supported the will for further growth, all the more as it overtook its main competitor, Deckel, in turnover owing to its production of high-value machine tools, whereas Deckel stayed with low-value standardized ones. So Maho began investment in a further modern plant in Kempten, in 1989, which was characterized by extended automation and was able to produce large parts for all the firm's German assembly plants. One of the major aims of automation was to decrease throughput time by 80%, thus running the whole firm even more competitively. To this end, DM150 million were invested but with the employment of only approximately 100 people. This investment decision was considered to be the key for Maho's further growth towards a high-tech company, enabling a new spatial division of labour between parts production in Kempten and machine-tool assembly in all older plants of the firm (see Figure 3.5).

Failures in product development, however, could not be avoided. So at the beginning of the 1980s, Maho tried to extend into related products and started to produce robots for charging machine tools, but stopped after one year. In the mid-1980s, Maho designed a flexible production system whose production start, according to Maho's distribution officer in 1986, was considered as 'a decision for the 1990s'. Increasingly, however, the fast progress in microelectronics forced the machine-tool firm into tremendous expenditure on R & D. Babel, who was elected chairman of the technical committee of the Association of German Machine Tool Firms (VDMA) during the 1980s, pointed to the increasingly shortening product cycles of hardware. The enormous progress that was made in hardware capacities and in standardization caused rapidly rising costs for the adaption of customized software. According to Babel (1986, p. 68), costs for hardware were halved within ten years, whereas software costs increased tenfold. For 1990, he estimated a share in costs of 25% for hardware and 75% for software in control development (Babel, 1989, p. 67). In establishing a software subsidiary in 1987 (joining an engineer at Eltville, near Wiesbaden, who had previously delivered to Maho), Babel tried to diversify into different software products related to machine tools, whereas software development for current products remained at the different plants. Finally, in 1988–9, Maho introduced laser techniques into its milling machines thus following, for instance, the German lathe producer Traub. Laser techniques were considered such a high priority for future technical development in the machine-tool sector that even in times of financial stress at the beginning of the 1990s research was continued.

Capital and finance
Growth and force for technological renewal of both firms were mainly determined by their capability to open up financial sources. In the early 1990s, both firms belonged to the largest of the sectors which, historically, were able to make their way despite severe competition from other firms in Germany. At first sight, Gildemeister AG was ahead of Maho, as it had been a joint-stock company for 90 years and was thus able to obtain new capital through the stock exchange while Maho had been, until recently, a private company and family enterprise. The management enterprise, Gildemeister, however, did not grow without difficulties. Thus, in 1962, the company's capital had to be reduced from DM4 million to DM3.7 million, but shortly after was increased to DM5 million. It may be assumed that the firm, at that date, had reached a certain growth threshold which was overcome by the decision of the major shareholder and chairman, Grautoff, both to invest vertically and to acquire horizontally, thus making the firm a large diversified company. In the 1970s, Gildemeister changed into a management enterprise, supported by a strong bank and trying to grow by acquisitions. This strategy, however, failed, and, for more than a decade, management tried both to continue the growth strategy via acquisitions and to sort out the consequences of unsuccessful decision-making. During the 1970s, nominal capital was increased several times – particularly in 1974 (DM20 million) – and reached DM30 million in 1980. This was primarily owing to the fact that the firm could not use self-finance in the face of long-standing losses since 1974. The resources for new strategies, such as the penetration of new markets (e.g. the USA) or the development of new products, could only be gained through new shareholders and increase of capital. Yet the firm could not expect to get new shareholders inside the stock exchange because of the 15-year period without dividends. In consequence, it had to look for shareholders outside.

In the crisis at the end of the 1970s there was a new major shareholder, Sauer Getriebe KG, which brought new capital to the firm. This was a medium-sized mechanical engineering enterprise with an annual turnover of some DM200 million (Gildemeister in 1980: DM441 million). As WestLB was a major sharehold of Sauer, together with Bosch GmbH and the later president of the Association of German Employers – Klaus Murmann – the bank increased its equity participation at Gildemeister against its own will (Fleming, 1983). But Gildemeister AG was not successful in making profits in the following years. In

1982, the firm had to reduce employment once more by 340 out of 2,800 employees. It clearly suffered from the high costs of finance, the interest costs reaching 7.8% of annual turnover in 1982, so over-riding R & D expenditures considerably. WestLB and Sauer KG managed, however, to sell a part of their equity shares in 1984 to the American Litton group, with an increase in nominal capital. In this way, in continuing its expansion path, management hoped to improve its market penetration of the USA. Both efforts made to increase sales in the USA and change the organization of the firm from a functional to a divisional one, however, were not able to make the firm profitable. As a response, a further restructuring in 1985 changed Gildemeister AG into a holding company with independent subsidiaries. Only two years later, in the middle of an outstanding boom, was Gildemeister AG able to pay off losses and to distribute a dividend some two years later.

The situation was totally different in the family enterprise Maho. Even during the crisis of the German machine-tool sector, in 1980 and 1981, the enterprise did not make losses. Often, the return on turnover was higher than the average of German manufacturing firms. Hence, growth could be financed mainly out of profits. The location of the main plant in Pfronten played a major role in financing, as it was situated in an assisted area so that the firm could profit from lower interest rates. Public assistance made easier investment decisions, such as, in earlier times, the new plant at Wertach (in 1972), the new plant (no. 2) in Pfronten and the acquisition of the Gebrüder Thiel firm in Emstal near Kassel (see Figure 3.1).

None the less, possibilities for finance out of profits are relatively restricted in a medium-sized family enterprise. For long, the nominal capital of Maho stayed at DM10 million, while the partners had given some credit to their own firm. These were used in 1985 to increase nominal capital to DM30 million and to change Maho into a joint-stock company which went to the stock exchange, one year later, to increase its capital further to DM44 million. Although Werner Babel had to buy out his brother, some DM52 million remained which could be used for an unprecedented expansion. This capital was used to invest in the new plant in Kempten, to modernize all older plants – particularly in changing production into the assembly of machine tools – and to improve foreign distribution.

Expanding and strengthening distribution
For decades Gildemeister AG, as well as Maho, had exported without any particular foreign organization, although the share of exports had been high (see Figure 3.4). Machine tools, however, became increasingly complex, particularly with the use of computers; sales, therefore, had to be supported increasingly by consultancy and eventually, training. Consequently, Gildemeister AG started the reorganization of foreign distribution in the 1970s, at the same time as it switched to the growth strategy towards becoming a large company. The first steps in internationalization were made in its most important markets: in 1967, a production plant was taken over in Italy (whose name

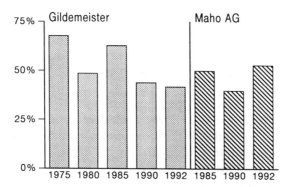

Figure 3.4 Export shares in annual turnover for Gildemeister and Maho, 1975–92 (*Source*: Firm reports)

had been changed into Gildemeister Italiana) and sales agencies were founded in the UK (1971), France, Switzerland and Austria (1977) and, finally, in South Africa (1981). During the 1980s, the firm expanded its foreign distribution network further, and recently (1991) in Spain and Sweden. Gildemeister, however, remained largely an exporter only to European countries and, particularly, to the USSR.

Though the American market was of particular importance for exports of machine tools, sales from Gildemeister remained modest. In 1984, Gildemeister went into co-operation with the machine-tool department of the American Litton company, which took a minor share in the capital of Gildemeister and acquired a licence to produce Gildemeister machine tools in the USA. Increasing sales in the USA were anticipated. As repeatedly in the history of this firm, however, the decision soon was revised as the expected success did not occur immediately; Gildemeister withdrew from the contract after three years. Although the firm tried to have a presence in the American market via the subsidiary of a smaller German machine-tool firm, H.Pfauter GmbH & Co. KG (Ludwigsburg), it never managed to be successful in the USA. In contrast to major capitalist markets, no particular sales organization was necessary for the firm's large exports to the USSR. After the breakdown of the socialist system, however, the firm had to pay for this. It had to reorganize its distribution in eastern Europe completely until this market totally broke down.

The younger firm Maho started its reorganization of distribution later, but took a more global perspective while trying to open up markets in the 'triad'. Possibly this was easier for Maho compared to Gildemeister, as Maho was selling machine tools in a high-value market segment not really affected by Japanese competition (Garnett, 1986). Rather, it was Deckel AG from Munich, at times Europe's largest producer of milling machines, who was an important competitor. Being mainly orientated towards the domestic market, it was not until the first crisis in 1980 ('second oil crisis') that Maho began to invest in an international distribution network of its own. The firm started in the USA in 1980 but this was more the result of the strategic will of opening up a large market than to actual sales figures. In 1988–9, orders from the USA only amounted to 6% whereas the bulk of orders came from West Germany (42%) and western Europe (40%); orders from eastern Europe and particularly from the USSR were 5% in that year. Consequently, further foreign sales agencies were established in the USA (1980), the UK (1981), France (1984) and Italy (1985). Quite early, Maho realized the growing importance of east Asian markets and opened up a sales centre for all southeast Asian countries in Singapore (1984). In 1989, a sales agency in Beijing and a service centre in Shanghai – together with three German partners – were established. Maho completed this strategy in the triad by the improvement of its European sales organization, investing in new sales centres in Italy, France, The Netherlands (in 1988) and Spain (in 1991).

Although the domestic market still accounted for the most important share of annual turnover, both firms managed without a sophisticated domestic sales organization for a long time. Gildemeister AG founded a subsidiary company responsible for domestic sales only in 1986, in Hannover, where production sites are located. This was completed by training facilities in Hannover and a joint leasing company for financing sales in Mainz, i.e. where the partner company DAL was located. Whereas world market demand dropped considerably and foreign turnover decreased by 16% in 1989, 1% in 1990, 5% in 1991 but 18% in 1992, German unification caused a particular boom, with domestic growth rates of 46% and 22% in 1989 and 1990, respectively. In these years, Gildemeister AG set up its own regional sales organizations in Munich (1990), Wuppertal and Berlin (1991) (see Figure 3.6).

Maho was earlier in intensifying its domestic sales organization. As a sales contract with the machine-tool merchant Hahn & Kolb in Stuttgart had existed for a long time for the distribution of the bulk of Maho's products, Maho started to set up its own sales organization either for parts or totally new products, such as Rotatec Vertriebs-GmbH in Pfronten selling ball threads (in 1983) or Maho System Pfronten for selling flexible production systems (1985). It was only during the new upswing of the machinery sector in the later 1980s that Maho established domestic distribution centres for those products which were more complex and needed further explanation: in 1986 in Kornwestheim/Baden-Württemberg, in 1988 in Hilden/Rhineland and in 1989 in Erlangen and Emstal/Northern Hesse. Thus the main regional markets of southern, western and central Germany received distribution centres. The next step towards deepening market penetration was the opening of a training centre at the firm's headquarter (Pfronten) in 1988 (see Figure 3.6). This was a sign of a further phase of expansion and, to underline the new market policy, Werner Babel changed the hitherto green colour which was so familiar for Maho machine tools into grey and purple.

Reinforcement of the functional and spatial division of labour
Despite their rather different development histories, both firms were somewhat similar at the end of the 1980s. Both were among the largest enterprises in their

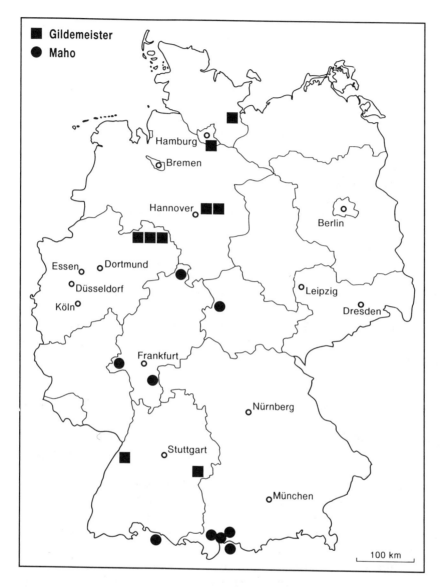

Figure 3.5 Spatial pattern of Gildemeister AG and Maho AG, 1992

market segment in Europe, both had been changed into joint-stock companies, both were mainly orientated towards the domestic and European market, including eastern Europe, both had expanded into a differentiated spatial division of labour, and both had developed into diversified products. Gildemeister AG, however, seemed to be organized more flexibly, with its holding structure, whereas Maho remained a functionally organized enterprise possessing dependent plants.

Earlier, compared to Maho, Gildemeister had used the different acquisitions for a strategy of a clear spatial division of labour. For instance, in 1982 the firm entered into co-operation and a minor shareholding with its most important domestic competitor in multiple spindle lathes, Pittler AG in Langen (south of Frankfurt) and immediately closed down final production and reduced employment by 800 employees in Langen. Pittler was reduced to the level of a parts-producing plant, but some years later (1984) Gildemeister was forced to sell it to a management buy-out owing to considerable losses. Witzig & Frank-Martin in Offenburg, however, an acquired subsidiary with the Pittler acquisition and a producer of special machines making profits, remained with Gildemeister. As has been said earlier, machine-tool production of H&H at Hamburg was also sold to the Japanese partner Makino Milling Machine Co. (in 1983), and Gildemeister kept only its foundry at Mölln. A clear vertical division of labour was introduced: the capital-intensive large casts came from the H&H foundry at Mölln, controls and software from Gildemeister Automation at Hannover, mechanical parts partly from NEF Drehmaschinen (where lathes are also assembled), and tools from Gildemeister de Vlieg GmbH in Sennestadt. These were assembled either by NEF Drehmaschinen or Gildemeister Automatische Drehmaschinen (as far as CNC lathes are concerned) in Sennestadt. Although Gildemeister had tried several times to integrate more distant plants via acquisition, the firm still concentrated its production core in the northwest German region (see Figure 3.6) and regarded itself as a local production unit. For example, management attached importance to a maximum one-hour journey by car to its Hannover plants in order to be able to visit them daily without announcement. Diversified products, however, were produced in more remote plants, such as large machine tools (Gildemeister Max Müller, until 1991), special machines (Witzig & Frank) and deep-drilling technique (TBT). Gildemeister Projecta, which was responsible for projecting, planning and realizing large equipment, is located at Sennestadt. This locational pattern of production plants was supplemented by regional sales agencies both in Germany and overseas countries (Figure 3.6).

Compared to Gildemeister AG, the locational pattern of Maho AG is even more clearly restricted to the original region of the firm. During the 1960s and 1970s, the firm developed into a small multiplant enterprise by establishing new plants for parts production in the neighbouring municipalities of Vils, Austria (1964) and Wertach (1971). For a long time, Maho left its original region only once by acquiring Gebrüder Thiel in Northern Hesse state for parts production (in 1972 – see Figure 3.1). The CIM-orientated technological modernization of production was implemented, however, only in its original region when Maho established a second plant at Pfronten at the beginning of the 1980s and a fully automated plant at Kempten at the end of the decade. Together with the decision taken to invest in this plant and the experience of growing sales figures, Maho management introduced a complete reorganization of production in 1989, separating parts production (at Pfronten plant 2, Vils, Wertach and – later on – Kempten) clearly from assembly (at Pfronten

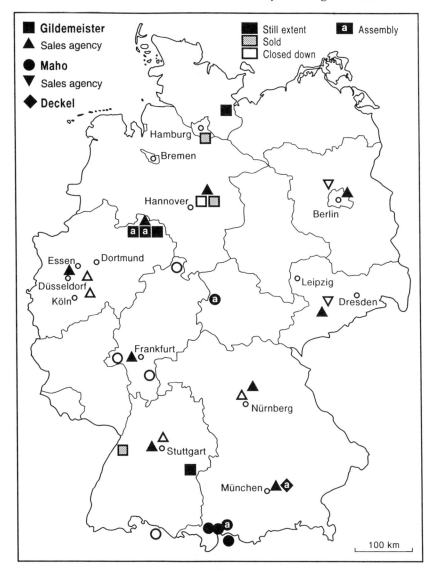

Figure 3.6 Domestic sales network and production network of Gildemeister, Deckel and Maho, 1993

plant 1 and Emstal). Earlier, in 1985, Maho had entered into co-operation with Traub AG, the major competitor to Gildemeister AG, for the Brazilian market, through personal contacts between the two major shareholders of the firms, but this co-operation never gained importance in exports. As part of the expansive strategy following the step to the stock exchange (1986), Maho, however, started internationalization of production in 1987 with the takeover of an Italian enterprise producing lathes and the establishment of a new plant for milling machines in the USA (Naugatuck, CT). Maho, furthermore, diversified in 1989 via the acquisition of the Swiss firm, Hansen, which produced spark erosion machine tools. Maho immediately started reorganization of this subsidiary, investing in a new plant for assembly near Frankfurt/Main via finance by leasing (in 1991) and focusing the Swiss plant at Wattwil on parts production. As was the case with Gildemeister, however, the production of the firm's core products remained in the original region.

Global growth euphoria and crash

The silent revolution in eastern Europe and the dissolution of the former USSR posed a unique challenge for those firms which traditionally made a considerable share of their turnover in those countries. In 1989 and 1990, opportunities for a tremendous expansion to the east seemed to open up as everybody expected that the sudden entry of these countries into the capitalist world system would force them quickly to renew their production equipment, given the enormous deficiency in production technology both in East Germany and, particularly, in the USSR.

In consequence, both firms tried to exploit the new opportunities. Gildemeister AG principally sought to improve distribution into Russia by acquiring shares of a machine-tool merchant. Maho took over a plant in East Germany which, historically, belonged to the firm's roots. Originally, Gebrüder Thiel, which had been acquired in 1972 by Maho, had been founded in Seebach, Thuringia, in 1862. It had grown up to become a well-known producer of milling machines before fleeing the soviet sphere of influence after the Second World War. Maho invested some DM25 million for the acquisition of this plant and a further DM25 million for its modernization. However, a reduction in employees from 900 during socialist times to 500 became necessary. Additionally, Maho opened up a sales agency in Berlin and a sales centre in Chemnitz, and entered into a joint venture with the former Hungarian state producer of machine tools, Szim in Budapest, in order both to open up the east European markets and to produce at cheap costs ordinary machines.

At the end of 1989, however, demand for machine tools had fallen considerably, particularly in foreign markets. Although domestic orders could compensate for this for a while, the stock of orders decreased, and even faster in 1990 (see Figure 3.2). First, the competitor Deckel AG ran into difficulties and lowered the prices of its products in 1990. In consequence, Maho AG was forced to follow. Subsequently, demand fell dramatically; while Gildemeister AG faced a reduction in annual turnover of 4% 1991 and 16% in 1992, Maho AG faced a decrease in annual turnover of 38% caused, *inter alia*, by a drastic investment decline in West German industries, particularly in car manufacturing.

Many different reasons account for this collapse. First, the domestic boom after unification of the two Germanies offset the recession in the world market. Secondly, investments in the former GDR after 1989 were much lower than expected and, furthermore, the West German boom collapsed in 1992. At the same time, the considerable increase in government debts and the anti-inflatory policy of the Federal Reserve Bank caused increasing interest rates, thus bringing about the decrease in investment in most sectors. Hence, the most important market area for both machine-tool firms was hit. But thirdly, increasing interest rates had effects comparable to revaluation and, thus, affected the competitiveness of both firms in their main west European markets. In order to maintain the European currency system, France brought its interest rates into line with Germany, thus causing a domestic recession; Italy and the UK drastically devalued in September 1992. Consequently, German machine tools were no longer competitive on both markets. Fourthly, contrary to optimistic expectations, economic and political turbulence in the CIS resulted in seriously dwindling demand; and, fifthly, both firms had far too optimistically expanded capacities and neglected decisions for rationalization. In consequence, Maho AG faced an enormous financial burden which has not been mitigated by using leasing for financing recent investments in the new plants of Kempten and Gross-Umstadt.

The consequences for both firms were extremely serious. For the first time in its history, Maho AG made huge losses of DM159 million in 1991–2. Gildemeister AG lost some DM70 million in 1992 and stopped its dividend, probably again for long time. Both firms now tried to get the crisis under control via contraction of production and co-operation in international distribution.

Contraction means concentration of both firms on their core products and a reduction of employment via rationalizing and selling or closing down plants. The spatial division of labour was reduced. Maho AG, reducing worldwide employment by 1,132 (to 2,327 in 1992), sold the software department in 1991, closed the new American plant, sold spark-erosion machine-tool plants in Switzerland and Gross-Umstadt (where, in consequence, production was closed down by the acquiring firm) and relocated assembly in 1992 from Emstal (complete closure) to the Thuringian Seebach. In the same year, the joint venture in Budapest, Hungary, ceased. Werner Babel lost his enterprise. First, he had to abandon a part of his shares of capital and to give up the chair of the executive board, but changed into the supervisory board; then, at the end of 1992, he lost his function, too, as a result of the reduction of the firm's nominal capital. The banks, among them the leading German bank, Deutsche Bank AG, appointed a specialist in reorganization, but did not yet solve the problem of the enormous losses caused by the Italian subsidiary and the new plant at Kempten, where capacities were underutilized by 60%.

Gildemeister also closed down a plant in 1991 (Max Müller in Hannover), relocated its production to the main lathe-producing subsidiary at Sennestadt and sold production of large machines. Furthermore, some diversifying production had been hived off: in 1992, a share of Witzig & Frank had been sold and in 1993 Gildemeister AG put control production in Hannover into a new joint venture with the major shareholder Grundig AG, which was a major competitor in controls production. In 1994, finally, the foundry in Mölln was sold in a management buy-out. Obviously, Gildemeister AG followed a holding company's strategy in not giving up completely some activities but in trying to join with other firms.

Contraction has been supplemented by new forms of co-operation with other large German machine-tool firms, particularly in foreign distribution. In February 1993, the lathe producer Gildemeister AG joined the milling-machine producer Deckel AG in the Deckel-Gildemeister Vertriebs GmbH for the reorganization of its domestic and international distribution network. A short intermezzo of co-operation between the milling-machine producer Maho and the drilling-machine producer Traub was concluded two months later when it came to negotiations among the major shareholders and the banks involved to merge both milling-machine producers Deckel and Maho. Co-operation between Maho AG and Traub AG would not have solved the problem of enormous overcapacities in the new Kempten plant, resulting in a continuous high-cost burden (Fischer, 1993). At the end of 1993, the Deckel/Maho merger was confirmed.

But this did not solve the problem of extreme overcapacities and high debt burden. In fact, settlement agreements in early 1994 failed and Deckel/Maho went into bankruptcy in June, with a total debt burden of DM530 million and further annual losses of DM140 million – compared to an annual turnover of DM340 million in 1993–4. In order to save the core facilities, decisions were made to close down the Kempten plant (ex-Maho) and the Munich plant (ex-Deckel) and to make an attempt to merge the remaining Seebach, Pfronten (ex-Maho) and Geretsried (ex-Deckel) plants, keeping together 1,000 workplaces, with another machine-tool firm.

This seemed to provide an opportunity for the creation of a larger corporation in the German machine-tool sector which would be better suited for global competition. As nearly all firms in the sector made losses in recent years, however, the building of larger organizations became a matter for the banks involved. For the moment, there were two competitive models of reorganization: integrating the rest of Deckel/Maho either into the newly emerging large machine-tool corporation around Traub, Heckert and Hermle, which was mainly backed up by Deutsche Bank, or into Gildemeister, whose major shareholder was WestLB (20%). Both corporations suffered from lack of capital, but Gildemeister profited from a bank which followed a clear industrial policy, from surety given by the state of Northrhine Westphalia and, finally, from the extant joint venture in distribution with Deckel. As a result, Gildemeister AG took over Deckel/Maho in 1994.

Although there was some overlap in the firms' foreign sales-agency networks, international distribution, which had become so costly owing to rising publicity, training and service expenditures, was strengthened in total. Gildemeister AG was strong on European markets, Deckel AG was mainly present in Japan, India, Iran and South America, and Maho AG had already entered southeast Asian markets. A truly international distribution network of Gildemeister AG thus recently emerged.

Largely reduced in capacities, partly released from debt burden from the past but disposing of a broad spectrum of different machine-tool products,

Gildemeister may have chances to survive and grow into the role of a global player. Capital, however, was still too scarce for the merger and internationalization and, consequently and once more in its life, Gildemeister looked for new capital at the stock exchange at the end of 1994. The crisis in the German machine-tool sector, however, had given rise to the emergence of some other large corporations owing to mergers, such as Traub and Bremer Vulkan. Market segments are no longer fragmented, as those firms now offer the total range of products. Hence, competition will increase even when expectancies of a new uprise in global markets are fulfilled. Gildemeister's position still continues to be precarious.

Conclusions

In the long history of both firms, the driving forces for internationalization have been weak, in spite of the high export rates in both firms, owing to the technologically driven strategies based on local competence and as a result of an important domestic market. The machine-tool sector gives a clear example of international competitiveness via geographical concentration, at least for some time, as has been pointed out by Porter (1990). The large number of domestic competitors in Germany, innovations stemming from related sectors, strong and challenging client sectors such as car manufacturing, and a particular kind of production factor both in the machine-tool sector and among clients, namely, the well qualified 'Facharbeiter' (skilled worker), enabled the firms to adapt to meet increasing technical requirements. Both firms constantly 'upgraded' their products into higher-value ones.

As far as they still produced low-value machine tools they tried to get access to particular markets such as the USSR. With high-value products, they increasingly became competitive on west European markets. In the long run, however, they moved into market niches which became increasingly narrow. In focusing on domestic production and the domestic market, but growing into a largely export-orientated firm at the same time, both firms went into what could be called an internationalization gap. Their exports increasingly became vulnerable owing to rising production costs in Germany, the rising value of products, but rising exchange rates in the German currency as well. The first steps towards internationalization of production by Maho followed a diversifying strategy: whereas high-value machine-tool production was pushed in Germany, production of lower-value machine tools for local markets was started in Italy and the USA in 1987. Neither firm reduced vertical integration of production considerably and tried to relocate parts production into low-wage countries, however. Instead, both expanded into new sectors in their domestic market in the search for further growth.

Given the fact that they grew up independently from medium size to large firms, they both faced restrictions in financial resources. Furthermore, these had to be split up into financial requirements for technical improvements and domestic growth and the establishment of an international distribution network. Both proved to become increasingly expensive. Thus the crisis on world markets at the end of the 1980s, in the domestic and east European markets in the early 1990s, only made it clear that both firms had come to a growth threshold.

The present process of restructuring resembles a ridge walk between safe-guarding the production home base of the firm and a fast internationalization in distribution in order to penetrate the global market. According to different observers, production costs and capacities in the German machine-tool sector have to be reduced, while safeguarding technological competence at the same time. Joint R & D centres, standardization of components production and out-sourcing of parts production to low-wage countries nearby, such as the Czech Republic, are suggested. Indeed, this is what Deckel AG had already started to do. Additionally, distribution on a global scale must be improved, particularly in large and fast-growing markets such as the USA and southeast Asia (Garbe, 1992; Fischer, 1993). For those sophisticated machine tools which are sold by the Gildemeister and Deckel/Maho merger, increasing de-mand for consultancy, training and services renders a presence in local markets absolutely necessary. As a conclusion, it was finally the general crisis which forced the firm to new efforts in internationalization. But still, then, produc-tion will largely remain embedded in its home base while Gildemeister will act globally both on the supply and sales side.

Note

1.   NEF stands for the technically progressive history of the firm. With the takeover of Heidenreich & Harbeck (H&H), Gildemeister had acquired a product called the NE machine tool (numerisch einspindlig, ie numerical one-spindle). Gildemeister, in coop-eration with the Japanese firm Fanuc, added a particular Fanuc computer steering device to it. This became the NEF machine tool which later became a multiple-spindle machine tool with universal steering device. As such, it is still a major product of the firm today.

4

SmithKline Beecham: global push and repositioning

Jeremy R. Howells

Introduction

In July 1989, SmithKline Beecham was created from the merger of SmithKline Beckman, based in Philadelphia in the USA, and Beecham, a UK company headquartered in London. Virtually overnight, although after a year-long series of negotiations, a new company emerged which was ranked third in global pharmaceutical sales revenues from the merging of two already significant players who were ranked eleventh (SmithKline) and twenty-second (Beecham), respectively, a year earlier. Although world shares of the drug market by individual companies are still low, with Merck & Co., the world leader, still only accounting for 4.5% of world sales, the merger between SmithKline Beckman and Beecham (and in the same year Bristol Myers and Squibb) set off speculation that times were changing. New 'mega' pharmaceutical companies were seen as emerging which would gradually set about dominating the formerly fragmented national pharmaceutical markets and set out on a strategy of global integration and advancement. Was size the only factor in the merger and, if so, what were its implications for the industry as a whole in terms of global development? The following discussion seeks to address this issue and investigate it within the wider context of the process of internationalization in the premerger companies and in its postmerger form.

The premerger years

SmithKline Beckman

SmithKline Beckman's origins date back to 1830, when a John Smith and a John Gilbert set up a drugstore in Philadelphia making pills and elixirs to their own formulae. In 1875 a Mahlun Kline joined the company, establishing its first pharmaceutical laboratory in 1893 (Liebenau, 1984, p. 334), followed in 1891 by the absorption of a drug wholesaler, French, Richards & Co. These additions gave rise to a new company name, Smith Kline & French (SK&F), a name which was carried under its pharmaceutical operations right up to the 1989 merger. The company was one of the few firms that had a proper analytical laboratory, but it did little in the way of original R & D. It was not until the interwar period, when sales had grown to around US$8–9 million (Swann, 1988, p. 22), that it began to take research more seriously, although even then it had only eight researchers with an annual budget of some US$70,000.

The interwar years also marked a period of embryonic overseas expansion. One of the first was a licensing agreement in 1927 with A.J. White, a small manufacturing chemist, which produced and distributed its goods in Britain. However, it was not until after the Second World War that overseas investment really emerged. Thus in 1956 A.J. White was acquired and, three years later, the UK operations were moved out of London and located at a new site in Welwyn Garden City. Thirteen years later, in 1969, a Belgian company, Recherche et Industrie Thérapeutiques (RIT), with two sites in Belgium, Genval and Rixensart was acquired. Meanwhile the UK became a key worldwide centre for SK&F in terms of research and production as well as a 'regional' headquarters base for Europe, Russia, Africa and parts of the British Commonwealth, with an administrative operation, SmithKline Offshore Ltd, located in the City of London. The Belgian operations also took on an expanded role within the company, becoming a lead venture for SK&F in research and production of vaccines and antibiotics both for human and animal consumption.

It was the late 1970s, however, that saw the major transformation of the company when, in 1976, Tagamet, an anti-ulcer drug discovered by James Black in the Welwyn Garden City research laboratories, was first launched on to the market. By 1979 sales had grown to US$450 million and, in 1983, when the drug was launched on to the major US market, Tagamet's sales had already approached US$1 billion and accounted for over half the company's profits. With such a strong cash flow the company tried to diversify by acquiring, in 1980, Allergan, an opthalmic company, and Beckman, a medical instruments company, in 1982. It also expanded its research activity, increasing R & D expenditure from US$99 million in 1978 to some US$424 million by 1987. Further global expansion was associated with these moves. For example, a new greenfield plant at Cork in Ireland was established to produce the main ingredient for Tagamet for the European and other markets. With the Allergan and Beckman acquisitions came two further plants in Ireland, located in the counties of Mayo and Galway. The company also used the cash to gain control of its joint venture in Japan, SmithKline and Fujisawa KK, from its partner Fujisawa. This international spread was reflected in the rapid growth in the overall number of employees from the late 1970s: from 21,893 employees in 1978 rising to 30,438 just five years later (1982) and on to 36,323 by 1987.

For a variety of reasons, however, SmithKline started to face a number of problems in the early 1980s. By 1983 Tagamet was competing with Glaxo's Zantac in the crucial anti-ulcer market. More particularly, by 1988 the sales of Tagamet had started to tail off and, critically, the company was faced with the loss of patent protection for the drug. Between 1987 and 1988 profits began to decline and the company had no new products in the immediate pipeline to meet the gap left by Tagamet. From a period of unhindered growth, dating back to the late 1970s, the company belatedly realized by 1988 that restructuring and cutbacks were required. A restructuring programme was announced, largely centred on its domestic operations, involving the write-down of assets, the closure of a plant in Philadelphia, with the loss of 800 jobs, and staff reductions in other areas amounting to further job losses of some 800 people. Overseas cutbacks were centred on the UK, where 125 R & D staff were made redundant via the closure of toxicology and pathology departments and another 180 administrative staff at the Welwyn site. Many analysts did not think these cuts went far enough.

Beecham: delayed expansion
Beecham had a similarly long history, dating back to 1842 when Thomas Beecham sold pills in Wigan. The business moved to St Helens in 1858, with a major factory being established there in 1887. The company concentrated on consumer drugs which could be purchased over the counter (OTC) from the pharmacist without a doctor's prescription. A major change in the company came in 1938. Beecham acquired another consumer drug and products firm, Macleans.

Shortly after the Second World War, in 1945, Beecham established research laboratories at Brockham Park (Lazell, 1975). For Beecham this was to be a significant departure, since it had undertaken little or no research before that date. More particularly, the research proved to be very successful. Thus in 1952 Beecham decided to get involved in penicillin research and production, and eventually by 1959 through its research efforts had discovered 200 new penicillins. With advice from Bristol Myers (under an agreement signed in 1959), it started production of penicillins in 1960, moving to a new purpose-built plant in Worthing in 1961. This was to be an important period for the company; in 1960 and 1961 respectively, it launched two major new products, Celbemin and Penbritin, the latter being a new broad-spectrum antibiotic. During the 1960s Beecham grew rapidly from £2.8 million worth of pharmaceutical sales in 1961 to £32.8 million by 1969. In 1970 a second factory was erected in Irvine and further factories in Piscataway (USA), Heppigives (Belgium) and Singapore were also built. Other penicillins followed with Orbenin in 1962 and Pyoben in 1967. In 1981 it launched a new generation penicillin, Augmentin, in the UK.

However, by the mid-1980s the company was coming under criticism for its heavy reliance on antibiotics, an increasingly mature and competitive therapeutic market, which accounted for approximately 80% of its pharmaceutical turnover. In addition it was seen to have a gap in its new-product pipeline which would not be filled until the 1990s. Nevertheless, Beecham underwent a major restructuring programme from 1986 onwards, involving numerous disposals and refocusing on its core activities: pharmaceuticals and consumer products. In addition, in 1988 it launched a major new (non-antibiotic) drug,

Eminase, to treat heart attacks, and Relifex, a medicine to treat inflammatory disease. Although sales fell slightly because of disposals over the latter half of the 1980s, its profits and net income continued to grow, whilst at the same time it had managed to reduce its debt ratio. Prospects looked increasingly good for Beecham.

The merger

In the year of 1988–9, the two companies faced contrasting scenarios. Beecham had an average profit margin level of up to 17.9%, whilst Smith-Kline's was 5.7% (Briggs, 1990, p. 13). Beecham was on an upward growth spiral whilst SmithKline was facing a downturn in its fortunes. Nevertheless, both companies felt that they were neither of sufficient size nor possessed adequate financial strength to compete in the global pharmaceutical market. Thus, as noted earlier, although leading drugs companies only hold a relatively small share of the world market (the top ten some 27%), there have been increasing pressures within the industry that have made life increasingly difficult for even medium to large-sized players.

A key area in this force for change has been R & D. In the pharmaceutical industry, as in other research-intensive industries, the task of R & D is becoming much harder. Increasingly, medical research is having to be directed to much more complex and ill-understood systems in the physiochemical processes which control the operation of the human body. As a result the rate of pharmaceutical innovation, as represented by the introduction of new chemical entities (NCEs) worldwide, has steadily dropped from a yearly average of 86.2 during the period 1961–5 to only 55.6 between 1980 and 1985 (Reis Arndt, 1987, p. 107).

The length of time needed to develop an innovation and the costs of undertaking R & D rose dramatically during the 1970s and 1980s, as the scale and complexity of research, safety, testing and validation requirement increased. Data collected by the Centre for Medicines Research indicate that development times for NCEs have increased from an average of 7.7 years in 1970 to some 12.8 years in 1990 (*Scrip.* 1993, p. 22). However, as development times lengthened, they in turn helped to reduce the lifespan of new drugs that are protected by patents. Thus, although patent cover for innovative new drugs is for twenty years from date of application, the effective patent life of a new drug has been steadily reduced to only eight years.

The increasing length and cost of product development, combined with shortening product lifespans, have put pressure on all firms in the industry and have, in turn, had ramifications for other functions within the firm, in particular *sales and marketing*. In order to amortize the high research costs as rapidly as possible (whilst still retaining their monopolistic position), firms have sought to launch their new products in as wide a geographical market area as possible – increasingly on a global market basis. For large firms this is via the development or extension of their multinational sales networks. In the pharmaceutical industry such pressures have been reflected in recent merger and acquisition activity, of which SmithKline Beecham has been a part. This activity was aimed at building up a stronger research base as well as at gaining a truly international sales and marketing network. Major merger acquisition activities in the late 1980s and early 1990s have included Monsanto and G.D. Searle, Eastman Kodak and Sterling, American Home Products and A.H. Robins, Bristol Myers and Squibb, Marion and Merrell Dow, Rhone Poulenc and Rorer.

Another factor encouraging mergers has been the opportunity for *cost and efficiency savings* in both administrative and manufacturing activities. In administration, this has involved cutbacks in clerical staff of up to 10–15%, generally excluding key sales and marketing personnel. In the context of costs, manufacturing costs typically represented only between 10 and 20% of total sales of the company and were not seen as a key function in terms of competitiveness at least in ethical pharmaceuticals (i.e. those drugs only prescribed by a doctor). Indeed, most major multinational companies have been encouraged to establish pharmaceutical plants in each individual national market to gain preferential pricing structures for their products. This, however, has led many plants to operate at levels well below maximum capacity. One estimate suggests capacity utilization levels in secondary[1] manufacturing operations rarely exceeds 55–60% in Europe (Polastro and Mellor, 1992, p. 39). This, together with the growing complexity of pharmaceutical manufacturing, in terms of increased range and numbers of product formulations, technological changes requiring 'one-use', bespoke equipment and ever-increasing environmental and regulatory standards, has meant that manufacturing costs are now around 20–5% of total sales value and are still rising (Byrne, 1993, p. 31).

There has been much discussion in the corporate literature of the relative benefits of size via merger and acquisition versus opportunities associated with collaboration and joint ventures with other companies. Both Beecham and Upjohn (Eminase) and SmithKline Beckman with Du Pont (Tagamet) had been involved in major comarketing deals. However, neither company, even given their competitive size, felt that it could remain competitive without full integration with another major company. On the announcement of the merger, many commentators and analysts remained sceptical of the benefits in terms of scale, joint synergies, efficiency and cost savings that were supposed to occur with the merger.

The merger has, however, proved remarkably successful, allowing the firm not only to achieve many of the benefits it expected but also to undertake more significant long-term restructuring. This is aside from the direct effects of the merger which allow it to be more in tune with its changing technical and economic environment. In R & D, its four main US research sites were reduced to one, and in the UK nine sites were reduced to seven, although no major job losses were announced and the company had a combined R & D workforce of some 5,000 (Figure 4.1). In 1992 it announced 150 redundancies in the UK, although overall R & D spending continued to grow strongly so

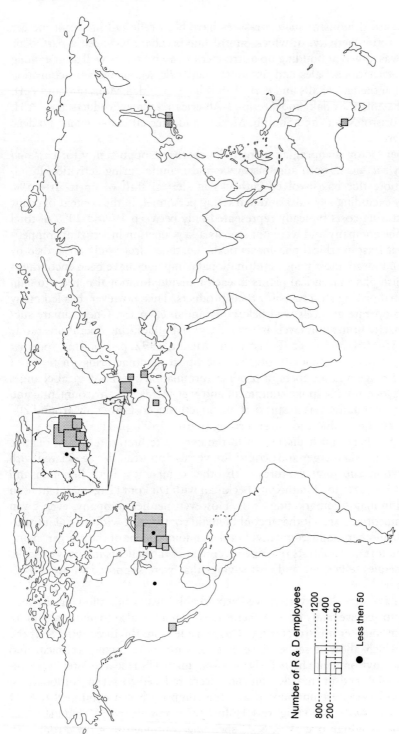

Figure 4.1   Global R & D network of SmithKline Beecham

Number of R & D employees

1200
800
400
200
50

● Less then 50

that the 1992 research budget amounted to £478 million (compared with a figure of £337 million in 1989). More recently, towards the end of 1993, the company announced further rationalization of its R & D facilities by purchasing a site in Harlow, Essex, adjacent to an existing SB facility, to consolidate most of its research facilities. By 1997 the firm intends to locate the bulk (over 1,000 employees) of its UK research staff at the new Harlow location, closing the Brockham Park, Great Burgh, Reigate and Worthing laboratories, but keeping, at least for a time, the Welwyn and Tonbridge research and technical establishments. Ultimately the nine UK laboratories may be reduced to a single facility.

In the context of sales and marketing, the emphasis was on merging the two sales teams as effectively and quickly as possible to allow cross-selling of the two companies' products, leading to the creation of a salesforce of some 6,000 people. In administrative and clerical activities, some 20 offices were designated for closure in 1989 as well as 25 distribution points. Overall employment fell by 3,200 between 1989 and 1990, and a total of some 60 operations were closed.

However, the merger allowed the company to take an opportunity for repositioning over and above the simple restructuring benefits that were associated with the mechanisms of the merger. These were as follows:

1. To undertake a strategic rethink and refocusing of the company's R & D, leading to the eventual targeting of five therapeutic research fields.
2. To take the rationalization of manufacturing much further, not just reducing initial overlap and inefficiency but to reposition the company through more substantial closures that would make the company significantly more cost efficient than its competitors.
3. To create a single operation to cover the European pharmaceutical market in preparation for the single European market.
4. To pay for financing of the deal and for restructuring costs, the new company was forced to sell many of its peripheral businesses. However, this allowed the company to become more focused, enabling it to gain global leadership in a selected range of key markets.

In the context of research targeting, the company initially announced a realignment of research activity into six fields, but in September 1992 it went further and decided that basic drug research should be focused on five: anti-infectives; cardiopulmonary; neuroscience; inflammation/tissue repair; and vaccines. Gastrointestinal research, which led to Tagamet, has now been dropped.

In manufacturing, SB has sought to take rationalization much further than the initial tidying up of duplicate plants. This was particularly true in the EU, where the eventual creation of a single European market in pharmaceuticals will eliminate the need for plants for each individual national market. At the merger in 1989, there were some 55 pharmaceutical plants; by 1991 these had been reduced to under 20, with the ultimate objective to have fewer than half this number again. The company will not only benefit from scale and capacity utilization in production via this concentration but it will also gain additional advantages via indirect benefits associated with, for example, lower pro rata overheads on the ever-increasing expenditure required for environmental compliance and cost savings derived from reductions on interplant product shipments (Polastro and Mellor, 1992, p. 39).

As with other companies that have sought to refocus on their core operations, the financial necessity of the merged company to sell off many of its peripheral activities gave it the impetus to consider its strategic core strengths. Before the merger, Beecham's activities covered not only pharmaceuticals but also a wide range of consumer products (42% of 1989 turnover) ranging from glue to toiletries and health foods. SmithKline Beckman, aside from its pharmaceutical operations, was more focused on scientific healthcare applications. However, it was still involved in quite a wide range of activities, including eye care/contact lenses (Allergan), scientific instruments (Beckman Instruments) and clinical laboratories. Soon after the merger, UHV Adhesives was sold for £97.5 million to HSG-Vermogensverwaltungs, North American Household Products to Bernickiser (for £66 million), and a series of food products (Ambrosia, Bovril and Marmite) went to CPC International (for £157 million). Cosmetics businesses, including Yardley and Lenthéric, were sold to Old Bond Street Corporation for £110 million. The company was restructured to four core businesses: ethical pharmaceuticals, consumer brands (OTC pharmaceuticals, personal care and health food/drinks), animal health and clinical laboratories.[2]

Global advance

Ongoing restructuring and repositioning has meant that, on the operational side, the company has continued to undergo dynamic change, which has not just been in terms of closure. Significant investments and acquisitions have continued to be made in its core sectors and geographical markets. In 1992 it announced the purchase of Sächsisches Serumwerk, based in Dresden in east Germany, from the Treuhandstalt to bolster its vaccine operations which are based in Belgium. In Japan it is nearing the completion of integrating its operations. It now has a combined salesforce of over 500 people and, in R & D, it is integrating its development and clinical trial activities based in Fuchu and Takasaki within its worldwide R & D operations.

However, although the merger was in part a response to creating a global presence, this has not meant that collaborations with other companies have been abandoned. In the context of licensing agreements it has signed two deals with Merck & Co., one for Merck to copromote its hepatitis vaccine in 1990 and in 1991 for SB to copromote Merck's anti-cholesterol drug, Zocor. Even for two drug companies ranked respectively first (Merck) and seventh (SB), the need to obtain speedy global marketing of key products still remains a major problem. Even more significantly, in the latter half of 1992 came the announcement that SB and Marion Merrell Dow were to create a joint venture in

OTC medicines. The new company is 90% controlled by SB and had pro-forma sales of £345.5 million in 1991. Both companies seek to market products in the new venture that are coming off-patent, such as Tagamet.

SB has also continued to develop collaborative links with other companies in the field of R & D. The company is collaborating with, for example, Hoffman-La Roche on PCR technology for virus detection; Genelabs technologies on hepatitis C and E; British Biotechnology on arithritis and cancer compounds; and IDEC Pharmaceuticals on monoclonal anti-bodies. In the context of academic collaboration, SB has links with Oxford University and Yale University on neuropsychobiology and vaccine development respectively.

The creation of strong international operations depends not only on extending and deepening the company's global network and linkage system, i.e. its *global configuration*, but also on being able to *co-ordinate* effectively these operations on a global basis (Howells and Wood, 1993). Many companies have sought to move away from a rigid centralized control system towards a structure which allows for differences in local capabilities and strategic importance in a more effective co-ordinated network (Doz, 1986; Bartlett and Ghoshal, 1989). As Håkanson (1990, p. 272) notes, the purpose of *co-ordination* in a transnational organization is twofold: 1) to avoid unnecessary duplication of effort; and 2) to ensure that available capabilities and locally developed initiatives are efficiently exploited. In addition, not only do companies have to concern themselves with co-ordinating their own internal functions but also with establishing and monitoring interorganizational linkages and partnerships (Håkansson, 1987).

Within SB, control and decision-making for the various sectors and functions had become in a locational sense more decentralized by the very nature of the merger. Thus, although the group headquarters is located in Brentford, London, co-ordination of pharmaceutical activities is split between Brentford and Philadelphia. Animal health activities are controlled from Philadelphia; vaccines operations from Belgium; clinical laboratories from Philadelphia; and pharmaceutical R & D from Great Burgh, UK, and Philadelphia. Moreover, the main motive for the merger was to achieve critical scale and to establish an effective global operational network. The company has therefore become a much more complex operation to co-ordinate. Nevertheless, the restructuring and reconfiguration of the combined operations have done much to simplify the basic structures of the firm and its four businesses. The rationalization has led to the company *concentrating* its operations on to fewer, larger sites but within the context of gaining global reach via a final and relative *dispersion* of units that cover the key markets of the world. A central issue here is that this geographical reconfiguration has taken place within the existing structures of two former separate companies, in turn relating back to their historical origins and development. Brentford, which became the group headquarters, was the original site for Macleans; the Philadelphia base, with its nineteenth-century origins, still remains a major functional base in terms of R & D and marketing for the company and is its North American headquarters site.

As noted earlier, the company has continued to extend its operations in scientific and product sectors or geographical markets where it considers itself to be underweight, providing a continuing dynamic to the company. Paradoxically, however, the *concentrated global dispersal* strategy of the company through its repositioning and restructuring of its existing facilities will make the geographical pattern of its overall operational framework more rigid. For the local economies where these remaining facilities are located, this will be advantageous. Those operations that remain will undoubtedly expand, taking on board functions and facilities shed from units that are closing or restructuring. In addition they will, through the concentrated nature of the capital expenditure programme, receive much richer flows of capital investment and be associated with ongoing physical, environmental and technical upgrades. This virtuous circle of increasing concentration of investment on to fewer, but larger, sites will also make the company increasingly reluctant to close these remaining facilities. Prospects for such establishments and their local communities look extremely good.

What this is likely to mean in the future is that the spatial dynamic of the company will become more static and potentially less flexible, at least in the economies where it is already well established. Closures will become a much more significant but rarer decision, since the 'sunk' costs associated within the plant and/or facilities will be much larger and of more direct significance to the company in terms of their operational role. Thus the closure of plant when the company still had six others manufacturing ingredients or products in the same product group is not the same as when it decides to close a plant leaving only one or two factories producing that particular product line.

The increasing static structure of the company in terms of its spatial structure may not be of great significance in a competitive sense, particularly when new investment is going into new markets in the far east, eastern Europe and South America. However, outside these markets, especially in Europe and North America, where the company is already well established, opportunities for attracting new investment are likely to be extremely limited.

Conclusion

The process of internationalization within the two companies and within the postmerger company has revealed a number of important points. The first is that the two firms, SmithKline and Beecham, historically displayed quite different internationalization processes. SmithKline's overseas expansion occurred earlier, in the 1950s, and was associated with initial takeover activity – 'brownfield' investment – which then led to subsequent investment in these acquired companies. By contrast, Beecham's overseas activity in pharmaceuticals did not effectively begin until the 1970s and was marked, at least initially, by direct 'greenfield' investment in new manufacturing facilities. None the less, much of the subsequent expansion abroad for both firms followed some kind of evolutionary process (however, see Buckley, 1988, pp. 136–7). SmithKline's main overseas acquisition targets were firms with which it already had well established links, whilst for Beecham new greenfield locations were chosen on the basis of existing trading and market knowledge. A production presence in such countries therefore marked the final stages of market servicing and establishment.

Much of the main expansion phase of overseas activities for both companies was partly an indirect outcome of their diversification away from their traditional core activities. SmithKline acquired substantial foreign operations with its takeover of Allergon and Beckman Instruments, whilst Beecham similarly gained substantial overseas activities with its household and consumer acquisitions. Diversification was therefore a process leading to further international growth.

However, just as diversification was associated with internationalization, moves to refocus on core sectors and products led to a strategic withdrawal or slimming down of overseas operations. The process of foreign divestment (Boddewynn, 1979) and 'deinternationalization' has been inadequately covered by studies investigating multinational companies (see also Doz, 1978). There is no inevitability about the continuance of globalization once a firm has embarked on the process (Welch and Luostarinen, 1988, p. 37). A great deal more work needs to be done in this area, as this process of strategic international withdrawal has had an important part to play in the shaping of SB's present global configuration.

Lastly, for companies which have truly global ambitions, such as SB, there has been a realization that to be effective, efficient and competitive, an appropriate global presence cannot be left as an *ad hoc* global sprawl. Global housekeeping is required on an ongoing basis; assets which no longer fit need to be disposed of. Rationalization and restructuring are needed to build an adequate global network, concentrated on fewer, larger sites. This global refocusing is necessary if multinational companies are to remain effective, but it may bring subsequent problems of reducing the flexibility of such corporations in the long term. As noted earlier, the sunk costs of any particular site become greater, and outright closure or withdrawal becomes much harder.

What are the more general issues facing SB in the future? In the context of manufacturing there has been increasing discussion about whether drug companies will still seek to be involved in primary bulk production of fine chemical and pharmaceutical intermediates or will instead move towards a more vertically disintegrated system of production, buying in these chemicals and intermediates from specialist producers. Although there are significant technical and economic factors weighted in favour of inhouse production, many companies, including SB, have become increasingly concerned to increase efficiency and reduce costs, particularly with mature products, and they have been increasingly willing to purchase in ingredients from contract manufacturers (Barber, 1993, p. 38).

In production, intracorporate trade linkages are still crucial. For key ingredients used to manufacture major revenue-earning drugs, most companies operate a dual-sourcing policy within the company so that the company has at least two plants that can manufacture the vital ingredients. If any problems occur in one plant, therefore, production can continue or be expanded in the other. Companies that have not operated such a policy, such as Fisons, can find themselves in major difficulties if a single source plant is required to shut down. Because of the sophistication of the products involved, many of the key supplies are only available from one or two sources worldwide and local linkages are unlikely, except for the more basic raw materials. The high value-to-weight ratios of pharmaceutical products makes global sourcing possible, whilst the high value-added nature of the final product enables and requires companies to retain comparatively high stock levels. Timing is becoming a factor, although even here the high value of the shipments means that they can bear high handling charges in recompense for speedy delivery. One pharmaceutical company in Ireland, for example, shipped a key pharmaceutical intermediate on Monday afternoon for delivery to a US plant on the Wednesday morning. For SB, though, which has undergone significant restructuring in this area, many of issues relating to manufacturing have been taken much further than most of its major competitors.

However, a key aspect of the development of the drugs industry is in the knowledge and information-intensive activities, more specifically in R & D and sales and marketing. There has been much discussion about the rise of new biotechnology firms (NBFs) ousting established pharmaceutical majors. However what has happened is that NBFs and pharmaceuticals are increasingly working together in a 'relational' context (Dore, 1986), in joint ventures, collaborative deals or through licensing agreements, as most NBFs lack the necessary financial and marketing strength to launch new products (Howells, 1992). Indeed, a number of key NBFs have been acquired. As we have seen, SB continues to establish such linkages with NBFs and to invest in such companies via its own venture capital company, SR One. At the same time it has sought to focus down and speed up its research operations, seeking to reduce costs, to increase the chances of producing successful new products and to shorten the development cycle of such operations. This is now increasingly managed and operated within a global context.

The crucial strategic question for the firm is how it will achieve an effective geographical co-ordination of these core activities in a timely and successful manner. The use of information and communication technologies represents a potential facilitating factor in global co-ordination, though in the crucial but largely non-programmed activities, such as R & D, its use in most companies has been limited (Howells, 1995). More significantly, companies such as SB will continue to experiment with and develop new managerial systems and techniques that allow individual businesses, operations and teams considerable autonomy and initiative but, in turn, within a framework of global interaction, co-ordination and support (empowerment). This will be the challenge of the twenty-first century for companies such as SmithKline Beecham.

Notes

1.   There are basically two types of manufacturing activity in pharmaceuticals: *primary production*, which involves the bulk manufacture of pharmaceutical ingredients, generally associated with capital intensive, process plant and equipment; and *secondary production*, comprising the process of transforming, via less complex physical operations, the active ingredients produced by the first stage and involving more labour-intensive technically less demanding operations of compounding, granulation, tabletting and packaging.

2.   The two companies Allergon Inc. and Beckman Instruments Inc. were floated off from SmithKline before the merger with Beecham.

5

Arthur Andersen: from national accountancy to international management consultancy firm

Frank Moulaert

Introduction

Until recently, Arthur Andersen (AA) was mainly known as an accounting, financial audit and tax advice firm. Today, management and information technology consulting activities represent more than 50% of the firm's turnover and personnel. The history of the company goes back to the eve of the First World War. In 1913, Arthur Andersen, a Norwegian immigrant, and Clarence Delany purchased the Audit Company of Illinois, located in Chicago. In 1918, they opened a second office in Milwaukee, Wisconsin. When in the same year, Clarence Delany resigned from the partnership, the name of the firm became Arthur Andersen and Co. Offices in New York and Washington were established in 1921.

When Arthur Andersen died in 1947, the firm's locations were still entirely on US territory. The first foreign offices were created in the 1950s, mainly in Europe. In 1962, a Japanese office was established in Tokyo, signalling the start of a rapid Asian expansion, partly through external growth, in which the merger with SGV in the Philippines in 1985 played a significant part. Today, AA is a transnational organization in the true sense of the term. In 1991, it had 307 offices in 67 countries as well as correspondent relationships with (other) national firms operating in 40 cities in 34 additional countries. In 1992, the number of offices had increased to 318, and the international coverage to 72 countries.

Historically speaking, AA's internationalization process can be divided into four phases:

- 1930s–early 1950s: development of accountancy and audit services to international clients on the basis of transnational correspondent relationships.
- Mid-1950s–mid-1980s: development of local practices instead of correspondent relationships; growing importance of management consulting services; establishment of a network of offices in European markets; the first direct investments in Asian markets (Japan).

- Mid-1980s–end of 1980s: growing importance of mergers and acquisitions; further penetration of Asian markets; growing importance of international human resources management.
- End of 1980s–present: opening of offices in capital cities of east and central European countries.

Originally, AA was mainly an accountancy, audit and tax service firm. Still, this does not mean that management consulting was completely absent from the firm's early history. In 1918, AA established an industrial engineering group which specialized in business consultancy. During the 1930s, it slowly developed its activities in management consultancy. In the 1940s, the firm profiled itself as a forerunner in machine-run accounting systems. It acquired knowledge in punch-card technology as a way to increase productivity in standard accounting practice (Rassam and Oates, 1991), and it became a forerunner in the use of magnetic tape as an information carrier. In the 1950s, it introduced the UNIVAC computer for applications in administrations (Iwabuchi, 1992). And during the 1980s, it became the world's leading information systems integration firm. Since 1989, AA Worldwide Organization has been divided into two business units: Arthur Andersen (accounting financial audit and tax advice) and Andersen Consulting (management consulting).[1] Today, its management consulting activities, predominantly centred around business and systems integration, earn more than half the firm's revenues.

AA: which type of business services?

The identification of the activities of firms operating in the field of business services is a well known, but unresolved, problem. The range of business services is so wide and the innovations in products and processes so rapid and massive (Gallouj, 1992), the tendency towards diversification by major service firms so large and the knowledge about the different markets so limited (Hindle, 1990) that only insiders have an accurate idea of the nature and reach of the different supply structures and market segments. This qualitative identity question is also visible in the classical methodological observation that services in general, and business services in particular, are hard to grasp statistically (Moulaert and Tödtling, 1995). In the case of AA, a hasty interpretation of diversification strategies could read like 'an accountancy firm shifting to software services and management consultancy'. In the statistics, AA would then be classified as an accountancy firm or as a professional software services firm. As an accountancy firm, in 1990, it ranked fourth at the world level (*International Accounting Bulletin*, 1991). And as a professional software services firm, it occupied the thirteenth position in western Europe (Input, 1990). But this aggregate or even professionally biased statistical appraisal would completely misrepresent the real picture of 'Arthur in serviceland'.

A statistical evaluation of the professional importance of AA can only be made by determining the status of the firm within each of the professions it operates within and for each of the markets where it plays a significant part. Take Andersen Consuting, which is our main focus in this chapter. Management consulting is a collective term referring to different consulting activities. Its definition is not clear cut. Following Tordoir (1992) and Greiner and Metzger (1983), 'management consulting [is] all advisory services provided to organizations by trained and qualified individuals who, in an independent and objective way, help the client organization to identify its management problems, to analyze them, to develop solutions or, if requested so, to implement them'. This broad definition has a particular interpretation for almost every important management consultancy firm. For AA, the only large Anglo-Saxon accountancy and financial audit firm which was involved in management consulting from the early days (the 1920s), it means business integration (see below), with a strong emphasis on integration of business and information systems, and on integration of office, factory systems and logistics networks (*Logistiques Magazine*, Issues 38, 47, 55). If one considers the markets for these activities only, knowing that they cover 80–90% of Andersen Consulting's turnover (US$2.8 billion in 1993), then we observe that AC is among the market leaders in the USA and Europe (Input Corporation).

Even with their limited reliability and contradictory outcomes, these statistical observations lift a tip of the AC strategy veil: AC is an innovator in professional services. And it accomplishes these innovations through its successful combination of new technology, new orgware, new management principles, new approaches to human resources. By applying the innovations it offers to its clients to its own organizational structure, AA has managed to develop a worldwide structure of offices realizing growth figures of 20–30% annually over the last ten years. Over this period, AA has become a global international service firm in the real sense of the term. Within the class of management consulting firms, it ranks first in the USA as well as worldwide. Of all US consultancy firms, it has also the largest turnover outside the USA (*Consultants News*).

Functional organization and internationalization of AA

Today, three levels exist in the spatial organization of the firm: the world or international, the regional or the continental, and the national or the local level. AA and Co. is organized as a worldwide co-operative organization, co-ordinated from Geneva and Chicago and consisting of two business units: Arthur Andersen (AA) and Andersen Consulting (AC). Both realize about half of their turnover outside the USA. A number of activities are co-ordinated at the world level, such as group corporate strategy (with respect to finance and investment, technology, human resources, etc.), R & D (consulting and training methodology, information and media technology, software development methodology) and training.

Operations are organized along two dividing lines: markets and products. Markets are generally defined in terms of client sectors: manufacturing products, financial services, administrative services and public sector. Products concern the types of services provided. Today, four service lines can be distinguished: strategic services, systems building/systems integration services, systems management services and change management services. In addition, AC also develops software. But there is a tendency towards multiproducts (global products) consisting of the complete range of services from all service lines.

Depending on the nature of the national or local market (sectoral composition of demand, technological and organizational maturity of the economic system, economic culture, density of the demand), local partnerships and offices will be organized differently. Also, support functions (technology, methodology, strategic analysis, training and selection, marketing) will be represented with different intensities at the different offices or shared between different offices and local markets. Four illustrations of 'local' markets should illustrate this.

A dense urban market, with a diversified industry mix, like the Chicago region, has no problems in maintaining specialized strategic analysis offices, with vast support functions. These offices are now principal suppliers of business integration services, with a strong emphasis on strategic consulting. The market can be subdivided into 10–12 client branches, and several high-technology products. Implementation of information systems plays an increasing part in the business, so that all stages in the systems integration process are provided.

In the Italian market, with systems integration needs for different types of manufacturing and service clients, located around different major cities of north and central Italy, AC displays an organizational pattern with spatial specialization, and transversal support functions. Main office locations are Milan (large manufacturing and service clients), Rome (serving the centre and the south) and Turin (automobile industry). Smaller offices are located in Treviso, Bologna and Verona, and there is a staff location in Florence. Offices have a large degree of autonomy, but for specific skills, partners and managers are temporarily moved from more important offices. With the exception of sectoral specificities, there is no regional specialization of offices. Northern locations are predominantly orientated towards manufacturing industry and its service support structure, while Rome depends more on the demand from the public administration sector. The local presence of offices or staff is important for cultural reasons. Not only SMEs, but also large enterprises want to talk to regionally rooted professionals. This is the case for a firm like Benetton, which wants to talk to a partner in the Veneto region.

AC France, with 1,350 staff and professionals nationwide, shows a locational pattern which reflects the main growth markets for business integration: Paris, as the all-round office, offering the general co-ordination and most of the support functions for the Strasbourg, Lyon and Toulouse offices. The Lyon office (about 100 professionals) is specialized in management consulting and information systems, serving the rapidly growing markets of the Rhone–Midi axis of the French economy (high-technology and high-level professional service industries). The rapidly growing, but also the most recent office, i.e. the Toulouse office (about 35 professionals), serves the large southwest region, with predominantly medium-sized enterprises in private services. In contrast to other technology-based industries, the access to the aerospatial industry market is difficult: this industry has a tradition of inhouse, large computer systems and shows resistance to the introduction of the more flexible distributed systems. An additional problem here is that the Toulouse office is specialized in the provision of management software development tools, and much less in its technical counterpart.

The Strasbourg office (30 professionals) relates to the expansion of the professional service sector in this urban region (European Parliament and Court, gateway to Germany) but also, be it modestly, to its growing role in high-technology industry. Still, the Strasbourg market for AA remains predominantly an audit and accountancy market. Most of the AC products delivered in France are of the business integration type, strategic in nature. Software development is not provided inhouse, but by two specialized wholly owned software subsidiaries. There is a growing tendency towards software development tools, involving a training of professionals and clients in the use of the AC software development tools.

In the Spanish market, AC meets little competition in the management consulting field. It has found a place in all market segments of this business, ranging from high-level strategic consulting to standard information technology services. Therefore, contrary to France, and for different reasons than in Italy, where the decentralized industrial structure explains the dispersed geography of offices, AA is present in most of the important cities in Spain.

The structure of AC demand in Japan is somewhat similar to that in France: the stress is on systems integration, with a strong tendency to become a business integrator in the near future. Software activities remain limited and are subcontracted to the AC Advanced Systems Center in the Philippines. Offices are confined to three locations (Tokyo, Nagoya, Osaka), all specialized in high-level consulting.

Although the structure of markets can be quite similar among countries (see, e.g. the west European national economies), consultancy practices can adopt different legal forms. In every country AA has one or more autonomous legal entities, usually partnerships. These legal entities correspond with the institutional specificities of each country. But they also usually represent the local market needs. In France, for example, AC and its different activities are covered by a number of legal entities which must be different from the international generic name: AA Informatique, AA et Compagnie, AA et Associés, AA Conseil en Organisation and, for the audit activities, Guy Barbier et Associés, Guy Barbier et autres. In GB, legal constraints are less stringent, and all activities are grouped under the heading, AA.

Between the level of the worldwide organization and the national partnerships, an intermediate 'regional' level was introduced in 1987–8. At

Table 5.1 Revenues and US/non-US professional personnel (AA consolidated)

	1975	1980	1985	1992
Revenue (US$million)				
USA	290.4	550.4	1,182.0	2,680.1
non-USA	95.9	255.1	391.9	2,897.2
Professional personnel (head count)				
USA	9,258	13,015	18,858	27,037
non-USA	1,124	6,921	10,944	35,097

Source: AA and Co.

present, the AA worldwide network is divided into three regions: the Americas, Europe, middle east, India and Africa and Asia/Pacific. Regions have not been created to take autonomy away from the national and local offices. In fact, regions have been created to improve communication between national operations, to define common marketing policies and to strengthen internationalization strategies. In this respect specialized market sector groups are created, which are managed by a partner (for example, the automobile group for the European region) and which follow market development for specific sectors and their business integration needs quite closely.

Another form of regional initiative which strengthens the internationalization dynamics is the collaboration between 'assisting' and 'assisted' countries. On the European scene, Scandinavia would support the Benelux, Germany would support Switzerland and Austria, and Great Britain would come to the

Table 5.2 Personnel (head count)

Professional personnel	1975	1980	1985	1992
Auditing and accounting	7,211	9,339	10,968	18,177
Consulting	1,790	3,642	7,150	22,495
Tax	1,679	2,646	4,078	6,729
Total	10,680	15,627	22,196	47,101
All personnel[a]				
Partners	844	1,170	1,630[b]	2,454
Other professionals	9,836	14,457	20,736	44,995
Administration	2,702	4,309	7,436	14,685
Total	13,382	19,936	29,802	62,134

Notes:
[a] Includes practice management personnel.
[b] Includes practice management partners.

Source: AA and Co.

Table 5.3   AC revenues by geographical area, 1992

	US $million	Share (%)
Americas		
USA	1,204.5	91.0
Canada	60.4	4.6
Latin America	7.3	0.5
Total	1,324.3	100.0
Europe, Middle east, Africa and India		
UK	324.4	30.4
Spain	204.0	19.1
France	141.5	13.3
Italy	132.0	12.4
Germany	86.3	8.1
Other Europe	154.4	14.5
Middle east, Africa and India	23.6	2.2
Total	1,066.2	100.0
Asia/Pacific		
Japan	88.3	45.9
Australia	67.0	34.8
Philippines	10.7	5.5
Other Pacific basin	26.5	13.8
Total	192.5	100.0

Source: AA Worldwide Organization, *Annual Report*, 1992.

help of Russia and Poland. This support usually takes the form of human resources. But for beginning markets, it can also mean a financial input, enabling the firm to attract the first important clients. The latter is quite important for establishing relationships with central and east European economies.

Tables 5.1, 5.2 and 5.3 provide some basic statistical information on AA and Co. (Tables 5.1 and 5.2) and on AC solely (Table 5.3). Table 5.1 illustrates the spectacular growth of revenues and professional personnel of AA and Co. in the period 1975–92. Table 5.2 shows the big leap ahead of consulting in the most recent period (1985–92). Table 5.3 provides an up-to-date summary of the geographical distribution of consulting revenues over the three regions and their main national markets. Several observations can be made from this summary. First, the USA still represents over 46% of AC's world market. Secondly, the UK is second in the list of most important national markets. Discounted in terms of population density and relative income, this market is even more important than the USA. Thirdly, the European region is almost as important as the American. Finally, AC's Japanese market is still not very developed.

Regional organization of AC outside the Americas

The Europe/Middle east/Africa and India region

This region is co-ordinated from the regional office located in London (1989). The activities are organized in three types of markets or industry groups: financial markets/industrial and consumer industries/government services. Various functional groups have been established at the regional level: software, technology and the three support services, finance, human resources and marketing. A partner is responsible for each of these groups. Partners who are industry group heads spend, in principle, 50% of their time on work outside their home-base country (Iwabuchi, 1992). In the fiscal year 1992, the region had a turnover of US$1,066.2 million (growth of 61% compared with 1990). The region's share in worldwide revenue is 41.3% (32% in 1989). At the end of August 1990, AC had 169 partners and 7,690 employees in the region (1970: 11 and 188, respectively; 1980: 40 and 671, respectively).

The French practice has offices in Paris, Lyon, Strasbourg and Toulouse. Total staffing, including office support personnel, is 1,350. At Sophia Antipolis, 120 people develop software tools and systems architecture, especially for France and the rest of Europe. The organization in France is divided into consulting services, data-processing/technical services and the software group. With approximately 500 professionals, the consulting services group is the largest such organization in France. The software group markets AC software development tools FOUNDATION and MAC–PAC. The data-processing and technical services group has about 600 staff members, and does a good deal of customized software production (Iwabuchi, 1992).[2] In 1990, 95% of turnover of AC France (FF768 million) was involved in systems engineering and other consultancy and systems implementation, and only 5% in software production. Of the clients, 40% came from manufacturing industry, 29% from banking and insurance, 12% from the public sector and 19% from other service activities. The UK alone represents one-quarter of the region's market. In 1990, turnover was US$173 million; in 1992 it had increased to US$324 million (+ 87%). The concentration on the client side of the market is very strong. In 1990, the ten most important clients accounted for over 60% of revenues. Growth is particularly strong in systems and change management services.

The Asia-Pacific region

This region is co-ordinated from Tokyo. Its functional organization is comparable with that of the European region. But, with the exception of Japan, the share of systems development and software production is larger than in Europe, where systems integration and business integration are the fastest growers. The first AA office in Japan opened in 1962. In 1966, consulting activities got off the ground. In 1991, AC in Japan already employed over 800

people. In the 1970s, consulting work was strongly concentrated in the manufacturing industry. By the 1980s, the financial sector (e.g. Mitsubishi Bank)
became an important client sector. At present, AC Japan is working hard to
become a business integrator in the strategic sense of the term. Collaboration
with Europe and with the Philippines (software production) plays an important part in this transition.

The Manila office of AC, the largest management information consulting firm
in the Philippines, had its origin as the consulting division of SyCip, Gorres,
Velayo & Company (SGV), which in 1985 joined the AA Worldwide Organization. SGV grew out of an accounting firm established in March 1946 by Washington SyCip, a US-trained accountant. SGV developed accounting activities
first, but as early as 1956 started providing management consulting services.
Later on, offices in Taiwan, Hong Kong, Malaysia, Indonesia, Thailand,
Singapore, South Korea, Brunei and elsewhere were opened. In the Philippines
alone, in 1990, SGV had 1,200 people. The AC Manila office consists of four
industry/functional groups: 1) the financial group serving the banking and insurance industries; 2) the product group for the manufacturing and distribution
industries; 3) the government services group; and 4) the advanced systems group.
Each group accounts for 20–30% of the office's revenue. The primary AC
service lines in the Philippines are information technology, change management
services and strategic services. About 400 people are assigned to work on IT-
related services, while a total of 300 work on the other service lines.

Given the very low labour cost for programming, AC has engaged in considerable offshore software development activities for foreign customers. For
this purpose, the Advanced Systems Center (ASC) was opened in Manila in
1986. Investments ranging from US$30 to US$40 million were made over the
last five years. There is a close collaboration for systems development between
the Philippines and Japan. Not only cost arguments but also shortage of human resources for systems development in Japan make the Japanese-based
offices appeal to the ASC in Manila. SGV also does consulting work for
Japanese subsidiaries in the Philippines, Indonesia and Malaysia.

Internationalization as an integral part of the 'one-firm concept' strategy

Today, the internationalization strategy is an integral part of the globalization
strategy of the AA organization (see Moulaert and Martinelli, 1992). For AA,
globalization means the application of the 'one-firm concept' in different types
of client markets, on a worldwide scale. It would be beyond reality to identify
AA as the only international management consulting firm applying a global
strategy. Still, AA as a forerunner in human resources management, in information technology and consultancy methodology, seems to be leading in comparison to other globalizing consultancies. Its innovative role in the previous
three domains, together with its flexible organizational structure and network-
ing, make AA the service firm to be observed closely by TNCs in various other
economic activities.

AA's 'one-firm concept' (Iwabuchi, 1992) is based on the development of human resources, consultancy methods and products and organizational flexibility which applies for the whole worldwide AA organization. This is only possible with an enterprise culture which by-passes the limits of interpersonal and intraprofessional networks. These types of networks are, for example, typical of the French management consultancies, based on common educational and professional backgrounds of consultants (Sauviat, 1992). The AA firm culture has no prior conditions *vis-à-vis* specificities of markets, professional careers and partnerships, as long as the organization's quality norms and methodological criteria are accepted by all agents involved in the consultancy process.

An organization-wide human resources policy
The firm's labour-market channels combine direct hiring from high-level universities with internal career tracks, going from staff members (years 1–3), senior (3–5), manager (5–9), associate partner (9–11) to finally becoming a partner. The training programme, which is common for all AA professionals, has been developed in accordance with this career track. As of the 1940s, AA has centralized its training programmes (Rassam and Oates, 1991) and, starting in the 1950s, programmers and computers specialists have been trained inhouse. Today, all AA personnel pass through the firm's 'professional university' of St-Charles located in the suburbs of Chicago. At this Center for Professional Education, graduates are trained to foster industry skills and management problem-solving capacities (Iwabuchi, 1992, p. 34). St-Charles was opened in 1971; it has a capacity to receive 1,500 students at all levels of the AC training trajectory. All the approximately 4,000 newly hired employees a year pass through the school.

Training at St-Charles basically includes the teaching and practising of the AC integral-consulting method foundation and its systems development methodology, Method 1. Foundation also contains its own training package and procedures. Training programmes and course contents are regularly reconsidered. Two elements, crucial to the reproduction of personnel operating in a global firm, are stressed in the most recent revision of the training strategy: 1) inclusion of all service lines into one programme and methodology; and 2) an increase in the share of decentralized training, i.e. at the local offices and in the local market practice. These only apparently contradictory developments must also guarantee that in the future 'the one firm' remains effective in 'the numerous markets'. As a consequence of the reinforced interaction between 'centralized' and 'grassroots training', to become a senior staff member, juniors have to pass through St-Charles many times in the first five years of their career. Later on, they return to the school for continuing education.

Another important aspect of the global human resources policy of AC, and which is common for the AA organization, is the constitution of project teams: the mobility of personnel from one project to another, and multiprofessional, multinational composition of teams with the required technical competencies and knowledge of national and local markets, are current practices within the AC organization.

A common, integrated methodology of service provision
The same concern to combine specificity of markets with generality of consulting culture and methodology, in the setting of a spectacularly growing network of partnerships, led AC to develop an integrated and codified consulting methodology. The Andersen consulting methodology has developed in accordance with the stages of development of consulting products themselves. According to AC, consulting services are now in their third generation (Iwabuchi, 1992, p. 65). After an early period of *ad hoc* consulting practice in the first half of the century, the first generation of consulting in which basic information systems development took place goes from the 1950s until the end of the 1970s. The second generation, that of systems integration, which aims at the development of integrated multifunctional client systems, runs through the 1980s; the third or the business integration era has just started. Business integration views a company as a single organization, with many components; still, consulting services must treat this organization and the many global and partial problems it poses as if they were one service or one 'service process'. This integrated approach to consulting services was already present in AA philosophy of systems integration used in the second half of the 1980s

	Strategic services
	Competitive and market
	  strategy
	Organization and change
	  strategy
	Business operation
	  strategy
	Information and
	  technology strategy	

Change management *services* Organization change Technology assimilation Knowledge transfer		*Systems integration* Systems planning Systems design Systems building Systems implementation

	Systems management
	Operations and network
	  services
	Facilities management
	  services
	Applications
	  management
	Back-up/recovery services	

Figure 5.1   Andersen Consulting Service lines (*Source*: Iwabuchi, 1992)

(Moulaert, Martinelli and Djellal, 1991). But it has only been marketed as 'business integration', with its four service lines, as of the early 1990s. The four business lines are shown in Figure 5.1. Although this figure is at the core of AC advertisement strategies, it is also helpful to understand some of the regional specialization of this consultancy.

Strategic services, based on strategic business analysis combined with AC's advanced knowledge of the organizational and strategic possibilities of information systems and technology, are of the utmost importance in maintaining the lead in west European and US markets. Systems integration is a general AC activity throughout the regions, with the exception of countries with a lower purchasing power, such as the Philippines or Indonesia, where the focus is more on systems construction and software, both for its development (for example, offshore software production in Manilla) and for its integration into information systems of client firms and institutions. Systems managements, which could be regarded as a higher-level rebirth of facility management, has seen a strong development in the USA, where AC aims at providing the whole chain of services to its client organizations, more than is the case in other regions. Still, systems management has a growing importance in Japan. Change management adopts particular forms according to the state of development of the market economies in which the consultants are active. In Japan, change management concerns technology assimilation and human resources management at the most advanced level. In east and central European countries, in contrast, emphasis is more on the transformation of elementary logistics and telecommunucations.

The integrated approach to consulting is supported by an integrated methodology, Method 1, covering all stages in the consulting process, going from strategic and functional analysis, through design and development (Moulaert, Martinelli and Djellal, 1990). Method 1 is in its eleventh version now. It was preceded by less integrated, less sophisticated methods, still in advance of those of most competitors. Progress in consulting methodologies has closely followed developments in the life cycle of consulting outlined above. The detailed description and manual of Method 1, version 8, including a training package for the AC professionals, provide the methodology with a worldwide utility. AC likes to say that any consultant from any country can step into any project in any country, and will immediately understand the 'language' that is spoken, the methodology that is used and the stage in the problem-solving process that is reached. This general accessibility of the consulting process is considered as another factor of globality in the Andersen system.

Organizational and spatial flexibility
The functional and spatial organization of consulting activities are determined by the geographical and sectoral character of the markets, as well as by the different forms of competition in the markets for accountancy and management consulting services. In this way, strong differences between countries in

the spatial organization of AA may occur (for example, compare Italy with France, or Japan with the Philippines).

At the national level, and depending on the scale of the markets, there is a trend away from the all-purpose shop approach towards sectoral and methodological specialization as a function of client needs in particular cities and regions. This professional flexibility or flexible specialization at the local level is possible not only because of the human resources policy and the methodological approach but also because of the flexibility of organization within the AA organization. It is guaranteed through the application of a number of principles which could be considered as proper of the adhocratic business structure (Mintzberg, 1988). Among these principles are the lightness of administration, the horizontality of communication and co-operation, and the creation or dismantling of business functions, task units or groups depending on the objectives of AA as a worldwide organization.

Markets sector groups, product groups and strategy groups can be organized at all three spatial levels. But such groups have no permanent administrative support structure. Most of the time, they are led by a partner on a part-time basis, have an international and changing membership and will be abolished or reorientated when the need arises.

Evidently, this flexibility of organization would not be possible without effective international strategic functions like R & D, training and methodology. Moreover, these functions themselves must be organized according to the rules of flexible organization. Having talked about training and methodology before, the flexibility of organization can be illustrated for R & D. R & D must obviously deal with the challenges of innovation for AC. These challenges concern consulting methodology, systems development tools, training methods and technology.

R & D can be divided into a generic component and an application-orientated component. The application-orientated component is largely focused towards the need of the local market. Therefore, it can best be left to the responsibility of the national offices. The generic part of the research must anticipate future developments in different local markets, but also in the global markets where this part of R & D is co-ordinated by the worldwide organization. Developments are followed and analysed in different transnational committees, the most important concerning technology, management, human resources and different market sectors. Such committees meet at a frequency of, say, three times a year. Their mission is to forecast developments in their domains for the next ten years. There is systematic exchange of information between committees, allowing the definition of interdisciplinary research priorities at the group level. Through a group-wide 'consulting' procedure, priorities are checked with partners throughout the world.

R & D is mainly performed at two locations: Chicago and Sophia Antipolis in the south of France. Chicago specializes in fundamental and generic research. Today, this means consulting methodology, image development systems, multimedia systems and artificial intelligence. Of course, methodological developments are also an issue for the training centre in St-Charles. Sophia Antipolis is more focused on 'applied' research: software development and open systems, but also telematics, a market for which France scores very highly worldwide. This organization of research in two main centres does not mean that there is no research taking place elsewhere. AC CIM centres, existing in most developed markets, are involved in research as well; and so are advanced consulting departments, involved with concrete problem solutions.

Therefore, although R & D is centralized in Chicago and Sophia Antipolis, the innovation process of AC pervades all aspects of the market and all its offices worldwide. This pervasiveness of organizational dynamics is part of the 'one-firm concept' strategy of AA and concerns most functions in the AA business. As argued before, this concept could never be realized without organizational flexibility, a light administrative structure, effective horizontal communication channels and a common business culture, based on a strong belief in technological and organizational progress and hard and competent work of all AC professionals in a multicultural environment. Such an entrepreneurial ideology can only be shared by all members of the organization, because of the uniform approach to methodology, training and professional organization. In this respect, AA is reluctant to pursue external growth strategies, and avoids acquisitions and hiring of professionals who have a long history with other firms, as much as market scarcity makes this possible.

Changing markets and the place of AA

AA, like no other international firm, manages to combine its business expertise with outstanding skills in the domain of information and communication. Its growth and globalization prospects are good. Of all its competitors, it has the most developed multinational supply structures. Its diversification strategy is supported by a coherent methodology, used by its offices worldwide. The uneven development of markets does not seem to hamper this uniform methodological approach; on the contrary, it produces important synergies in the chain of MC services ranging from strategic analysis to systems implementation and management, serving market segments which are sectorally, nationally and regionally differentiated. In several respects, AC marketing strategies follow the spatial life-cycle theory of markets quite well.

AC is a world leader in the domain of systems integration, both in services and manufacturing. But will it remain so? Will hardware producers, software and systems houses increase their part of the (still fast-growing) business integration cake? Will AC continue to valorize its integration of business and IT knowledge? Can its R & D capacities stand up against those of the large-scale hardware suppliers (IBM, AT&T, Alcatel) and systems houses (EDS, Cap Gemini Sogeti)? As the financial concentration movement in the sector moves on, the latter may become a problem. The participation in 1992 of Daimler Benz in Cap Sogeti, the US joint venture between Coopers and Lybrand and IBM (Merutus Consulting Services) in the very business integration market where AC is so strong, the creation of IBM Consulting (with offices in the USA, Germany, France, Japan, etc.), the purchase of or collaboration with software firms by a number of immediate competitors of AA (like KPMG, Ernst Young) and the diversification towards business integration of Cap Gemini Sogeti, Cap Group, all illustrate the tensions in the systems and business integration market which AC has to face.

Still, AC has a number of convincing comparative advantages *vis-à-vis* its (potential) competitors. For all these service and IT hardware firms, with a different sectoral origin, how to become both good systems integrators and management consultants in the short tun is not evident. Although their financial reserves are often superior to those of AA, their probability is lower. The problems of hardware producers like IBM are well known; but even flourishing systems houses like Cap Gemini Sogeti, which are supposed to know the IT consulting market better than IBM, performed poorly in 1992. Moreover, even if the financial basis for a continuing creative R & D endeavour is present, it can only succeed if sufficient know-how about business integration is available in combination with technological and organizational innovation. In this respect, AC scores quite well in comparison to large systems houses and hardware producers. Because of the absence of internal expertise, the latter depend on joint ventures and the hiring of professionals in the external labour market to develop their business integration skills. But experience shows the tremendous risk of external growth in this management consulting profession. External growth strategies usually suffer from the loss of business culture and of methodological and organizational clarity. In a business such as business integration, this is a real problem.

Therefore, for AC, one of the main challenges for the future is the dilemma of external versus internal growth. The absolute preference for internal growth, in order to preserve methodological uniformity and professional flexibility, may constrain the possibilities to penetrate even more national markets and to increase the financial basis of the worldwide organization. For certain markets, like the Philippines, external growth was the only real entry possibility. For other markets, and despite deregulation of certain professions, association with local offices and consultancies will remain the rule. The real success of further globalization will then be to reconcile the adoption of business culture and consulting methodology by all partners and professional staff with the particular economic and institutional requirements of office creation in promising, new, national markets. The lessons from the Japanese experience will be very instructive in this respect.

Acknowledgements

Information for this chapter was obtained from several interviews with J.C. Guez, partner AC France (interviewers: F. Catrice, F. Djellal, J. Gadrey, F. Moulaert), St L. Cornelison and E.F. Lakes, AA Chicago (interviewer: J. Gadrey), Dr Sinicorni and Dr Ambrossini, AA Italy (interviewer:

F. Martinelli), as well as from data provided by the AA Chicago office and maps by the Paris office. I am indebted to J.C. Guez and Flavia Martinelli for their comments on this chapter and to Faridah Djellal for her research assistance.

Notes

1   There are several reasons for this division: deontological and ethical considerations, tensions between consultants and accountants, different market perspectives for different service lines and, perhaps most important, the need to provide the firm's fastest-growing business, i.e. management consulting, with a clear identity *vis-à-vis* the 'accountant profile'. For reasons of deontology and/or regulation of the profession, client markets only partly overlap. In the USA, the UK and Italy, AA and Co. refuses clients in one discipline, because it already serves them in the other. In France, the segmentation of markets is extreme. Only 10% of the consulting clients are also audit firms (in the USA, this percentage is estimated at 50–60%). Data 1987.

2   In 1990 it was considered as France's second-largest software house.

6

Thomson Consumer Electronics: from national champion to global contender

Julien Savary

Introduction

Thomson Consumer Electronics (TCE) is a subsidiary of Thomson. TCE's growth has to be explained as one part of the overall strategy of Thomson group. Created in 1893, the Thomson private group grew by acquiring several French firms in the electric industry. In 1980 it was a diversified group, managing more than 16 different activities, mainly professional electronics, home appliance and consumer electronics, civilian telecommunications, medical systems, lighting, cables and armaments, but also several less important activities.

From 1982 to 1992 Thomson, which had been nationalized in 1982 by the French government, made important changes in its activities. The two main dates are 1983 and 1987. In 1983, Thomson disinvested from civilian telecommunications, which were taken by CGE within a national industrial plan (see Chapter 2 by Charles in this volume). In 1987, Thomson sold its medical systems business (Compagnie Générale de Radiologie) to General Electric (USA), and bought from the same group its American consumer electronics business, RCA, ranked number one in the US TV market. But the movement of acquisitions and divestitures was a continuous and strong one. Other divestments included lamps, postal equipment, copper wire, freezing equipment, microcomputers and specialized activities in defence electronics.

Within ten years Thomson managed a complete shift from nearly 22 activities in 1982 to three major activities, run by three subsidiaries in 1991: 1) defence electronics, with Thomson CSF, 48% of revenue; 2) consumer electronics, with TCE, 45% of revenue; and 3) home appliances, with Thomson Electroménager, 7% of revenue. One support activity, electronic components, is managed within a joint venture, but Thomson produces itself some specialized components for defence systems. Some analysts regard this choice of non-integration in components and computer industries to be risky, and to be weakening TCE, because the consumer electronics industry uses more and more chips and software. In 1993 this specialization process increased, as Thomson finally sold its home appliance subsidiary, Thomson Electroménager, to the Italian group, Elfi. The intention here was to reduce the group's high-level indebtedness, incurred following heavy losses in consumer electronics.

This focusing of activities corresponds to a clear strategic choice: to concentrate Thomson investments on activities in which the group can be a world leader. TCE is today ranked fourth in the world consumer-electronics industry, and Thomson CSF is ranked second in the world defence-electronics industry. That choice applies within the defence electronics activities where Thomson tries to be a dominant player in every product segment (first rank for air-traffic control and ground-air defence systems, second for battlefield detection, third for undersea activities).

In 1980, Thomson was mainly a French-based group. Its international sales were 45.5% of total sales. However, 31.6% of total sales were direct exports from France, while only 13.8% were products manufactured in foreign subsidiaries. Telecommunications and defence electronics were mostly exporting activities. The consumer electronics business had just begun its internationalization and the German and Singapore subsidiaries accounted for some 30% of the total Thomson employees in that business. The medical systems division was the sole truly multinational activity, with Compagnie Générale de Radiologie manufacturing abroad more than 57% of its total production. By 1991, Thomson had improved its total internationalization, though its most multinational activity, medical systems business, has been sold. Today international sales are 70% of the total sales, and quite half of these overall sales are manufactured in foreign subsidiaries (see Table 6.1). These sales are mainly made in west Europe: France 31%, other west European countries 26%, North America 25%, middle east 10%. The far east accounts for only 3% of total sales.

As Table 6.2 shows, rates of internationalization are very different between the three activities. Defence electronics are mainly export activities, but foreign manufacturing does represent about 18% of the total, because Thomson has acquired companies in Europe and North America. Consumer electronics is a highly internationalized activity, with both foreign markets and foreign production representing 90% of the total. Home appliance production is a French-based activity, with few exports and no foreign manufacturing (but agreements with European firms).

The numerous changes in Thomson's activities between 1980 and 1992 have often been related to French national industrial policy, because Thomson was

Table 6.1 Internationalization of Thomson group, 1974–91

	International sales as a share of total group sales	Employees in foreign subsidiaries as a share of total group employment
1974	34.1	14.4
1982	45.0	15.4
1991	68.6	54.3

Source: Thomson *Annual Reports* and author's estimates.

Table 6.2   Internationalization of Thomson by product group, 1991

	International sales as a share of total group sales	Employees in foreign subsidiaries as a share of total group employment
Defence systems and electronics	58.0	18.4
Consumer electronics	89.1	90.2
Home appliances	n.a.	1.6

Source: Thomson *Annual Reports*.

nationalized in 1982 by the socialist government. The French government decided to sell the profitable telecommunications operations to CGE. It also required Thomson to invest in electronics components until 1987, and then accepted the creation of a joint venture between Thomson and the Italian company, SGS. Since 1980, the French government has also sustained Thomson's efforts and investments in consumer electronics and provided funds to help Thomson to fight against the Japanese leaders. A. Gomez, CEO of Thomson, says: 'State ownership provided Thomson with the funds it needed for its come-back. It was what allowed us to move up into the first division of consumer electronics companies by acquiring General Electric's GE/RCA consumer electronics business. Backing that required a very brave, very long term investor' (interview in McCormick and Stone, 1990).

The strategic choice of focusing Thomson on two activities, defence electronics and consumer electronics, reflects both a historical trend and a new choice. With its subsidiary, Thomson CSF, defence electronics always played a central role in Thomson: it is an activity focused on government-related markets in France and abroad, receiving state grants for R & D programmes, and it provides good margins and profits. But, consumer electronics appears far from Thomson's corporate culture: it is a risky activity, implying important investment, with low profits or losses. It is developed in competitive markets, and marketing innovation is as important as purely technological innovation. For Thomson, investing in consumer electronics was therefore a new choice, strongly sustained by the French government.

The national and international growth of TCE is clearly related to the strategic choices of the Thomson group and of the French government. But the *specific* patterns of TCE's internationalization depend on changes in the driving forces of internationalization within consumer electronics. In the following discussion, a distinction is made between three 'growth eras' in Thomson's corporate evolution.

The French era: creating a French leader

Until 1970–3, Thomson's growth in consumer electronics was important, but limited to its French home market. Indeed, from the 1950s the market demand for consumer electronic products exploded. Its continuous growth was based on the launching of new innovative products. In the 1920s was the gramophone. Next in the 1930s came the radio. After the Second World War in the 1950s came black-and-white television (60% of total market in 1960, a few percent today). Then came colour television (1960s), followed by hi-fi equipment (1970s). In that industry the creation and launching of new products have played a major role in competition. But the concentration of French, European and world industry remained low as every national competitor grew mainly inside its own protected national market. In this typically multidomestic industry, the general strategies run by competitors were centred on domestic growth and, for the most innovative groups, on international licensing. For instance, the American group RCA, which discovered colour TV, signed several licensing agreements all round the world.

The Thomson group was internationalized from the beginning. Indeed, in 1893 some private French managers set up the Compagnie Française Thomson-Houston (CFTH) in order to develop in France the patents of Thomson Houston Electric Corp., USA. This is the origin of the Thomson group, which became independent and grew by acquiring several French firms:

- In 1929, CFTH took over the French company, Etablissements Ducretet, manufacturer of radio sets ('postes de TSF'), which was the starting point of Thomson's business in radio and TV.
- In 1936, CFTH took over the French company, Etablissements Kraemer, which became its first activity in broadcast equipment and further in professional equipment activities.
- After the Second World War, Thomson consumer-electronics production developed strongly. In 1959, CFTH became one of the main French radio and TV manufacturers, through an agreement with the French company, Pathé-Marconi.
- In 1966, the merger between CFTH and Hotchkiss-Brandt created the new parent company of the group: Thomson-Brandt, in which consumer electronics activities were managed until 1978, when the specialized consumer electronics subsidiary TCE was founded.
- In 1968, Thomson acquired the French company CSF (Compagnie Générale de TSF), which had itself developed since 1918 in professional electronics and particularly in radio transmissions.

Before 1970–3, therefore, Thomson's strategy in consumer electronics had been growth in its home market. It was very successful. In the 1970s, Thomson became the only French manufacturer of radio and TV. But as the colour TV market was growing fast, Thomson had a gap in colour TV technology. In 1965 it bought the RCA patent for manufacturing TV tubes in Europe. But until 1971 it had produced only 60,000 colour TVs. This explains the future agreement strategy of Thomson, implemented during the European era.

At the beginning of the 1970s, Thomson was a French manufacturer of consumer electronics products, with significant market shares in the French

Table 6.3   Thomson market share in selected consumer durables, France and Europe, 1974

Product	Market share in France (%)	Rank in European market
Washing machines	50	1
Refrigerators	45	4
Dishwashers	38	
Freezers	20	
Televisions	33	
Television tubes	low	2

Source: *Usine Nouvelle*, author.

market, but few sales in the rest of Europe and no sales or production in North America and Asia. Thomson was a domestic non-internationalized competitor, which in 1974 held 33% of the French TV market and 22% of the European colour TV tubes market, through its joint venture, Vidéocolor (see Table 6.3). Before 1974, Thomson's international sales in consumer durables accounted for less than 10% of total sales in that product segment, and the firm had no foreign manufacturing subsidiaries in consumer electronics.

The European era: reaching efficient scale

Since 1970 competition has increased through strong innovations and the launching of new products: hi-fi equipment in the 1970s, followed by the videocassette recorder (VCR) in the 1980s. For these new products, as for the colour TV whose market expanded, the competition quickly became price sensitive. All products followed the stages described by product life-cycle analysis, and more precisely by the international product life-cycle theory (see Vernon, 1966). Each new product allows the innovative firm to sell at good prices and high margins during the few years of the first launching period. Quickly, the growth of demand and the entry of imitators leads to mass production and a price war during the following growth and maturity periods. Then the competition is brisk on cost (and price), and the only firms which are able to survive in the market are those selling quantities large enough to achieve scale economies, and those increasing manufacturing efficiency and relocating some manufacturing operations in low-wage countries in order to reduce costs. Indeed, all leading firms were, during the 1970s and the 1980s, moving part of their manufacturing capacity abroad to countries like Mexico, South Korea, Taiwan and, especially, Singapore, Malaysia, Thailand, Indonesia and China. These shifts of production involved low-skilled operations, while the more technological and skilled components remained in developed countries.

This innovation race implies huge R & D expenses, and that gives advantages to integrated groups producing electronics components and computers,

Table 6.4   Leading groups in world colour TV production, 1983

Rank	Group	Country	Annual production (million units)
1	Philips	The Netherlands	5.5
2	Matsushita	Japan	5.0
3	Sony	Japan	3.0
4	Hitachi	Japan	2.7
5	Toshiba	Japan	2.6
6	Sanyo	Japan	2.5
7	RCA	USA	2.3
8	Zenith	USA	2.3
9	Thomson	France	1.7
10	Grundig	Germany	1.7
11	Telefunken	Germany	0.7

Source: Eurostaf DAFSA 1988.

and to those spending the greatest amounts in R & D. Large sales volumes facilitate both R & D investments and scale economies, and appear as a necessary strategic aim for all companies. They expand at home and in foreign markets. International competition also increased in the 1970s and the 1980s because reduced trade barriers opened the market to new Japanese competitors. Furthermore, when national protectionist policies remain, the foreign competitors make direct investments, as do more and more the Japanese groups in the USA and in Europe. During the period the Japanese groups became the dominant players in consumer electronics at a worldwide level. Indeed, since 1980 the Japanese groups have been the world leaders in the colour TV market, which still represents the main product segment (see Table 6.4).

In the 1970s and the 1980s, innovation, international trade and foreign direct investments changed the consumer electronics industry from a multi-domestic industry, divided between several protected national markets, to a global industry, with worldwide products and competition. The European integration process created, in the same period, a unified market. This European market has been partly protected from Asian imports by quotas and tariffs. That led the main Japanese and Korean firms to establish manufacturing operations within the EU. The trend towards harmonization of European norms and standards allowed the development of pan-European customer segments and the standardization of products sold throughout EU countries. The opening up of that unified European market to imports and to direct foreign investment increased competition.

Between 1965 and 1979 Thomson managed a strategy of technological agreements in order to try to fill the gap in two major product areas. In 1965 it had bought the RCA patent for manufacturing TV tubes in Europe. In 1971 it created a joint venture with that American group RCA, which had invented the colour tube in the early 1950s. That joint subsidiary, Vidéocolor, established a TV tubes plant in Anagni (Italy) in 1972, and set up a second plant in Lyon (France) in 1976. In 1978, it was the second-largest European manufacturer with 22% of the market. In 1979, Thomson-Brandt and AEG Telefunken jointly acquired 58% of Vidéocolor's capital stake, and in 1981 Thomson became the sole owner. Today Thomson is able to develop new technologies in TV tubes, after this 'shrewd follower' strategy.[1] In 1979 Thomson also decided to learn how to produce VCRs through a licensing agreement and a joint venture with the Japanese company, JVC, called J2T. It created a plant for mechadesks in Tonnerre (France), and a plant for assembling VCRs in Berlin (Germany). That allowed Thomson later to develop its own inhouse production capacity.[2]

In an interview published in 1978, Jean Marie Fourier, General Director of Thomson-Brandt, explained the new international strategy of Thomson in consumer electronics (Fourier, 1978, p. 11): 'By becoming the only French manufacturer of radio and TV, Thomson first wanted to conquer an important share of the French market. That was the necessary basis to gain, later, a European position.' He also explained that Thomson would one day have to invest in North America – where half of the market is located – and may have to relocate some production in low-wages countries. He clearly reflected what would be the major internationalization strategy for Thomson during the following decade (1978–88): international acquisitions in Europe to reach efficient size which enable heavy expenses in R & D and low production costs through the effects of scale economies.[3]

Germany was the major country in which Thomson implemented its international strategy of acquisitions, because it was the biggest market in Europe and it had a fragmented industry. The German consumer electronics industry was divided into more than seven manufacturing companies, often with overcapacities, overemployment and negative financial results.[4] Indeed, several acquisitions were made, as follows:

- 1974: Thomson took over the TV activities of General Electric in Spain.
- 1977: Thomson bought a majority capital stake of Nordmende, third German TV producer.
- 1979: Thomson, through its joint venture Vidéocolor, took the control of the Telefunken TV tubes plant in Ulm, Germany (2,700 employees).
- 1980: Thomson bought from GTE Sylvania, USA, the German company Saba GmbH, which was producing TVs and VCRs and facing difficulties (5,300 employees in 1978; 2,500 employees in 1983).
- 1982: Thomson took over the last important European manufacturer of hi-fi products, the German company Dual, which had important losses (2,000 employees).
- 1982 (end year): Thomson decided to take the control of Grundig, the important family-owned German company, number one in colour TV with

21% of the German market. Even if the Grundig chairman agreed with that takeover, the federal office interdiction and the trade unions' opposition forbade an acquisition which would have enabled Thomson to grow faster in consumer electronics (finally in 1984 Philips took a 31% stake in Grundig's capital) (see Quatrepoint, 1984).

- 1983: as the group AEG-Telefunken was in receivership, Thomson bought a 75% capital stake in Telefunken Ferseh and Rundfunk GmbH and raised its participation to 100% in 1984. This German company was facing major difficulties and had already reduced its total labour force from 5,300 to 3,200 employees between 1981 and 1983.
- 1987: Thomson took control of the Ferguson consumer electronics business of Thorn EMI in the UK.

All these international acquisitions in Europe changed the total size of TCE and gave it a truly international scope, with sales and manufacturing spread throughout Europe. TCE international sales as a percentage of total sales rose step by step from 9% in 1974 to 63% in 1987. But in 1986–7 TCE had no presence in North America and only a small manufacturing base in Asia. It was still primarily a European group. However, in the 1980s Thomson began the restructuring of its European operations, and the relocating of low-cost production to Asia. Thomson's first Asian plant was established in 1975: European Standard Electronic (ESE) in Singapore produced components for radio and TV (and washing machines) for the French and German Thomson plants. later, in 1984–6, it ceased its French (Moulins plant) and German (Dual plants) production of hi-fi equipment, and shifted them to a new Malaysian plant.

The restructuring operations occurred mainly in Germany, which was the major country for Thomson investments. First, after having taken over Nordmende in 1977, Thomson restructured its operations. It closed four plants near Bremen, stopping the manufacturing of black-and-white TVs and audio products. The total labour force was reduced from 5,200 employees in 1977 to 2,000 employees in 1983. After having taken over Saba in 1980, Thomson closed its plant in Friedrichshafen (black-and-white TVs and hi-fi). In 1982, Thomson closed the former AEG Vidéocolor plant of TV tubes in Ulm, which had then 1,700 jobs. This choice was one aspect of a restructuring plan which also led Thomson to close the French plant in Lyon and to shift all the German and French tube production to the Italian plant in Anagni. That sudden and brutal closure continued to give Thomson a bad reputation as 'job-killer' in Germany. After having taken over Dual, with losses reaching 10% of its annual turnover, Thomson first restarted production in 1982 with 600 employees (among 2,000 former employees). Then it closed the hi-fi manufacturing facilities of Dual, and decided to serve all the European markets from its Asian plants. Meanwhile it also decided to stop its French production of hi-fi products in Moulins.

In TV production, Thomson specialized the plants of Nordmende, Saba and Telefunken. Small and medium TV production was stopped in Germany and shifted to the Asian subsidiaries. Investments were focused on the Celle plant (near Bremen), which became one of the two European assembly plants of large colour TVs, and on the Villingen plant for printed circuit boards. The total effects of these restructuring operations clearly appears in the employment figures. In 1983, Thomson was managing 8,379 employees within its German subsidiaries, and at the end of 1990 that number was reduced to 4,800 employees. In 1985, Thomson also decided to focus all its research activities for hi-fi, video and television on its Villingen laboratory by transferring the major R & D activities of Angers (France), with 100 employees, to Villingen. Germany is clearly today the leading area for the management of all worldwide activities of TCE. In the UK, after the takeover of Ferguson, a subsidiary of Thorn EMI, the group closed the J2T video plant in New Haven in April 1988. This closure was explained by the slackening of demand growth in the UK market, and by the existence of overcapacity in Europe.

After 1977 Thomson's strategy in consumer electronics changed. It had financial difficulties and made several technological mistakes, for example, missing the VCR and compact-disc technologies. International acquisitions in Europe and international agreements became the two main choices of the company. This led to conflicts with French industrial policy, which was becoming more and more interventionist after the left came into power in 1981 and the nationalization of Thomson in 1982. Between 1981 and 1985, the main interactions between Thomson and the French government included the following (see Eurostaf-DAFSA, 1988, pp. 130–3):

- In November 1981, the French government forbade Thomson's participation in the international agreement J3T among JVC, Thorn EMI, Telefunken and Thomson, which involved manufacturing VCRs in Germany, video disks in the UK and video cameras in France (see Collins and Doorley, 1992, p. 62).
- In 1982, Thomson had to discuss a 'plan contract' with the French government, including two strategic choices for consumer electronics: manufacturing hi-fi products in France and looking for a European partner.
- In October 1982, the French government decided to limit VCR imports. This 'Incident of Poitiers' restrained Thomson's imports of JVC products.
- In 1983, the French government helped Thomson to buy the German company Grundig to create a French-based European leader. After the failure of that acquisition, the French government gave its agreement to the acquisition of Telefunken,[5] and to the J2T agreement among JVC (Japan), Thorn EMI and Thomson to produce VCRs in Europe with the JVC technology.
- In 1986, a new conflict appeared about the location of the new J2T plant to assemble one million mechadesks of VCRs a year. The French government preferred Longwy in the depressed area of Lorraine; Thomson preferred Tonnerre, a former black-and-white TV site of the group, which was finally chosen.

• The French government also asked Thomson to produce hi-fi products in France in Moulins. But these manufacturing operations caused Thomson heavy losses. So they were stopped and shifted to Asian plants.

Finally, these six or seven years of important interaction between French government policy and Thomson's strategy had two main results. First, the French government orientated and supported the basic choice of staying and investing heavily in the consumer electronics industry during the 1980–90 period. It supported R & D expenses in video and TV products through capital increases and state grants, and the strategy of international acquisitions in Europe and the USA. Secondly, the French regulations slowed – but did not stop – the shift of hi-fi production to Asian plants. They also constrained the manufacturing of VCRs in Europe (at Tonnerre and Berlin) through a joint venture with a Japanese group, JVC.

The world era: towards globalization

Consumer electronics has been a global industry since the 1980s, with world products, rapid innovation, important international trade and foreign direct investments, and a Japanese domination. During the 1990s, changes in the industry's environment increased that global competition in a number of ways.

First, the worldwide demand for consumer electronics products is slackening, as consumers in the wealthier parts of the world already own very basic products and are growing older and choosier. In Japan, 99% of all households now have a colour television set, 80% a VCR, 61% a stereo system and 42% a CD player. The American and European markets are not far behind. And no product seems able, in the 1990s, to play the locomotive for the whole industry, as the VCR did in the 1980s. So the annual growth rates, which were of above 50% for many years of the 1960s and 1970s, are far lower. In that saturated market, good years now are measured more in terms of a 10–15% growth for the best firms. In 1990, the Japanese consumer electronics industry as a whole saw its output rise by 3.8%, and its forecast for 1991 was a mere 3%. In Europe, the market growth showed a negative trend of –6% in 1991, following annual rates of about 10%. Secondly, in recent years this sudden maturing of the markets increased the intensity of price competition, and accelerated the shifts of production towards low-cost countries.

Thirdly, companies are recently pushing many new products, from pocket-sized video cameras to digital tape recorders, satellite dishes and large-screen television sets. The trend is to use numerical sounds and images, as did the CD, launched by Sony and Philips in 1982, and as will do the digital audiotape (DAT) recorder. But today the industry is in an intermediate phase between products using analog technology and new products using digital technology, which would integrate several functions (sound, image, etc.), and consumer demand remains low. Fourthly, all groups are investing heavily in a new product which may allow a recovery in sales: the high-definition television

Table 6.5   Leading groups in world consumer electronics industry, 1990

Rank	Group	Country	Annual production (million units)
1	Matsushita	Japan	15.9
2	Sony	Japan	15.8
3	Philips-Grundig	The Netherlands	9.3
4	TCE	France	6.2
5	Hitachi	Japan	4.3
6	Toshiba	Japan	4.1

Source: TCE, 1991.

(HDTV). But that challenge needs very important R & D investments, which are very risky, because different standards for HDTV exist in America, Europe and Japan. Large size is thus more and more necessary to be able to incur such huge R & D expenses.

All these trends have led to increasing concentration in the consumer electronics industry. Thomson made several acquisitions. Philips bought a minority stake in Grundig in 1984. So three of the former eleven leading groups in the colour TV industry no longer exist today. The Japanese domination has increased, and two giants of consumer electronics, Matsushita and Sony, now tower above the rest of the industry (see Table 6.5). TCE has surged to the fourth rank. American groups no longer remain in the list, and today only Zenith appears as a significant indigenous manufacturer in the USA. In Germany, only two medium-sized independent producers remain. The major European groups are Philips, TCE and Nokia, a Finnish firm, which also reached that third rank through acquisitions.

In recent years this trend towards increased concentration has also reached the Japanese industry itself. JVC is 51% owned by Matsushita, Akaï had to be rescued by the Mitsubishi group, Sansui collapsed into Polly Peck's group and Aïwa is now little more than a subcontractor for Sony. Sanyo and Sony, which still remain today independent firms, are facing huge difficulties. Some analysts forecast that only three Japanese groups could survive in the long run, because they are able to generate operating profits that are 5% of consolidated sales: Matsushita, Sony and Sharp (*The Economist*, 13 April 1991).

Another trend is that vertical integration within an electronics group is obviously today a key to success for consumer electronics firms. The Japanese leaders are the most vertically integrated. Matsushita, for instance, buys two-thirds of its electronics components within the group subsidiaries, whereas TCE buys no more than 5% of its chips from its French–Italian joint venture, SGS-Thomson (*Les Echos*, 10 April 1991).

The deepening of European integration also has consequences for corporate strategies, which are increasingly integrating at a European level. So the non-

European groups which have invested in Europe, and the two European leaders, Philips and TCE, are increasingly integrating their European operations, specializing plants in order to reach economies of scale, and selling homogeneous products throughout the European market. Within Europe, national regulations are weakening, but the EU as a whole is playing a growing role in competition. It is helping Philips and Thomson to create a European standard for HDTV.

In 1987, Thomson acquired the consumer electronics activities of General Electric in the USA. GE/RCA had recently been created by the merger of General Electric's business with RCA. This important acquisition doubled the total size of TCE. TCE reached the second rank of world TV producers, and the first rank of TV tube producers, and it won 22.5% of the US TV market. The rate of international sales rose from 63% in 1987 to 79% in 1988, and TCE became able to compete within two of the three main world areas of the triad – Europe and North America. In the USA, General Electric had formerly restructured and cut down the workforce within RCA: between 1986 and 1988 the number of plants fell from 23 to 17 and the workforce from 36,000 to 30,000. Thomson continued to close down plants and restructure operations. In 1990 it managed only seven plants with 9,700 employees in the USA and Canada, and five plants with 6,900 employees in Mexico. The main factories are one TV assembly plant (3 million units a year), and two plants producing TV tubes.

Since 1975, Thomson has begun to relocate components and low-cost products manufacturing to far east-Asian countries. That policy had intensified in the late 1980s and the 1990s. Shifting production from Europe and the USA to developing countries, southeast Asian countries and Mexico has been a main strategic issue for TCE. All European operations of low-cost products, such as audio products, black-and-white TVs and small-screen colour TVs, have been shifted from west Europe to Asian countries, such as Singapore, Thailand and Malaysia, in order to attain cost competitiveness.

That huge shift was, in recent years, the only way for TCE to be able to continue to sell these products in Europe under its brands, and to offer all the range of consumer electronics products. Recent significant investments in Asia include the following:

- In 1989 a new low-cost TV manufacturing facility in Bangkok (Thailand) was completed for producing small-sized TVs for the world market, and in 1991 its capacity was increased to one million units a year.
- In 1989, the capital of IVP in Singapore was doubled. IVP is a joint venture with Toshiba, producing 500,000 VCRs in 1989.
- Also during 1989, audio-products plants in Malaysia expanded their production facilities for US products, and the business increased the number of assembly lines in the Shenzhen facility in China, which re-exports all its production of audio products. Another contract was signed with the Chinese authorities for the construction of a coil plant in Shenzhen.

- In 1991, TCE opened a new plant in Batam, Indonesia, to assemble TV components. In 1991, TCE's audio facility in Shenzen, China, doubled its size.
- In 1992 the Thailand TV plant was also the site for another important development, the introduction of the TX 80/81 chassis, a global product designed to maximize corporate synergies and economies of scale.

Today TCE manages more than 13 plants in Singapore, Thailand, Malaysia, Taiwan, Indonesia and China (and many in Mexico), with more than 18,100 employees, and five plants in Mexico with more than 7,700 employees.[6]

Since the early 1980s, important restructuring has been made within Europe to build a more integrated structure. Many low-cost activities have been shifted to Asia. Many plants were also shut down.[7] For the manufacturing operations which were maintained within Europe, that is to say for the production of colour TVs, production was shifted between European plants in order to create specialized plants. As the tube is the most technologically sophisticated part of a colour TV, representing around one-third value of the final product (McCormick and Stone, 1990, p. 130) and as important scale economies do exist, TCE has concentrated its production in a single plant, at Anagni near Rome. This location was initially chosen by the American group RCA in 1970 as one part of Vidéocolor, because the Italian government provided substantial grants and incentives to create jobs in this area of southern Italy. The relatively low level of wages in that region may also have played a role. In 1981, Thomson became the sole owner of Vidéocolor, which had three plants producing TV tubes in France (in Lyon, with about 1,000 employees), Germany (in Ulm, where 1,600 employees produced 600,000 tubes in 1981, in a plant with a production capacity of 1,200,000 tubes) and Italy (in Anagni, where 2,000 employees produced over one million tubes, and the plant had a production capacity of 1,500,000 tubes in 1981), but which at that time had a total production volume of only 2.5 million tubes a year.

In order to increase the volume of its production to three million TV tubes a year, Thomson then invested heavily in the Anagni plant which had a high technological capability and skilled workforce, and which was thus closest to the optimal size. This production volume of three million tubes today corresponds to the minimum technical efficient scale in this activity. During the 1980s, the two other TV tubes plants in Europe (at Ulm and at Lyon) were closed down. The Anagni plant consequently became a key element in the company's integrated system of European production.

This system implies both a specialization of plants by products, with one plant making VCRs (Berlin), two plants producing TVs (Angers in France and Celle in Germany, Tarancon producing only for the Spanish market), and a specialization along the value chain, by components, just one European plant making TV tubes in Italy, and seven manufacturing TV components. Of course, the Angers and Celle plants do not produce the same kind of TV: each plant specializes in certain sizes and brands of TV (TCE is responsible for six brands in Europe). This system is also based on plants which are of efficient size. That may imply that TCE sells outside the group the production volumes that cannot be used within its own products. For instance, the Anagni plant produces about 3.4 million TV tubes a year and this volume is probably close to the minimum efficient technical scale. The three TCE plants of Celle, Angers and Madrid use about 2.15 million units, and the difference – about 1.2 million units – is sold to non-TCE assembly plants of colour TVs in Europe, including some Japanese plants.

However, another trend is the production of world products which permits economies of scale in production and huge R & D expenditures. That trend begins with the production of components that are common for all production in North America and Europe. That process started in 1989: 'The year 1989 also saw an important step in global products concepts for TCE. An international chassis, the TX 80/81, produced in Thailand, was launched for introduction in markets around the world. It takes advantage of development, production, and distribution synergies of the world-wide TV Group' (1989 *Annual Report*, p. 15). That trend in world production, if it is to develop, will lead to a worldwide integration. This integration will be different from the present European one in medium and large-sized TVs.

The international organization of TCE's R & D is already integrated on a worldwide basis; it was built in the 1980s by the rationalization and co-ordination of the R & D centres in 17 countries (expensive duplications of research were eliminated). For instance, 'the concentration of technical means in Genlis-France has created an important centre of expertise in optical electronics and a world class centre for TCE research' (*ibid.*, p. 21). In 1985 Thomson had transferred the major R & D of its French laboratory in Angers to Villingen in Germany, which became the single world centre for research on video and television. The main R & D centres of TCE are located in Europe: in Villingen (Germany) where the headquarters for worldwide R & D with 600 to 700 researchers (audio, video, TV) are; in Hanover (Germany) with 60 people (numeric signals for audiovideo); and at Strasbourg (France) with 60 people (HDTV) transmission signals). In the USA, the GE and RCA centres are specialized on American specific standards and products (new TV, HDTV standards). They are located in Syracuse (audio and communications), Lancaster and Los Angeles. In Asia, the R & D centres, which are located close to the TCE plants, specialize in specific problems related to local production (small-screen TV, audio products, etc.). These R & D programmes in developing countries will not decrease. For instance in 1989, the new factory built by IVP in Singapore contained an R & D and engineering centre.

International marketing is also already integrated in two subsystems, an American one, with two brands, RCA and General Electric, mainly in the Americas and other countries, and a European one. Within Europe, TCE owns six brands: Ferguson (a British market brand), Saba, Nordmende and Telefunken, mainly in Germany but also elsewhere in Europe, and Thomson and Brandt, mainly in France but also elsewhere in Europe. TCE could, in the near future, reduce the number of its brands in Europe. But it will continue to spread European brands through European countries, because the European integration process is facilitating this global marketing. The European integration process is causing a reorganization of TCE's distribution networks in the EU, from a national to a regional orientation. Two reasons explain that necessary restructuring. First, the Europe of 1992 made standardized europroducts and eurobranding easier. Secondly, the concentration and the internationalization of independent distributors of TCE products imply that TCE's own sales network is also an international one.

International TCE management had already been globalized at a worldwide level. The TCE organization is based on worldwide product divisions: Television, Video (VCRs and camcorders), Audio and Communication (hi-fi, CD products, telephone products), Tubes and Display. As the trend is to globalize production on a worldwide basis, this product-driven structure is useful to co-ordinate plants, R & D centres and marketing (40 plants in 17 countries). TCE is also increasing the integration between its R & D centres and its plants (each R & D centre is already located within a major plant). In 1991, TCE is improving the integration between the design of its products and the semi-conductors they require. It created a joint venture between TCE and SGS-Thomson, and centralized the teams which were previously dispersed throughout the different divisions (*Annual Report*, 1991, p. 13).

In 1992, TCE decided to set up a common communication system, which will link TCE's major worldwide locations. The system will offer direct links for voice, fax and data between the company's principal sites. It will begin with an axis between Indianapolis (and, thereby, all the USA), Paris and Villingen. Afterwards other sites (Tokyo, Singapore, Hanover, Genlis, Anagni and Angers) will be linked. The lines will also carry data between TCE's local area networks, terminals and computers (*TCE World*, May 1992). This worldwide internal communication system is necessary to improve the efficiency of the management of such a global company, with several specialized and interdependent units spread throughout the world. This network will at the same time enable TCE to implement a more integrated global strategy.

Thomson today

Today international sales of TCE represent 90% of its total sales. TCE is ranked third in the world consumer electronics industry, first in North America and second in Europe. This is the result of a ten-year long international growth through acquisitions.

TCE is a highly multinationalized group, which is selling and manufacturing important volumes in the three main areas of the world economy: North America, Europe and Asia. In fact, TCE still remains a global group which is actually present in only two of the three triad areas. Indeed, TCE can be considered today as more a North American–European group, with strong manufacturing facilities in far eastern Asia, than a truly 'triad global competitor', with equal strengths in the three triad areas.

Indeed, international sales of TCE are focused in North America and Europe, which represent 92.5% of total sales. Conversely, an important share of world TCE production is manufactured in Asia. Employment in that area represents 39% of the company's total employment. By 1991 TCE was clearly managing an international division of labour: Asia is mainly a manufacturing basis for products which are exported to Europe and the Americas. Mexico plays a similar role of international sourcing. This international division of labour is related to the location of low-skilled tasks and labour-intensive components in low-cost countries, while the more technological and capital-intensive components and products are located in North America and Europe.

TCE is now a group which focuses on television products: TVs represent 63% of total TCE's sales, video products 20% and audio products 14%. TCE is today more focused on TVs than other competitors, like Sony, because TCE is weaker in video and audio products markets, in which it has been a follower. TCE is also a manufacturing group, because manufacturing operations employ 88% of total TCE employment. Manufacturing activities, managed inside the group, are very important for the overall profitability of TCE. This may explain – and be the result of – the shift to Asian plants of so much production.

The future division of labour

Today TCE operates a global strategy, as does Philips.[8] But the globalization of TCE's strategy and structure remains incomplete. Asia represents a main area for manufacturing (39% of total head count are located there) but only a weak area for sales (7.5% of total sales). To become a truly global competitor and fight against Japanese and far eastern groups within their own home markets, TCE decided to improve its investments in Asia and to increase its sales in that element of the triad.

A. Gomez said:

> TCE is global. We operate in all three parts of the triad. Our products are completely fungible. And they are no impediments to world-wide distribution. We must have an organization that can install and move the links of the business chain to any part of the world. Ten years ago, that meant moving assembly and production to low-cost areas such as Malaysia and Taiwan. Now it also means moving marketing and R & D to places like Singapore. Years from now, the wisest decision might be to bring production plants back to Europe and move the headquarters wherever the brightest, most hardworking people are.
> (Quoted in McCormick and Stone, 1990, p. 135)

In its industry survey, *The Economist* concludes: 'The best chance for America and Europe to compete with Japan is to compete in Japan' (13 April 1991). This is the way chosen by TCE.

East Europe is viewed by TCE as a future natural production base for west European manufacturers in consumer electronics. Today TCE has investment projects in Hungary and the Czech Republic, and a former TV plant project in the USSR. In June 1991, Vidéocolor, a French subsidiary of TCE, created a joint venture – Thomson-Polkolor – which will produce small colour TV tubes in Poland. This plant will be integrated within the European manufacturing system of TCE. It will reach the optimal size and become one of the three manufacturing sources of TCE for colour cathodic TV tubes in the world (see Savary, 1992b).

Thomson plans to increase the Thomson-Polkolor annual production volume from 700,000 to 3,000,000 tubes. This will be done progressively and with new production. In a first stage (July 1991), for a year maximum, the plant restarted and produced the former medium TV tubes of 22 inches for Polish firms. Then, in a second stage, the plan for 1992 was to transfer from Anagni to Piaseczno the production of a similar – but of better quality – medium TV tube, the 19V-20 inches. This tube will be sold in eastern markets (for the first-TV market). The third stage was planned to be the production of a new product within Vidéocolor plants, a small TV tube 13V-14inches. This tube will be produced in important volumes and sold in west European markets.[9] Indeed, in these countries the demand is growing quickly for small TVs which are second TV sets for the kitchen or the bedroom. Later, on a medium term, the production of the medium tube 51 FST could be transferred from Anagni to Poland, and this product could then be sold in east Europe where the demand for medium colour TVs could grow quickly. This new Polish plant will bring TCE four strategic advantages:

- The integration of Polkolor facilities within Thomson will increase the total production volume of TV tubes of Vidéocolor in Europe from 3.5 million to 6.5 million. That growth in size will give a competitive advantage to Thomson.
- Thomson-Polkolor will also allow Thomson to produce small TV tubes which were formerly imported to Europe from Korean competitors. That is important because that market segment is growing quickly. The low labour costs in Poland are planned to permit that production within Europe, at competitive costs compared to Korean products. 'Poland offers us the same costs as Thailand', says Bernard Varaut, Chairman of Thomson Polkolor (*Business Week*, 14 September 1992). Thomson-Polkolor will give Thomson a competitive basis of production of low-cost products sold in west Europe: that strategy corresponds to a production-orientated strategy.
- The control of Polkolor by Thomson is a means to prevent the increase of Korean competitors which would have been interested in controlling that plant within Europe. For Thomson, investing in Poland is a blow in an oligopoly rivalry game which is played on a worldwide level.
- Thomson-Polkolor also plans to produce important volumes of medium TV tubes for Polish and other east European markets. That is related to a more market-orientated strategy, even if low production costs are necessary to reach eastern consumers. The east European market in colour TVs is viewed

by TCE as a very fast-growing market, because 98% of the families own a TV, as in west Europe, but half of them possess only a black-and-white TV. Indeed, TCE has numerous investment projects to produce and assemble TVs in eastern countries.

Thomson investments in east Europe could increase in the near future, although a recent divestiture underlines the cost vulnerability of such investments. In 1991, TCE decided to close its VCR assembly plant located in Berlin, because the reunification process between West and East Germany was increasing wages and costs. That sudden and planned closure of the Berlin plant shows that TCE investments in east Europe are today cost driven, and therefore could be cancelled if their competitiveness was pulled down by wage increases.

Thomson has progressively obtained technology from its acquired firms and its partners. For example, in the 1970s Thomson made technological agreements with RCA (in TV tubes) and JVC (in VCRs), which allowed it to stay in the market. Indeed, these technological agreements were also developed in the 1980s, and they also took the form of simple commercial agreements. Yet the weakness of Thomson in technology is underlined in a recent industry survey:

> Thomson has been more aggressive in snapping up rivals than in developing its own engineering and pioneering new products. Unlike Philips, Thomson is a newcomer in VCR business. The video recorders it sells are Japanese. So are the DAT (digital audio tape) recorders that Thomson is planning to sell shortly. Its video disc players are supplied by Pioneer. The 8mm camcorders that Thomson sells in America as the RCA models are made by Hitachi. Thomson admits that it is unlikely to be in position to produce VCRs for high-definition broadcast before 1977. Industry pundits agree that Thomson has few chances of closing the gap with its Japanese rivals.
> (*The Economist*, 13 April 1991)

Today, another very risky challenge for TCE is the development of HDTV, which needs huge investments in product design, special semi-conductors chips and large screens. Indeed, Philips and Thomson are already conducing joint research on HDTV, and have received funds from EU programmes like Eureka, and indirectly through the protectionist EU rules: D2MAC Interim HDTV standards and imports quotas. But a new and more strategic co-operation between Philips and Thomson could be the next strategic choice for TCE: improve R & D co-operation, develop joint productions of TVs and related video products and undertake joint research and joint manufacturing in special semi-conductor chips for HDTV and other products.

Notes

1 'The picture tube accounts for about 30% of the cost of a TV. Less than 20 years ago, we did not know how to produce picture tubes. Now we are among the leaders. We had to learn how from RCA through a licensing agreement and a joint-venture that lasted most of the 1970s. Finally, by the end of that decade, we were autonomous. Now ten years later, we've launched a new movie-screen format tube called the 16/9. That represents an important step on the road to a high definition TV. Other companies are

manufacturing it too. But Thomson was the first to develop and produce it' (A. Gomez, Chairman and CEO of Thomson, interview in McCormick and Stone, 1990, p. 130).

2 'At the beginning of the 1980s we again started by distributing our competitors' products of VCRs. In fact, for years and years, all we heard was that we were people sticking labels on Japanese sets. But we had entered into technical agreements with JVC. Next we developed our own in-house production capacity. Now we have both a 50–50 venture with JVC in Berlin and a plant in Singapore where this year we will produce one million sets based on proprietary technology' (A. Gomez, Chairman and CEO of Thomson, interview in McCormick and Stone, 1990, p. 130; see also Collins and Doorley, 1992, p. 62).

3 In 1976, with about 500,000 TV sets assembled a year, Thomson was far from having an efficient size (in 1977 a BCG study of the British consumer electronics industry concluded that the Japanese superiority came from greater production volumes). The UK government then decided a national restructuring plan, aiming at reducing the number of TV plants from 16 to 6, and at increasing the average per plant annual production from 100,000 to 500,000 units (Eurostaf-DAFSA, 1988, p. 126).

4 'Seven important companies, Grundig, Telefunken, Philips, ITT, Nordmende, Saba and Blaupunkt, and six smaller firms were fighting for reaching critical size,' explains R. Kôberle, Director of Thomson-Brandt GmbH (*L'Expansion* 21 January 1983).

5 The acquisition of Telefunken gave Thomson a 33% stake in the plant which was assembling VCRs in Berlin (other owners: Thorn EMI and JVC). So in 1983, Thomson joined in the J3T agreement, and did what the French government had forbidden two years before.

6 Far east Asia is the main area where TCE invests, but it is not the only one. In the Mediterranean basin, it created two joint ventures in Turkey in 1989: one with Vestel, to produce TV tubes for local manufacturers, one with Telra, to produce TVs and VCRs. It also manages two TV-assembling plants in Morocco and in Tunisia. In Mexico the plant in Juarez produces TV chassis for US plants, the plant in Torreon produces yokes and the plant in Mexico City produces TV tubes. Finally, TCE sells TV kits for local assembling in numerous developing countries where direct imports are prohibited, for example, India and Pakistan.

7 In France (St Pierre Montlimart, Auxonne, Gray, Lons-Le-Saunier); Germany (Bremen, Sankt and Georgen; the total workforce fell between 1980 and 1990 from 17,000 to 4,800); Great Britain (Thorn EMI plant at Enfield closed in 1989, Gosport plant closed in 1991).

8 For twenty years Philips has been following an international strategy very similar to TCE's strategy. Philips has made many acquisitions in Europe and the USA. It has relocated several productions in east Asia, and is restructuring its European operations from a multidomestic structure to a more integrated one (see Dicken, 1992, p. 342).

9 That third stage had really started because, in 1992, TCE already was explaining: 'The Polish production will double in 1992 and will provide TCE with small low-cost TV tubes' (TCE *Annual Report*, June 1992).

7

Tootal: internationalization, corporate restructuring and 'hollowing out'

Jamie Peck and Peter Dicken

Introduction

In 1991 the textile giant Tootal closed its headquarters in Manchester. In the midst of the British recession, which had been gathering pace since early 1990, this may have seemed a comparatively minor incident. For Manchester, however, the event signified the end of an era: 'Cottonopolis' had lost its last major textiles headquarters. The city – in so many ways the paradigmatic industrial conurbation of the nineteenth century – had constructed its economy around cotton and textiles. With the closure of Tootal's Manchester headquarters, following the takeover of the company by London-based Coats Viyella, this link with the past was finally severed.

The significance of these events was arguably more symbolic than economic, however, for in some senses Tootal had already left Manchester a decade earlier. The company had begun to internationalize its operations in the 1960s: by the time of the Coats Viyella takeover, two-thirds of Tootal's workforce was located outside the UK and almost 90% of the company's trading profit originated from overseas, whilst its traditional production base in the north west of England had been run down to a fraction of its former size. By 1990–1, Tootal employed fewer than 7,000 people in the UK. If the company's huge network of overseas associate companies is included, overseas employment at this time stood at around 14,000. Tootal's major overseas interests were in southeast Asia and North America, although the company also had production sites and associated companies in Africa, in continental Europe and in Australasia.

The purpose of this chapter is to examine the processes behind the internationalization of Tootal. These are of wider significance in that they defy one of the most durable stereotypes of the internationalization literature – the argument, derived from the new international division of labour thesis (NIDL), that internationalization is driven by a search for cheap labour (Fröbel, Heinrichs and Kreye, 1980). Studies of internationalization in the textile industry have, with few exceptions (e.g. Elson, 1989; 1990), tended to explain the phenomenon primarily in terms of a search for low-cost production (i.e. labour) sites and arrangements. But the labour explanation of internationalization has been grossly exaggerated. Of course, it is all too easy to displace simple and elegant conceptual devices with counterfactual case studies which ritually emphasize complexity and idiosyncrasy (see Walker, 1989; Dicken and Thrift, 1992). But this is not our aim here; rather, we seek to explain the internationalization of Tootal with regard to two sets of inter-related processes: first, the 'pull' of overseas markets and, secondly, the relationship between the company's global reach and its positioning within the UK economy. In other words, the explanation of Tootal's internationalization will be couched largely in terms of the company's changing *market relations* – its relationships with supply markets and with product markets. Consequently, the logic of internationalization in this case is not to be found in the company's labour relations *per se*. Although the search for cheap and pliable labour certainly played a role in Tootal's decision-making, it was not the driving force for change, not did it produce the same locational effects as would have been predicted by the NIDL thesis. Internationalization strategies which are read off from NIDL stereotypes do not constitute an adequate explanation in this case.

Initially, the process of internationalization in Tootal was driven by the imperative of maintaining and gaining access to overseas markets, particularly in southeast Asia. Although this enabled Tootal to achieve a global presence, the company did not strive at this stage to *integrate* production on a global scale: overseas operations were functionally separate from the company's UK operations. Over time, though, the company began progressively to integrate production through global sourcing arrangements. Intersecting with, and later reinforcing, these developments was the changing position of Tootal within the UK economy. The company suffered heavy financial losses and was forced dramatically to restructure its UK operations during the damaging UK recession of the early 1980s. This, in turn, accelerated the process of internationalization as, in relative terms, Tootal's overseas interests assumed greater significance to the group as a whole.

The example of Tootal, however, is certainly not exceptional. Indeed, the experience of Tootal echoes that of Courtaulds, another British-owned textiles and clothing giant. In Courtaulds, too, the process of corporate restructuring has been shaped by the tension between the company's global interests and its position in the UK manufacturing sector. As we shall see in this chapter, in the process of internationalizing its activities Tootal has dramatically changed the balance of the functions it performs for itself both in general and, specifically, in its home base, the UK. In both senses, it can be argued that Tootal has become a 'hollow corporation'. In functional terms, Tootal has drastically reduced its inhouse manufacturing activities and commensurately increased its service activities. As a UK-based corporation, and especially in employment terms, it is now little more than a manufacturing shell although the profit-generating importance of its non-manufacturing functions to the UK economy should not be underestimated.

The competitive context: global shifts and global restructuring in the textile industry

Competitively, the textile industry is highly volatile; it also probably has the longest history as a *global* industry. During the past few decades there has been a very substantial global shift in textile production with pronounced relative decline in the older established countries of production and rapid growth in certain developing countries (Dicken, 1992). Between 1972 and 1987 – a period of particular relevance to Tootal, as we shall see – textile production grew at a much faster rate in Asia, parts of Latin America and in the Mediterranean rim than in western Europe where production levels remained stagnant or, in some cases, actually declined. This does not imply that western Europe is no longer a significant region for textile production. On the contrary, in 1989 western Europe accounted for 46% of world textile exports. However, three-quarters of these exports were intraregional. In contrast, the five leading east Asian suppliers (China, Hong Kong, South Korea and Taiwan), which together accounted for 32% of total world trade in textiles, were overwhelmingly orientated towards global markets (GATT, 1990).

These global shifts in textile production have been associated with very substantial changes in the way in which the industry is organized. Clairmonte and Cavanagh (1981) identified a 'world textile oligopoly' of some 35–40 firms which have been primarily responsible for shaping and reshaping the global industry. In 1986, nine of the twenty leading textile companies originated from the USA, two from the UK, five from Japan and two from France. Tootal, at that time, ranked third in the UK after Coats Viyella and Courtaulds. As a result of the 1991 merger (see below) Tootal is now part of the Coats Viyella group. This has reinforced the position of the UK as the world's most concentrated textile industry.

Competition and corporate restructuring in the global textile industry has to be seen within the very particular international regulatory framework – the Multi-Fibre Arrangement (MFA) – which has characterized the industry for the past two decades. The MFA has, without doubt, helped to create a global geography of textile production and trade which, in its absence, would have been very different. At the same time, the industry at the national level has been subjected to state policies aimed, in the case of the older industrialized countries, at restructuring and rationalizing the domestic industry.

Within the context of intensifying global competition and a highly regulated trading environment, the world's textile firms have evolved a variety of competitive strategies. In particular, a major feature of the industry is the widespread use of international subcontracting, licensing and joint ventures of various kinds. Indeed, internationalization through direct equity participation, as in the conventional definition of foreign direct investment, has been more limited than in most other global industries. Although European (including British) textile companies have a long history of international involvement in textile production and trade, the first really significant wave of such activity occurred in the early 1960s and was led by the Japanese textile firms and the Japanese general trading companies (the *sogo shosha*). The Japanese firms were already strongly vertically integrated in Japan itself and operated a dualistic-hierarchical network of domestic subcontractors. The *sogo shosha* were responsible for organizing a large proportion of Japanese imports and exports and already had an intricate and extensive international distribution network. When the USA first imposed protectionist measures against Japanese textile imports in 1962, this triggered the first major surge of overseas activity by Japanese textile firms. To avoid the problem of US-imposed quotas both the specialist textile firms and the *sogo shosha* set up international subcontracting networks in other east and southeast Asian countries. Relatively quickly, therefore, the Japanese textile industry became an international, vertically integrated operation which incorporated an extensive network of local Asian producers. According to Oman (1989), by 1980 Japan's nine leading *sogo shosha* were involved in some 150 textile ventures outside Japan. The leading vertically integrated Japanese textile companies (Toray, Asahi, Teijin, Toyo, Mitsubishi) were also involved in a vast array of international operations. Some of these took the form of direct investment but most were international subcontracting arrangements.

Compared with the Japanese companies, US and European textile firms are less internationalized. In the USA, the tendency has been to increase the degree of domestic concentration through acquisition and merger and to upgrade domestic productivity through heavy investment in new technology. Such strategies have also been pursued in Europe although some of the large textile companies have also internationalized extensively. Thus most firms have adopted a varying mixture of product rationalization and focus; technological innovation to reduce costs and increase flexibility; and reduction of domestic production capacity and the use of international subcontracting, licensing and other forms of relationship with local firms in both developed and developing countries. Tootal has been a prime mover in these rationalization, restructuring and internationalization strategies and, as a result, has been transformed as a company during the past three decades. It is to this tortuous evolution of Tootal as an internationalized company that we now turn.

Developing Tootal

Tootal, one of the world's most long-established textiles companies, concentrated through most of its long history on the spinning, weaving and knitting of artificial fibres. The company was in some sense multinational even in the nineteenth century, at which time it had interests in the USA and the far east. The process of internationalization in Tootal accelerated considerably in the period after the 1960s, a period which has witnessed changes not only in the degree but also in the qualitative nature of the company's overseas interests and global structure. Figure 7.1 summarizes the organizational history of Tootal and that of its recently acquired parent company, Coats Viyella.

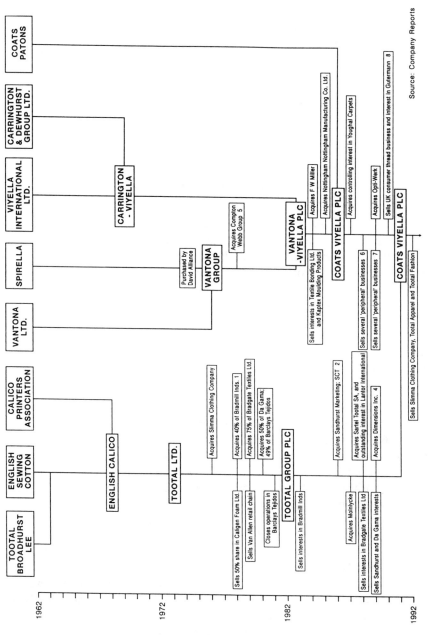

Figure 7.1 Organizational history of Tootal and Coats Viyella (*Source:* Company reports)

From its origins in Lancashire in 1799, Tootal's traditional base was the north west of England although, since the 1960s, the company has been engaged in an ongoing process of corporate restructuring and internationalization. The company operated as a family-controlled partnership for the first 90 years of its existence. Edward Tootal and Henry Broadhurst Lee were to establish Tootal Broadhurst Lee (TBL) as a limited company in 1888, a name which was retained until the early 1960s. The corporate structure of Tootal prior to the Coats Viyella takeover was forged in two critical phases in the company's history: the merger boom of the 1960s and the period of recession and restructuring of the early 1980s. The focus here is on the development of the company over the last 30 years.

The internationalization of Tootal can best be examined within a periodization framework. The company's recent history can be summarized as follows:

- 1963–73: *Corporate consolidation* through merger activity, during which the company 'took shape' as a corporate entity.
- 1973–9: *Global expansion* mainly by way of acquisitions, licensing agreements and expansion of associate companies.
- 1979–85: *Hollowing out* following recession and rationalization, largely as a reactive strategy.
- 1985–9: *Global integration* through strategic reorientation and a renewed emphasis on marketing, distribution and finance.
- 1989–92: *Corporate exposure* following financial vulnerability and ending in the Coats Viyella takeover.

Here, a brief overview of the company's development through these phases is provided. Subsequent sections will focus in greater detail on the processes of internationalization in Tootal and on its explanation.

The 1963–73 decade was a formative one for Tootal, in which the company sought to establish itself as an international producer. The company merged with English Sewing Cotton and with the Calico Printers Association during the 1960s with a view to establishing a more broadly based, vertically integrated production network. The striking feature of the company during this time was that, through its merger activities, it acquired a portfolio of overseas interests (mainly in the USA and the far east) which almost perfectly complemented the UK-orientated structure of TBL. In the 1950s TBL/Tootal was basically a British company with overseas interests. Through the 1960s, the company became international in its operations, but was never to achieve the status of an integrated global producer. Rather, the 1963–73 period should be seen as that in which Tootal's corporate 'shape' was established. Restructuring and rationalization would occur later, triggered initially by external pressures.

From the foundations established in the 1960s, the broadened Tootal group began slowly, and only partially, to integrate its global operations. The company pursued a strategy during the 1970s of extensive intragroup trading, coupled with a deepening of its overseas interests (Banyard, 1987). The main focus of employment expansion during this time was Tootal's overseas associate companies (in which Tootal would have a controlling, though usually less than 50% shareholding). Between 1973–4 and 1979–80, employment in its overseas associates rose by 118% (+7,000), while Tootal's UK employment fell by 22% (–4,000), all of which occurred in a major shakeout in 1979–80. Direct overseas employment within the Tootal group itself remained static. This growth in overseas employment in associate companies represented the beginning of a process of 'hollowing out' of the company's UK employment structure. In 1975–6, 57% of Tootal's employment was based in the UK; by the end of the 1970s, overseas employment outnumbered domestic employment and by 1990–1, only one-third of group employment (including associates) was based in the UK (authors' estimate). These trends reflect the fact that, for some time, Tootal's UK operations have been its least profitable.

It would be misleading, however, to present this 'hollowing out' of Tootal as an inevitable by-product of the company's internationalization strategy. This strategy was itself necessitated by changes in the structure of global competition in textiles, as the company's turbulent passage through the early 1980s demonstrates. The early 1980s recession in the UK had a devastating effect on the company's domestic operations and – as a result – on its global structure. Almost half of Tootal's UK workforce was shed in the space of four years, whilst overseas employment rose by one-third. Tootal emerged from this phase of rapid restructuring with a rather ragged assortment of activities, a rationalized management structure and a modernized, though slimmed down, production network. Through the turmoil of the early 1980s, the company had become more internationalized than ever before (Lloyd and Shutt, 1985; Elson, 1989).

By the mid-1980s, Tootal seemed to have recovered a stable footing. The group's profitability grew steadily for the remainder of the decade, the most profitable sectors being threads, international fabric sourcing and distribution and specialized materials. Over this period, Tootal's activities in Africa, Asia and North America consistently achieved the highest rates of profit on sales, whilst European and Australian operations continued to yield comparatively low profit levels. Employment stabilized, then began to increase again in the mid-1980s: the company's total employment (excluding associate companies) rose by 13% (+1,700) between 1986–7 and 1990–1, more than doubling in Asia (where more than 2,000 new jobs were created), but continuing to fall in the UK (where a further 1,100 were shed, a reduction of 14%).

After successfully thwarting an attempted takeover by the Australian textiles group, ENTRAD, in 1985, Tootal set about a strategic reorganization of its activities. The new strategy, announced in the 1986–7 *Annual Report*, involved the decentralization of management structures and the development of a marketing-led approach. As the report stated:

> After years of eliminating high-cost production capacity, the Tootal Group is increasingly placing emphasis on its market position . . . Our objective is to develop a worldwide marketing and distribution organisation in markets where we can achieve leading supplier status . . . [The] future of each of our business groups must be built

on providing excellent service and distribution skills to industrial users and retailers, thereby deriving higher value-added in the service component. This implies a concentration on customer service and distribution in the broadest sense, backed up by design and technical skills, by branded products and low-cost sourcing either from our own capacity or from other controlled sources around the world.

(Tootal, 1987, p. 7)

The company consequently sought to derive a higher value-added component from more sophisticated servicing at the same time as driving down production costs. Tootal further internationalized its operations during this period, making major new investments in China, Portugal and Turkey.

Tootal continued to develop its strategic reorientation through the late 1980s, but soon found itself again embroiled in takeover speculation. In 1989, ENTRAD proposed a merger, again rejected by Tootal, while later in the year Coats Viyella made its first bid to acquire the company. Coats Viyella, the largest textile company in Europe, possessed a portfolio of interests complementary with those of Tootal. Both sectorally and geographically, the two companies had a quite different structure of operations. Coats' activities were focused on southern Europe, Latin America and on the consumer threads sector in North America. However, this first bid was rejected by Tootal which announced plans to deepen its investments in the far east (*The Financial Times*, 21 December 1989). Over the following year, though, Tootal's performance weakened considerably as the British economy again began to slide into recession. Takeover interest was reawakened in Coats Viyella, which after some months of negotiations and exploratory bidding purchased Tootal in June 1991 (see below).

Internationalizing Tootal

Corporate consolidation: 1963–73
It was during the 1963–73 period that Tootal first 'took shape' as an international corporate entity. The company was involved in two significant mergers during the 1960s: first with English Sewing Cotton in 1963 and later with the Calico Printers Association in 1968 (Figure 7.1). These mergers enabled Tootal to extend and deepen its product base into cotton spinning and sewing thread (through the network of companies owned by English Sewing Cotton) and into weaving, dyeing and finishing (through the interests of the Calico Printers Association). The newly merged company (which for a time was known as English Calico, being renamed Tootal Ltd in 1973) was established as a vertically integrated textile conglomerate. This was a far cry from the relatively decentralized structure previously favoured by TBL. Tootal's evolution into a vertically integrated textile group was consequently achieved through two judicious mergers with complementary organizations, a mark of which was that no major restructuring of the company's operations took place in either the merger or the immediate postmerger period (Lloyd and Shutt, 1985; Banyard, 1987).

The 1960s was also the period in which the basis was laid for Tootal's emergence as a truly internationalized company. Both English Sewing Cotton and the Calico Printers Association possessed extensive overseas interests. English Sewing Cotton, for example, had owned a string of US spinning mills since the late nineteenth century, while the Calico Printers Association brought with it a network of subsidiary companies and export relationships in countries such as China, Egypt and India. Prior to the merger, TBL itself also had international links, although production remained predominantly UK-based prior to the 1960s. TBL's strategy in the 1950s had been to build from this UK base: in 1957, for example, a new mill in Bolton, north of Manchester, had been established through a joint venture arrangement with a US company (*Manchester Evening News*, 10 January 1957).

By virtue of its powerful market position at the time, Tootal was able to internationalize through mergers, simply extending its geographical reach and production portfolio without the attendant pain of rationalization, either in production or in management systems. This is not to say, of course, that the company would not have benefited from such restructuring. It was perhaps a combination of managerial conservatism and oligopolistic market conditions which enabled Tootal to expand its operations without rationalization. During this time, the company's key strategic goal was the development of a broadly based production network, though even at this early stage there is evidence of Tootal pursuing the expanding market in southeast Asia. In many ways, though, while the company was beginning to *act* globally, it was yet to start to *think* globally. The costs of this, perhaps understandable, corporate complacency were to be extracted in the turbulent years to follow.

Global expansion: 1973–9
During the 1970s, Tootal expanded and slowly began to integrate its global operations. At first this took the form of increased intragroup trading between the company's 11 operational divisions. In the mid-1970s, though, the company began to rationalize its labyrinthine organizational structure. The year 1975 saw the first internal reorganization of the company in the postmerger period, as some divisions were consolidated under a new management structure. Although still comparatively modest in scale and scope, these changes enabled Tootal to begin to integrate its overseas activities, although still very much from a UK base. The nature of the company's internationalization during this period, however, placed structural limits on the process of integration. Overseas plants tended to serve regional markets, while Tootal's UK operations served both the domestic and the export market.

Over the period 1973–4 to 1978–9, Tootal's UK workforce remained stable at around 20,000 employees, despite the fact that these had been turbulent years for the national economy. The company achieved record profits in 1973–4, but the advent of recession in the UK saw these fall to half this level over the following year. Although corporate profitability was restored over subsequent years, this was largely on the basis of the company's overseas operations (Tootal,

1976). The company was reluctant at the time to acknowledge the precise contribution of overseas production to group profitability, owing to the political sensitivities surrounding this issue. It is clear, though, from Tootal's activities that the once privileged place of UK production was no longer guaranteed.

During the mid-1970s, Tootal expanded and reinvested in its profitable overseas interests, while maintaining its UK operations at a stable level. This was, in effect, a period of 'relative' hollowing out. A new thread plant, for example, was opened in Malaysia in 1975, whilst in 1978 Tootal acquired the Australian textile producer, Bradmill (Figure 7.1). The company also sought to extend its overseas capacity through licensing agreements and through the acquisition of controlling stakes in associated companies. Indeed, employment in associates more than doubled in the four years following 1975–6, to account for one-third of group employment by the end of the decade.

This process of 'relative' hollowing out was driven only in part by geographical differentials in profitability. Tootal also realized that – in order to maintain export markets in the face of accelerating competition – it was necessary to relocate production closer to the source of demand. Hence, much of Tootal's expanding network of overseas production units was geared to supplying *regional* markets. It should not be confused with a system of global sourcing from low-cost production zones. The company's interests in southeast Asia, for example, were developed to serve the rapidly expanding *regional market* for thread, and were also consistent with the import-substitution policies of governments in the region (Elson, 1989; Dicken, 1992). This approach effectively placed limits on the process of global integration, as overseas operations tended to focus on regional markets rather than export markets or internal company transfers. Significantly, these overseas operations – at least those which were directly owned by the Tootal group – rarely conformed with the NIDL stereotype of the labour-hungry factory. Although production and profitability rose, employment in Tootal subsidiaries overseas (i.e. excluding associate companies) was static at around 9,000 workers throughout the 1973–9 period. Many of these plants were re-equipped and automated during the 1970s, shedding labour as a result (Elson, 1989). The stability of overseas employment during this time was, therefore, the result of new plants coming on stream at the same time as older plants were modernized.

The period 1973–9, then, was one in which Tootal began to define its internationalization strategy. Although the core of the company remained in the UK, Tootal's overseas interests were expanded considerably in order better to serve regional markets, particularly in southeast Asia. It was these overseas production sites which benefited from the company's investment programme during the 1970s on the expectation that they would yield the highest rates of return. Meanwhile UK production ossified, dependent as it was on a depressed domestic market and a highly competitive export market. So the process of hollowing out began, despite the company's protestations that it wished to retain its UK base in anticipation of the upturn in the domestic economy (Tootal, 1977).

This anticipated upturn did not occur. On the contrary, the UK economy was to enter another serious recession in the late 1970s which would bring about the virtual collapse of Tootal's UK operations. As a result, the company which, despite adverse domestic market conditions, high inflation and low profitability, had been prepared to maintain its UK production capacity and workforce during the 1970s was to find itself plunged into a period of intense rationalization and restructuring. The process of hollowing out was consequently taken one step further, as UK production and employment fell in real terms. Such was the seriousness of this situation that the viability of the entire Tootal group was to be compromised.

Hollowing out: 1979–85
Although Tootal had internationalized in a quite profound way during the 1970s, it remained at the end of the decade a company heavily dependent upon its domestic base. Because Tootal had eschewed global sourcing and functional integration in favour of a strategy of serving regional markets, its UK base remained the backbone of the company, sourcing as it did both the large domestic market and the export trade. The recession of the early 1980s was to witness a dramatic decline in the company's UK capacity, as Tootal was hollowed out in absolute terms: UK employment and capacity fell, while overseas employment – at least initially – continued to expand. A measure, though, of the damage suffered by Tootal during the early 1980s was that, after 1981–2, even overseas employment began to fall.

Over the period 1978–9 to 1984–5, Tootal's UK employment fell by 61% (–12,250), while overseas employment (excluding associates, for which the company ceased to publish information in 1984) rose strongly for three years before falling away sharply. Direct overseas employment in the company fell by 36% (–3,300) over this time. Employment in overseas associates grew very rapidly in the early 1980s, peaking at 23,500 in 1981–2 when it accounted for 57% of total employment in the group. Employment even in associates began to fall after this time, as the company sought to defend its core operations in the UK.

A combination of factors served to undermine Tootal's UK production base during the late 1970s and early 1980s. Rising energy costs depressed UK trading, while the strength of sterling – particularly between 1979 and 1981 – produced the twin effects of eroding the value of the company's export returns at the same time as the UK domestic market was becoming more lucrative for importers. Import penetration of the UK textiles market rose from 40% in 1980 to 57% in 1984. These pressures forced Tootal savagely to restructure its UK operations. Loss-making plant was eliminated, while some of the company's saleable assets were sold off in order to support cash flow. The scale and speed of these changes was without precedent in the company's history.

By 1982, the number of weaving looms operated by Tootal in the UK had fallen to just 24, having peaked at several thousand in the early 1970s (*The Financial Times*, 3 October 1982). The closure in the same year of Tootal's printing plant in Strines, Derbyshire, marked the end of fashion fabric printing in the UK (*The Financial Times*, 12 January 1982). The abandonment of Tootal's policy of vertical integration was signified by the sale of the retail chain, Van Allan (Tootal, 1980). Through this remorseless hollowing out of the company, the character of Tootal was being redefined:

> The aim of [the rationalization] policy is the elimination of all loss making plant in the UK. This will strengthen the UK base from which exploitation of the group's world activities can be best achieved.
>
> (Chairman, Tootal, 1980, p. 2)

> This group has altered considerably over recent years and no longer has any large involvement in the production of traditional basic textiles . . . Our wide geographic and product spread reduces our vulnerability to cyclical influences.
>
> (Chairman, Tootal, 1984, p. 2)

> There are opportunities for expansion of our thread production overseas but we won't be going back into basic textiles in the UK.
>
> (Chairman, Tootal, *Daily Express*, 7 December 1981)

Through the turmoil of the early 1980s, Tootal was becoming a globalized company. Global sourcing of thread, for example, began in 1980: no longer would Tootal's overseas operations be restricted to serving regional markets (*The Financial Times*, 30 September 1980). Following the run-down of British weaving capacity, cloth too was to be sourced from overseas at the most competitive prices which could be obtained (*The Financial Times*, 12 October 1981). In 1982, the company took its first step towards a globalized management structure when the headquarters of the key Threads Division was transferred to the USA (*The Financial Times*, 14 May 1982).

Emerging from this period of restructuring, Tootal's Chairman announced that 'the period of surgery and convalescence is now firmly behind us' (Tootal, 1985, p. 2). The company's rationalized UK base accounted for only 57% of direct group employment, though less than 30% if overseas associates are included (Tootal, 1984). As Table 7.1 shows, however, Tootal's UK operations remained its least profitable, despite the surgery of the early 1980. The company's interests in North America, in contrast, accounted for 31% of group profits, though only 18% of group employment, while its African operations yielded 9% of group profits from just 6% of group employment. Moreover, Table 7.1 reveals that the UK performed poorest in terms of profit yielded per employee, though it is also notable that Tootal's operations in Asia were also weak on this measure. Interestingly, it was the company's operations in continental Europe which yielded the best profit returns per employee: at £5,800 per worker in 1984–5, these operations were three times more productive than Tootal's Asian plants and four times more productive than its British plants.

Tootal in the mid-1980s could claim to have survived the worst ravages of recession and rationalization, but it had been left with an uneven and ill-balanced assortment of global interests. The company had internationalized over the 1979–85 period, but this should be seen as the outcome of Tootal's

Table 7.1   Global structure of Tootal activities, 1984–5

	Share of employment (%)*	Contribu- tion to sales (%)	Contribu- tion to profit (%)	Profit on sales (%)	Profit per employee (£000s)
UK	57	47	39	5	1.4
Other Europe	4	9	11	8	5.8
North America	18	26	31	8	3.5
Asia	12	9	11	8	1.9
Africa	6	4	9	14	2.9
Australasia	3	4	5	7	3.7
Divested activities			(6)		
Group total	100	100	100	6	2.0

Note:
*Excludes overseas associate companies.
Source: Tootal *Annual Report*, 1984–85.

struggle to survive rather than the realization of some preplanned and deliber- ately executed strategy. The costs of rationalization and capacity scrapping for the company had been extraordinarily high. Throughout this period, Tootal had been writing off huge sums in reorganization and closure costs. In 1979– 80, these amounted to £18.2 million; even as late as 1984–5, they amounted to £26.0 million, a year when the company's pretax profits were only £22.9 million (Tootal, 1980; 1985). Profits from overseas operations and from the sale of assets were used to cover these costs. For example, the sale of the Australian company Bradmill in 1984, despite being presented by the Tootal Chairman as 'a feature of our strategic thinking for some time', was clearly also necessary to cope with the costs of restructuring in the UK: the company acknowledged that the 'principal effects [of the Bradmill sale] were to improve UK cashflow and at the same time release funds for redeployment' (Tootal, 1984, p. 2).

Global integration: 1985–9
In contrast to the largely reactive approach of the company during the early 1980s, Tootal in the 1985–9 period was intent on developing a more strategic approach to its global operations. Under its new Chief Executive, Geoffrey Maddrell, the company sought to develop a new orientation based on tight financial stringency, market sensitivity and an explicitly stated strategy. There was to be an emphasis on global distribution networks. This followed a recog- nition that 70% of the value added in the key area of industrial sewing thread

derived from distribution rather than manufacturing (Banyard, 1987). No longer would Tootal simply be a textile manufacturer.

The new strategy proposed alterations to the company's senior management structure, increased investment in training, attempts to improve internal communications, the adoption of more flexible working patterns, and detailed plans to spruce up its clothing interests. It was felt to be especially important to implement this strategy in the area of industrial threads, a business where customers have very specific requirements, thus presenting an opportunity for the supplier to steal the competitive edge by offering a faster and more flexible service. Tootal planned to exploit this opportunity by concentrating its spinning activities in low-cost countries (specifically China). When new markets opened up it would be able to move in swiftly as a thread supplier at a relatively low cost. Acquisitions, such as that of Sandhurst Marketing, would form a major component of this strategy and it was hoped that they would perform a dual role – taking Tootal into more fertile fields, while also introducing new, marketing-orientated management approaches (*The Financial Times*, 28 August 1987).

This would represent a significant shift in the culture of the company as well as the structure of its operations. As stockbrokers BZW commented in a private assessment of the company's prospects: 'Tootal has never before had a totally coherent strategy, but this is now emerging strongly under Geoffrey Maddrell. It is market led, distribution orientated, and sourcing rather than manufacturing based . . . However, the Tootal Group as a whole is not entirely consistent with this main line strategy' (BZW, 1988, pp. 1–2). It was clear that, for Maddrell's strategy to be realized, further restructuring of the company's operations would be required.

This implied a reorientation of Tootal's global relations. Significant developments here included increased global sourcing, a deepening of the company's interests in Asia and continental Europe, and a refocusing of UK operations on more effective and responsive customer relations. Tootal sought increasingly to integrate functionally its operations over the 1985–9 period, sourcing thread, materials and garments on a global basis. The proportion of the company's garment sales sourced outside the UK, for example, rose from 13% in 1985–6 to 27% in 1989–90 (Tootal, 1986; 1990). The company also took steps to secure its position in the expanding markets of China and southern Europe. The further internationalization of Tootal was a prerequisite for realizing this strategy, a key development being the establishment – through a joint venture arrangement with the Chinese – of a new thread mill in Canton. The company also established two new 'fleximills' in Turkey and Portugal in order to provide finishing services for the expanding garment industries of southern Europe (*The Financial Times*, 4 October 1988). Thus, Tootal aimed to reap the benefits of low-cost production, at the same time as being poised to capitalize on the opening up of new markets.

Tootal's new interests in China played a particularly important role in the company's strategic vision. China is now the world's largest textile producer

Table 7.2   Global structure of Tootal activities, 1989–90

	Share of employment (%)*	Contribu-tion to sales (%)	Contribu-tion to profit (%)	Profit on sales (%)	Profit per employee (£000s)
UK	50	44	22	4	1.1
Other Europe	5	16	15	7	6.8
North America	16	21	32	11	5.1
Asia	21	11	19	12	2.2
Africa	6	2	5	15	2.0
Australasia	2	3	4	9	6.3
Divested activities		2	3		
Group total	100	100	100	7	2.4

Note:
*Excludes overseas associate companies.
Source: Tootal *Annual Report*, 1989–90.

(Dicken, 1992). The new mill in Canton would sell one-third of its output to this booming Chinese market, the remaining two-thirds being destined for other Tootal operations in southeast Asia (Elson, 1989). As Table 7.2 shows, the company's Asian operations had by the end of the 1980s come to represent a significant element in its global portfolio, accounting for 21% of group employment and 19% of group profits. Since 1984–5, the Asian operations' share of employment had risen by 75%, while its share of group profit had risen by 73% (Tables 7.1 and 7.2). Profit per employee in Asian plants re-mained below the group average in 1989–90, however, reflecting the fact that Tootal's interest in the region was not simply as a cheap production zone but also as a means of access to new and growing markets.

Despite the heavy investments made by Tootal in Asia during the second half of the 1980s, and despite the company's representation of itself as 'an interna-tional marketing-led group . . . drawing upon the most cost and quality effi-cient services in the world' (Tootal, 1990, p. 1), it still retained a substantial British presence. Half the company's workforce (excluding associates) and 44% of sales were accounted for by the UK in 1989–90 (Table 7.2). In the post-rationalization period, the nature of Tootal operations in the UK had changed significantly. This involved major new investments in plant and ma-chinery and an emphasis on quality, flexibility and responsiveness. In 1986, a state-of-the-art dyehouse operation had been opened in Glasgow, the largest of its kind in Europe (*The Financial Times*, 28 November 1986). In 1989, Tootal announced an alliance with two Japanese companies (Kurabo Industries and

Toyo Menka Kaisha) for the development of a new fabric-finishing plant in Dundee, seen at the time as a precursor to other joint ventures on the continent (*The Financial Times*, 21 January 1989). Tootal's clothing interests in the UK were also being modernized. Here, investments in new technology were accompanied by increased contracting out of work, although under strict quality control standards. Tootal had become one of the leading suppliers to the British retail giant, Marks & Spencer, renowned for its enormous market power, its close interest in supply arrangements and its exacting quality standards (Mitter, 1985; Elson, 1989). Tootal's network of contractors, according to the company itself, developed an approach which was 'bi-focal, scanning distant horizons for design ideas and low cost, quality fabrics, even sourcing blouses from Malaysia (not as easy as it sounds, given the Group's rigorous demands on quality), while maintaining a close-up focus on their customers' needs and choices' (Tootal, 1989, p. 17).

The company's internationalization strategy was summed up by Elson (1989) at the time as a two-pronged approach. On the one hand, emphasis was placed on commercial subcontracting, both within the UK and internationally. On the other hand, significant investments in new technology, particularly in Asia, the UK and southern Europe, enabled Tootal to improve quality while at the same time becoming more responsibe to customers' needs. In Asia, the strategy implied moving closer to industrial users, and continuing to serve regional as well as global markets.

Corporate exposure: 1989–92
During the mid-1980s, Tootal had recovered something of a firm footing and reasserted a strategic approach after the dislocations and upheavals of the beginning of the decade. However, it was the fact that a significant, albeit reduced, proportion of the company's operations remained British based which proved to be a key issue in its undoing. Changing macroeconomic conditions in the UK were to undermine Tootal's position, as sterling again began to strengthen. The overvaluation of the pound in the period following 1988 again exposed the UK's domestic market to far-eastern manufacturers. Import penetration rose by 14% in 1988 as overseas suppliers ate into Tootal's domestic market share. The concentration of retail purchasing power in the UK, where half of all clothing sales are controlled by just five companies, facilitated this sharp increase in import competition (*The Financial Times*, 13 September 1988).

Under this pressure, the stability of Tootal, developed since the arrival of Geoffrey Maddrell, soon began to weaken. The strength of sterling depressed Tootal's overseas profits, and its remaining textile interests suffered from the troubles of the UK industry outlined above. In addition, Sandhurst Marketing (acquired in 1986 – Figure 7.1) had also performed poorly, and was sold in July 1989 (*The Financial Times*, 21 December 1989). In May 1990, Tootal announced a 15% fall in pretax profits, its first decline for nine years. This performance was said to 'belie [the] Tootal chief's self-confident yarn that his

Table 7.3 Global structure of Tootal activities, 1990–1

	Share of employment (%)*	Contribution to sales (%)	Contribution to profit (%)	Profit on sales (%)	Profit per employee (£000s)
UK	45	46	17	2	0.8
Other Europe	6	17	19	7	7.0
North America	16	20	35	11	4.4
Asia	25	11	21	12	1.8
Africa	6	3	5	13	1.9
Australasia	2	3	3	6	3.7
Divested activities					
Group total	100	100	100	6	2.1

Note:
*Excludes overseas associate companies.
Source: Tootal *Annual Report*, 1990–1.

strategy of focus, scale, and internationalization would ensure the Tootal Group a secure future' (*Guardian*, 1 May 1990). Although profitability in Tootal's overseas operations remained sound, the contribution of the company's UK plants slumped by 23% between the years 1989–90 and 1990–91 (Tables 7.2 and 7.3). What remained of Tootal's UK operations proved in many ways to be the company's Achilles' heel.

As Tootal's position began to weaken, the company was again immersed in takeover speculation. The year 1989 witnessed further interest in the Tootal group from Abraham Goldberg. Goldberg's proposals involved a merger, whereby Tootal would acquire his Australian textile interests in return for his obtaining a sizeable shareholding in Tootal. This was rejected by Tootal, which made it clear that his advances were unwelcome (*The Financial Times*, 28 February 1989; 2 March 1989). Goldberg subsequently announced that his objective was to control Tootal, which would provide him with a platform for expansion into Europe at a time when the limits to growth in Australian markets had been reached (*The Financial Times*, 2 March 1989).

Later in 1989, Coats Viyella announced its intention to acquire Tootal with a £395 million bid, having acquired Goldberg's stake in the company. Both Coats and Tootal claimed that the merger would make strategic sense as the two had complementary interests. Tootal was strong in northern Europe, the far east and the industrial-thread business in North America, whilst Coats' major interests were mainly in southern Europe, Latin America and the consumer-thread business in North America. The merger, it was argued, would not only deliver economies of scale but also would provide Tootal with capital for expansion and enable shared development programmes to be established. It would also add a sorely needed critical mass to Tootal's weaker interests in sectors such as clothing (*The Financial Times*, 10 May 1989).

From the viewpoint of Coats, the rationale behind the merger bid lay in the twin goals of creating a global force in international sewing thread and giving the company an entrée into the strategically important southeast Asian market, where traditionally it had been weak (*The Financial Times*, 28 June 1989). Coats hoped to combine its own marketing strengths with Tootal's sourcing skills and clearly defined strategy in order to release organizational synergies and merge overlapping interests. Despite appearances at the time, it is questionable whether the desire to merge was genuinely mutual. The imperative of thwarting Goldberg's continuing interest may have been Tootal's over-riding motivation (Carr, Kitcat and Aitken, 1989).

In June 1989, the Coats bid was referred to the UK Monopolies and Mergers Commission (MMC) on the grounds that the merger would be anti-competitive: the two companies combined would command 42% of the UK market for industrial thread, 70% of the domestic thread market and control one-third of the haberdashery sector (*The Financial Times*, 28 May 1989). In October, the merger was approved by the MMC on the condition that Coats sold off its UK domestic thread business and its 20% holding in Gutermann (a Swiss/German thread company). Neither Courtaulds, the major rival to both Tootal and Coats, nor Marks & Spencer opposed the merger (*The Financial Times*, 27 October 1989). In December 1989, however, the merger broke down when Tootal rejected a new reduced offer from Coats of £315 million. Neither firm said that it had changed its view about the logic of a merger, although Tootal announced that it was to proceed with plans for independent development, especially in the far east (*The Financial Times*, 21 December 1989).

In August 1990, Coats satisfied the conditions required by the MMC for a takeover, thus raising the likelihood of there being a new merger bid (*The Times*, 4 August 1990). In January 1991, Geoffrey Maddrell resigned from Tootal's board, to be replaced as Chief Executive by Anthony Habgood. This was again viewed as being positive for a potential merger (Extel Financial, 1991; Henry Cooke Lumsden, 1991). Two months later a new bid, of £194 million, was indeed unveiled by Coats. This was immediately rejected by Tootal, which dismissed it as an 'unwelcome and unrealistic' attempt to take over the company 'on the cheap' (*The Financial Times*, 5 March 1991). Tootal claimed that conditions had changed markedly since the last takeover attempt in 1989, and that the 'compelling logic' for a merger no longer remained. Coats had the worst profit and sales record in the previous four years in the textile sector, and many of its major businesses had suffered commercial difficulties. In addition, it remained highly dependent on vulnerable South American markets.

Consequently, Tootal felt that the merger would no longer be beneficial to the company. Any cost savings would almost certainly be outweighed by a loss of sales, especially in the UK, the USA and the far east. The 1989 MMC report on the merger had indicated that 17% of industrial thread customers of the two companies would seek alternative suppliers if the takeover were to go ahead. Although the arguments about the global and sectoral complementarity of the two companies remained valid, as did the potential scale economies, Tootal was now recommending that its shareholders reject the bid. The future success of Tootal, the company now argued, would depend upon innovation, not simply upon size (Tootal Group, 1991; 1991b).

The high level of corporate activity in the textiles sector during this time was related to several factors. First, opportunities for organic growth were being restricted under static consumer market conditions, which made expansion by acquisition a more attractive possibility. Secondly, the falling market capitalization of many companies left them vulnerable to predators. Thirdly, some of the larger companies were also acting quickly in order to take full advantage of the next upturn in the trading cycle (Carr, Kitcat and Aitken, 1989). Coats' interest in Tootal consequently occurred at a time when the British textile industry was under increasingly intense pressure. Uncertainty concerning the gulf war aggravated the effects of the deepening domestic recession, while the continuing stalemate over world trading ageements continued to create problems. Retailers exploited these conditions to drive down margins, while there was also a downturn in demand from industrial customers for contract furnishings and hi-tech textiles (*The Financial Times*, 2 May 1991; 9 August 1991). These factors combined to leave Tootal particularly badly exposed.

Coats finally succeeded in acquiring Tootal with an improved bid in May 1991. This created a textile group with a combined annual turnover of over £2 billion (Extel Financial, 1991). Subsequently, Coats' strategy has been to merge its interests with those of Tootal, thereby aiming to boost profitability through achieving economies of scale in production and through pooling administration and distribution. The integration of consumer thread companies in the USA and Europe has already been achieved, through the combination of administration and sales functions and through the rationalization of production operations. The Coats group is now the market leader in threads and handknitting in the Asia-Pacific region, in addition to western Europe and North America, and also has a very strong position in South Africa, Turkey and Latin America (Payne, 1992).

It is too early, as yet, to assess the full impact of the Coats takeover of Tootal. Coats recently announced an increase in operating profits of 37% to June 1992 (*The Financial Times*, 11 September 1992). The synergies between the Coats and Tootal operations are already becoming apparent, particularly in North America where the industrial and consumer interests of the company have been merged with resultant gains both in market share and profitability. There are also signs that Coats will continue to build on the Tootal operations in Asia, extending global sourcing arrangements across the group as a whole.

Between 1990 and 1992, for example, Coats' sourcing of garments from out-side western Europe increased from zero to more than 20% (*The Financial Times*, 11 September 1992).

Soon after taking control of Tootal, Coats set about rationalizing and streamlining the company (Figure 7.1). Tootal's women's wear business, the Slimma company, was disposed of to avoid losing orders to Marks & Spencer although, in fact, no major contracts have been lost as a result of the acquisi-tion. In October 1991, Tootal Apparel and Tootal Fashion, both part of Tootal Clothing Ltd, were also sold. Coats is also restructuring and rationaliz-ing the overseas sourcing interests of the two groups to focus on clothing. The acquisition of Tootal has gone some way towards resolving the sourcing con-cerns of Coats' traditional operations. Having inherited Tootal's Chinese mills and trading links, it now has much better access to low-cost cotton fabrics (Payne, 1992). Other Tootal companies such as Specialized Materials and Tootal's non-woven business, Lantor, may also be sold.

The costs of integration and reorganization are put at over £60 million, a high figure indeed considering that Coats paid only £240 million for Tootal (*Guardian*, 5 September 1991). Coats, however, believes that once the integra-tion is complete, the company will achieve annual savings of £10–12 million (*The Financial Times*, 29 August 1991). These benefits are unlikely to be realized, though, until the British economy recovers from the recession. The significant rationalization carried out by the larger companies should enable them to withstand short-term difficulties and generate higher earnings as they gain a greater market share. Coats' strengthened management team and its dominant position in the world thread market is believed to augur well for the group's future (Carr, Kitcat and Aitken, 1991).

Conclusion

Tootal's evolution as an international company demonstrates the extreme complexity of the processes involved, even in an industry such as textiles in which most conventional wisdom has attributed internationalization to a simple search for cheap labour. In fact, as the Tootal case has demonstrated, the process of moving production offshore according to the supposed imper-atives of a new international division of labour may be of relatively little importance compared with other forces. Most significant of all have been the chase for markets, even in those parts of the world usually regarded simply as low-cost sites, and the need to respond to the volatility of currency exchange rates.

To understand the internationalization process within firms, therefore, it is essential to examine very carefully the firm's specific history and the changing competitive and regulatory environment in which it attempts to develop a coherent strategy. However, strategies are not always as coherent as the man-agement and business literature leads us to believe. Even when they are co-herent they do not necessarily succeed. The experience of Tootal through the five phases of its recent development – corporate consolidation, global expansion, hollowing out, global integration and corporate exposure – has been one of very considerable variation in fortunes. Tootal rarely seemed to outside observers to exhibit a coherent corporate strategy, often being forced to use reactive rather than proactive measures. The process of corporate restructuring in the company subsequently came to be shaped by, on the one hand, its 'inherited' form of internationalization and, on the other hand, by its vestigial dependence on the UK economy. Ultimately, despite the significant size and geographical extent of its international operations, the company was unable to survive as an independent entity and has now been absorbed within Europe's largest textile company, Coats Viyella.

Tootal's evolution as an international company has been deeply enmeshed with its changing functional and strategic orientations. The company has been hollowed out in both geographical and functional terms. Over the past three decades. Tootal has been transformed from being a conventional textile manufacturer to a service-led company which generates the bulk of its value-added revenue from the provision of distribution and service functions to its global customers in the textile and related industries. This structural transformation has been associated with a massive decline in the company's manufacturing operations worldwide but, especially, in its home base, the UK. Tootal has become, from a manufacturing perspective, a 'hollow corporation', a process which has had devastating effects upon the communities in which it was, for many years, a major employer. But, again, it is important to emphasize that this was not a simple outcome of 'runaway production' but, rather, the result of a very complex structural and geographical transformation. In fact, Tootal's experience, though specific in many respects, is not at all untypical of firms in a wide variety of industries. The trend towards a greater focus on the downstream functions within the production/value-added chain, the increasing involvement in international networks of relationships with a diversity of companies, and the growing emphasis on the co-ordinating function within business systems are all symptoms of pronounced structural changes in the organization of economic activities.

8

MoDo, SCA and STORA: from national pulp producers to European forestry companies

Jan-Evert Nilsson

Introduction

By the end of the nineteenth century, technology had advanced to the point where large-scale production of paper from wood pulp was possible. The demand for paper increased dramatically in both Europe and the USA, thereby creating a unique opportunity for the fledgling Swedish export industry. Sweden, with its extensive access to forests and expertise in the field, had extraordinarily good prerequisites for the satisfaction of the increasing European paper demand.

Pulp production increased rapidly in Sweden, with an increase from 200,000 to 1,200,000 tonnes during the 20-year period leading up to the First World War. With this production spurt, Sweden had become the world's second-largest pulp producer, behind only the USA. This expansion continued, and production rached 3,500,000 tonnes by the outbreak of the Second World War. Of the total Swedish pulp production, approximately three-quarters was exported, primarily to other European countries.

Three dominating firms

There were 150 pulp-producing companies in Sweden in 1945, with production occurring in around 250 pulp factories. Each of these factories normally constituted an independent company, but there was one noticeable exception: Svenska Cellulosa Aktiebolaget (SCA) owned a total of 19 factories (SCA, 1979, p. 166). The company was founded in 1929 through the fusion of existing companies, with a total of 16 companies making up the new one. The goal of the fusion was to create a large company which could play a leading role in the international pulp market. The actual integration of the member companies remained weak, however, until the 1950s. During this period SCA acted as a holding company, while decisions regarding strategy were made at the factories.

The 1950s saw the beginning of a process of structural change which is still going on today. The number of factories began to dwindle while the production capacity of those remaining was expanded. A result of this process was that pulp production increased from 4.4 million tonnes in 1953 to 11.2 million in 1990, while the number of factories declined from 129 to 55 in the same period (DS Ministry of Labour, 1991, p. 20).

There were approximately 130 companies in 1950, a number which had declined by 50 in 1970. The decline continued, leaving only around 20 companies today – three large ones with a few heavy production areas, four of medium size aimed at specific market segments and about ten small companies with specialized production (*ibid.*, p. 26).

The three largest Swedish forestry companies – SCA, STORA and MoDo – together own 25 pulp factories and paper mills in Sweden and account for three-quarters of the industry's sales. The three companies, while sharing similar positions today, have vastly different histories. SCA's history goes back to its conception in 1929, with only minor changes occurring thereafter. Munksund Ltd in Luleå was absorbed by the company in 1934, while Bergvik & Ala Ltd in Söderhamn was divested in 1943. The few purchases of forestry companies that were made after 1950 have either been intended to expand SCA's raw material base – such as Kungsgården-Mariebergs Ltd in 1955, Wifstavarvs Ltd in 1966 and Björkå Ltd in 1974 – or as a step in the company's diversification – Mölnlycke Ltd in 1975 (SCA, 1979, pp. 175, 457).

SCA had become Sweden's largest forestry company by the end of the 1960s. STORA was seen at the time, with its three steel mills, as more of a steel than a forestry industry, while MoDo was still purely a pulp producer. MoDo was the country's largest producer of pulp for sale, but its production capacity was only two-thirds that of SCA. It was not until the end of the 1980s that MoDo stepped up to a very large group with the acquisition of Iggesund and Holmen. Through these purchases the company more than doubled the production capacity of its paper division while simultaneously entering three new product areas: newsprint, cardboard and packing paper.

The steel industry's crisis led to the divestiture of the steel division in the mid-1970s, and STORA's interest in the forestry branch began to grow. Bergvik & Ala was purchased in 1976 as a step in the company's attempt to expand its domestic raw material base, a move which nearly doubled that base. The year 1984 saw the purchase of Billerud which had bought Uddeholm's forestry division six years earlier. Two years later, the firm purchased Papyrus which, through its own acquisition of Kopparfors and Nymölla, had become a large paper and pulp manufacturer in its own right. Through these two acquisitions, STORA took SCA's position as the country's largest forestry company.

The strategy for these three companies has been to exploit the scale economies created through technical and market developments. The increased internationalization of activities has been an important factor in the attainment of this goal. Today, 72,000 of the companies' 112,000 employees (64%) are in foreign units, a number which increased dramatically during the 1980s.

The desire to utilize economies of scale has been combined with the attempt to reduce the vulnerability to changes within specific product areas. In the attempt to achieve the latter, these companies have concenrated on the development of several equally strong product areas. STORA and MoDo have invested in uncoated wood-free fine paper, printing paper and cardboard while SCA has concentrated on printing paper, corrugated board and hygiene products.

The production orientation of the different companies is often directed by the decisions which laid the groundwork for the transition to integrated pulp and paper production. The newsprint production of STORA and SCA are examples of this. Production orientation can also reflect the takeovers which the three companies have made. STORA's production of fine paper and cardboard came about only after its purchase of Papyrus and Billerud in the 1980s, and SCA's hygiene products division was acquired in the purchase of Mölnlycke in 1975. MoDo also follows this pattern, with its production of newsprint and cardboard being a result of the takeover of Holmen's mill and Iggesund in the late 1980s.

The internationalization process

The Swedish forestry companies have had their activities firmly anchored in the international arena since the late nineteenth century, with the majority of production being exported. From this early international role, it took until the 1960s for these companies actually to produce abroad. Foreign production grew throughout the 1960s and 1970s, but remained relatively modest in the beginning of the 1980s, when SCA, STORA and MoDo together had only 8,200 foreign employees. The 1980s ushered in a whole new view of foreign activities, with employment at the 'big three' increasing nearly 800% between 1980 and 1991.

The forces behind internationalization have varied over time. Internationalization can be said partially to reflect changes in the competitiveness of the Swedish companies, and partially to reflect changes in corporate strategies. Three main goals of internationalization can be identified: to secure access to raw materials, to secure markets for the company's products and to achieve market dominance.

Securing access to raw materials
The first foreign expansions made in the mid-1960s were intended to expand the companies' raw material bases. STORA decided in 1962 to make a greenfield investment in North America. A pulp mill was built and Nova Scotia Pulp Ltd founded. At the beginning of the 1970s a paper machine was added to the pulp mill. SCA followed STORA to North America. In 1963 the firm started negotiations with a large American chemical corporation about building a pulp mill in British Columbia. The project was, for different reasons, delayed. Production eventually started in 1966. Owing to technical problems, it took another two years before production achieved established standards and it was not until 1968, five years after the planning started, that the new pulp mill

could deliver an acceptable product. In the mid-1960s Billerud (now a part of STORA) acquired pulp-production facilities in Celbi, Portugal (Rehn, 1992, pp. 40–2). Billerud's idea was to use eucalyptus to produce a new pulp quality. MoDo also had plans to invest in forest resources abroad. In their case an investment in Argentina was considered, but the plan was never realized. One factor behind these expansions was the growing concern during the 1960s that Sweden would soon experience a timber shortage. Wood prices were expected to rise, a situation which would considerably reduce the competitiveness of Swedish pulp producers. The investments in Canada and Portugal were intended to secure access to cheap timber.

Foreign expansion was seen as a sign of the great confidence Swedish pulp manufacturers had in their own abilities. The first research laboratory at a Swedish pulp mill had already been built at the turn of the century. In the following decades a growing number of Swedish pulp producers built up research facilities at their mills. The first professorships in cellulose technology were established in the 1930s, about the same time as the industry founded a number of central laboratories to solve the industry's technical problems. SCA and MoDo, among others, set up central research laboratories in the 1940s, something STORA had done as early as 1918. As a result, Swedish research into the production of both mechanical and chemical pulp had reached internationally advanced levels by the 1960s.

The investments in Canada never lived up to expectations. In 1970, only two years after the start of production, SCA pulled out of its project in British Columbia for economic reasons. It sold its share of Columbia Cellulose to its American partner. STORA, on the other hand, stayed with Nova Scotia Forest Industries despite poor profitability. The most successful of all these foreign investments was Celbi in Portugal, in spite of the fact that the chosen new pulp quality was never a success and Billerud had to change the production plans.

The fact that the above investments were not followed by more can be interpreted as a realization that the anticipated Swedish timber shortage did not become as bad as had been predicted. A more correct interpretation is probably that the shortage took a longer time to appear than expected. Logging activities in Sweden increased by nearly 100% between 1960 and 1974. This increased logging eventually resulted in the logging rate exceeding the replacement rate, thus causing shortages and increased wood prices. At this point, future expansion of Swedish pulp production seemed to have been stopped (Lönnstedt and Randers, 1979). To avoid overlogging, the Swedish government passed a law prohibiting factories from increasing their wood consumption without special permission.

Surprisingly, the timber shortage of the 1970s did not lead to an intensification of SCA's attempts to secure foreign raw materials. STORA and MoDo followed, on the other hand, the old pattern. They again started to invest abroad in order to secure their access to raw materials. STORA established, together with two smaller Swedish pulp producers, a forest plantation in Liberia. A revolution in Liberia prevented the Swedish firms from logging the forest. MoDo, on the other hand, did gain access to Brazilian forests by becoming a part owner in a Brazilian company in 1974.

The fact that the shortage did not result in increased foreign acquisitions can be explained by several factors. The first is that the poor experiences of the early Canadian ventures gave the companies a good idea of the difficulties involved in such activities – foreign establishment was no longer seen as a simple solution. The second factor is that the second half of the 1970s was characterized by poor profitability for Swedish companies. There was no financial foundation upon which to base new investments, and the companies chose to upgrade existing facilities rather than to invest in new capacity. The third factor was a change in corporate strategy. SCA and MoDo, ranked among the world's largest pulp producers in the 1960s, both invested in increasing the refinement of their products. For SCA, this meant investing in newsprint machinery and the expansion of kraftlinerboard production. SCA's purchase of Mölnlycke, with its hygiene products division, did much towards the achievement of this goal. MoDo invested in wood-free fine paper mills in connection with its pulp factory in Husum, and built three paper machines for the production of fine paper between 1972 and 1985 (Gårdlund, 1986, pp. 98–105).

The interest of these companies in securing access to raw materials has thus played a subordinate role in stimulating internationalization in recent years. It is possible, however, that the increased use of recycled fibre will once again increase the role of raw materials in this process. Access to such materials is concentrated in the densely populated regions outside Scandinavia, and increased recycling will force Swedish companies to build or to purchase facilities nearer to the large European cities. SCA's purchase of Reedpack in Britain in 1990 can be seen as a move in that direction. Included in this acquisition was Maybanks, Europe's second-largest recycled paper processor. SCA is now Europe's second-largest recycled paper handler, in addition to its position as Europe's largest private forest owner. Internationalization has in this way contributed to an expansion of the raw material base.

Securing markets abroad
All three of the companies discussed have invested in increasing the refinement levels of their products since the 1960s. The idea behind this move has been to reduce dependence on pulp sales. The reasons behind this shift are several: the first is that an increased refinement level decreases the vulnerability of Swedish products to the high cost of Swedish timber. Another benefit is that the increased refinement level buffers the companies from the price fluctuations of the pulp market. The third reason is that increased refinement allows the companies to experience integration economies, since integrated pulp-paper production has cost and quality advantages over unintegrated paper production. Pulp-producing Swedish paper companies thus have an edge over their pulp-purchasing competitors.

The implementation of the Swedish corporations' strategy to increase the refinement levels of their products was delayed by their concern about the role conflict introduced by increased production of paper. Pulp producers who started producing paper automatically became competitors to their pulp buyers. In this way increased refinement might have a negative impact on demand for the firm's major product. The corporations looked for ways to make use of Swedish firms' cost and quality advantages without building up a new role conflict. The central role of cost meant that the development of processing strategy was decided by production factors. Characteristics of the Swedish wood fibres and the ability to produce in large volume determined the specialization areas. The companies began by concentrating on bulk paper products, such as newsprint and kraftlinerboard. Both STORA and SCA invested in newsprint, while SCA also went into kraftliner production. Neither STORA nor SCA had any newsprint producers among their pulp customers and kraftliner was a new product imported from the USA. SCA's choice of kraftliner demanded efforts to develop a new market in Europe. In this way the two firms selected products which implied minimal competition with their old customers.

The bulk paper investments were a sign that the shift was primarily intended to reduce dependence on the pulp market. The intention was thus to find suitable paper types which could be produced in large volume, thereby using a great portion of the companies' pulp production. This increased integration did not, however, serve to change the character of the Swedish forestry industry – it remained a mass producer of standardized products (Rydberg, 1990, p. 118). The specializations were decided more by the characteristics of Swedish wood fibre than by the needs of the customers.

The transition from pulp production intended for sale to mass production of bulk paper products brought about new demands on the companies' marketing organization. Within production areas with only a few large customers (such as newsprint), it was necessary to win over customers from established paper manufacturers. The limited number of customers enabled direct contact between the manufacturers and the buyers. Within other areas with many small customers – like kraftliner and wood-free fine paper – the companies had different challenges. Here the need was to build up effective distribution and marketing channels in many countries to secure the sale of their products. Internationalization became an important element in this attempt.

Kraftlinerboard was a product which was sold to a large number of smaller box plants whose factories were located near their markets. With the development of SCA's kraftliner mill in Munksund, the company was forced to build up a marketing organization which would be able to work with the box plants in Europe's more densely populated areas. The question of how to secure the markets for kraftliner then arose within the company. A committee within the company arrived at the conclusion that 80% of the box plants were integrated with their liner mills. Within SCA, the expectations seemed to be that European manufacturers would continue along this path. There was also concern that the establishment of the EEC, with its free internal market and common trade barriers, would increase American kraftliner manufacturers' interest in the acquisition of European box plants. The conclusion reached by the company was that there existed no option except the purchase of European box plants if it was to secure a market for its product (SCA, 1979, pp. 193–4).

The first step came in 1961, with the purchase of 50% of Papela Navarra in Spain. In addition to its box plants, the company owned an integrated pulp-paper mill which supplied the cardboard section with liner and fluting. This purchase obviously did not fulfil SCA's needs for an outlet for its kraftliner board produced in Sweden, and it can primarily be seen as an attempt to keep American competitors out of the European market. Papela Navarra desperately needed a capital injection and so it turned to SCA and three American forestry companies with an offer. SCA's positive reply to this offer closed the door to the American companies' hopes of gaining a foothold in Europe. SCA's Spanish investment was followed by several more. A Danish corrugated board manufacturer, with a little over one-third of the home market, was purchased in 1963. After this, SCA purchased its largest liner customer in France, thereby acquiring two box plants in the country. Three years later, the company added another box plant in France to its holdings.

The experiences of the French factories had been good, and in 1974 the company proclaimed in a strategy document that internationalization would continue. SCA thus had a continuing interest in the purchase of foreign box plants in order to improve the sales potential of Swedish liner (*ibid.*, p. 474). Attention was now turned towards two other large European markets – Germany and Great Britain. SCA took a different path here than it had in France, choosing to co-operate with the German and British forestry companies instead.

In 1974, SCA became a half owner in the German forestry company Papierwerke Waldhof Aschenburg's (PWA) packaging division. After this, the division was re-established as an independent company under the name of Zewawell AG & Co. A similar arrangement was made in Great Britain in the late 1970s through a partial purchase of Jefferson Smurfit group's cardboard operations – a purchase which opened doors to corrugated board factories in Ireland and the UK. The result of these actions was that the SCA owned corrugated board factories in these countries with companies which were simultaneously its competitors. By the end of the 1970s, SCA was a full owner of corrugated board factories in Sweden and France and partial owner of factories in Germany, the UK, Ireland and Denmark. SCA divested itself of Papela Navarra SA during the 1970s, since it was never able to establish any real integration between the Swedish and Spanish units.

SCA's internationalization within the corrugated board sector continued during the second half of the 1980s. Six board companies were acquired in Great Britain, Belgium, France, Holland and Italy between 1987 and 1990. During the same period SCA pulled out of those companies which it owned together with its foreign competitors – Zewawell, Smurfit Corrugated and UK Corrugated. SCA today owns approximately 50 corrugated board and packaging companies in six European countries excluding Sweden.

MoDo began its integration towards paper production considerably later than SCA. As late as the end of the 1960s, MoDo was still primarily producing pulp for sale. A decision was made at the turn of the year 1969/70 that a fine paper machine with a capacity of 70,000 tonnes per year would be installed at the Husum mill. The intention here was to begin bulk production of wood-free, uncoated fine paper in large rolls (Gårdlund, 1986, p. 99). This change in direction constituted both a technical and a marketing challenge. The technical challenge was that the company's production method was new for large, rapid paper machines. The marketing challenge was how to gain access to the market with a large quantity of fine paper without affecting pulp sales. Integration meant that MoDo now played two parts – one as exporter of pulp to feed European fine-paper mills, and the other as a competitor of those same mills.

The investment in bulk rolled paper can be seen as a way to reduce the above conflict. The fine-paper mills of Europe were characterized by small paper machines and poor specialization. These machines were therefore used to produce a large number of products in short runs. MoDo's paper rolls would be sold to pulp-based paper mills in Europe, which would then convert the paper and sell it to the final consumer. It was in this way that MoDo's paper would not directly compete with that of its pulp customers. MoDo would remain a base raw-material supplier, while simultaneously offering more processed raw materials.

This strategy had two advantages beyond the reduced risk of conflict between MoDo as pulp producer and paper producer. The paper products could be sold to the same companies which previously bought pulp from the company, thereby reducing the demand for a new marketing organization. In addition, this solution would not require any fundamental organizational changes, since paper production could easily be assimilated by the pulp division. The plan had allowed for the paper production to be sold in roll form, and for the paper manufacturing to be incorporated into the pulp division. This, however, was not to be the case. The paper was eventually sold directly to the final consumer, and the manufacturing units were organized as an independent company called MoDo-Paper Ltd.

The chosen strategy had assumed a market-orientated organization. Following this strategy, the company strove to establish totally owned sales companies in the major European markets, with the long-term goal of becoming a power in the wholesaling arena as well. Entering the wholesale branch was seen to have many positive benefits, such as expanding the company's customer contact and access to a salesforce whose primary goal was the sale of its products. Completely owned wholesale activities were in this way seen as securing the company's markets abroad.

Efforts towards this end began as early as 1972, when the first fine paper machines went into service. In this year MoDo acquired Sweden's largest paper wholesaler – Svenskt Papper Ltd. The first move into the European market did not come until the 1980s, when the company took over three large wholesalers in Great Britain, Holland and France. In 1991, MoDo bought 40% of a Spanish wholesaler in an attempt to gain a foothold in that market.

Strengthening market positions

A driving force behind the industrialization of both MoDo and SCA during the 1970s and 1980s was the desire to ensure the sale of paper produced in their Swedish mills. The rate of internationalization was slowed somewhat during the 1970s owing to profitability problems caused by a weak market, high timber prices and an unfavourable exchange rate. This period was a time of consolidation rather than one of large new investments, and foreign investments were reduced accordingly. By the 1980s, a new element had appeared which affected the internationalization of Swedish forestry companies.

Non-European forestry companies had begun to show increased interest in their European counterparts, and a handful had already bought into pulp and paper companies on the continent. If this development had continued, there was a risk that the Swedish market position would be weakened. At about the same time the Swedish government removed currency regulations, and the Swedish companies gained new possibilities for the financing of foreign direct investments. SCA was the first to react to the new threats and possibilities.

In 1988 SCA purchased Laakirchen, an Austrian pulp and paper company which produced a special quality of printing paper (SC paper). With this acquisition SCA's printing paper line was broadened. The following year it made a bid for the giant German forestry company Feldmühle. Had this bid been accepted, SCA would have vastly reinforced its printing paper line, doubled its production of newsprint, become Europe's largest producer of LWC paper and become the market leader in printing paper. However, the bid was rejected and SCA was forced to turn its attentions elsewhere.

The next object of SCA's attentions was Reedpack in Great Britain, which it bought into instead. With this move, SCA acquired a recycled-fibre-based newsprint mill in England and two recycled-fibre-based testboardliner and fluting facilities in England and Holland. Several years earlier, the Italian cardboard producer Italcarta had been obtained, and with it access to recycled-fibre-based testliner and fluting capacity in Italy. Through the acquisition SCA became market leader on testliner and fluting in Italy. These two moves resulted in the foreign recycled-fibre-based testliner and fluting capacity exceeding the combined production of the companies two kraftliner mills in Sweden. SCA also acquired the French Peauduce. In this way the firm's market position on the French and British tissue markets was strengthened.

SCA's internationalization in the late 1980s cannot be said to have been motivated by the desire to secure markets for paper products manufactured in Sweden. The goal has rather been to strengthen the company's market position within certain prioritized product areas. This has been achieved by adding new products such as SC paper, LWC paper and testliner/fluting through the purchase of European competitors. These purchases have also served to make it more difficult for SCA's competitors to strengthen their market positions within this product area. Today, SCA is Europe's largest producer of corrugated board and related products. Wholly and partially owned box plants account for 75% of SCA production capacity of corrugated board. SCA's position in the printing paper market is somewhat weaker. With a production capacity of approximately one million tonnes per year, SCA ranks only ninth among Europe's producers of wood-containing paper. STORA has become the market leader in this area.

STORA's strong position can be seen as a partial result of SCA's aggressive purchasing strategy during the 1980s. SCA's bid for Feldmühle enabled STORA to purchase it instead. The process began when SCA bought 5% of the company's stocks, while showing interest in acquiring the entire company. The board at Feldmühle reacted negatively to this announcement, preferring to remain an independent German forestry company. At the same time, VEBA, which owned 50% of the company, exhibited an interest in divesting its shares, thereby reducing the board's chances of succeeding – the company was about to be bought. The board then reassessed the situation and felt that STORA would be a more interesting partner than SCA. This decision was probably the result of the fact that STORA and Feldmühle had dealt with each other for many years – being co-owners of a pulp factory and a newsprint mill in Sweden.

STORA was also interested. Since the mid-1980s the company's management had been stressing the value of scale to competitiveness. Modelling themselves after SCA, the company expanded its product line to include cardboard and uncoated wood-free fine paper through the purchases of Billerud in 1984 and Papyrus in 1986. With the purchase of Swedish Match in 1988, STORA added a number of other wood products to its product line – doors, flooring and kitchen interiors – as well as more paper products – packing products and packaging systems. Swedish Match also brought along a substantial international contact network. From STORA's point of view, the timing for a possible acquisition of Feldmühle was not good since it was busy assimilating its recent Swedish purchases, but this was an offer that could not be passed by when faced with the alternative of SCA getting Feldmühle instead. The acquisition meant that STORA doubled its sales volume and became the world's third-largest forestry company.

Through its purchase, STORA obtained two newsprint mills, a large LWC mill, a factory producing both LWC and fine paper, three units specializing in cardboard production and one fine paper mill. STORA's wholesale network also expanded, with sales of fine paper in Denmark, Norway, Finland, The Netherlands, Great Britain, Belgium and France now going primarily through wholly or partially owned wholesale companies.

MoDo's foreign investments were held at a relatively low level during the second half of the 1980s. The reason for this was that the acquisition of Holmen and Iggesund in 1988 limited the company's financial ability to expand abroad. The purchase of these two companies meant that MoDo added printing paper and cardboard as supplements to its fine paper production. These new companies did not do much to expand MoDo's foreign holdings. Holmen owned two bag factories in Britain and Germany, and bought two more, one in Germany in 1989 and one in Britain in 1991. Iggesund owned one cardboard factory in Britain. MoDo had also owned a French fine-paper mill since the end of the 1960s. As can be seen, MoDo's foreign production was still relatively limited. The purchase of Alicel/Alipap in 1991 boosted the market position of MoDo's fine paper division, making it the second largest in Europe.

The recent international expansion of the big three Swedish forestry companies has been characterized by a desire to strengthen market positions throughout Europe. Large direct investments abroad, a long international upswing and a favourable exchange rate have all led to unusually high profitability. The result of this period has been that STORA is Europe's largest producer of printing paper, SCA leads Europe in corrugated board production and MoDo is Europe's second-largest manufacturer of uncoated wood-free fine paper. These companies have been successful in using the acquisition of foreign companies and facilities to gain market position and increase competitiveness.

The geography of transnational forestry companies

The international expansion carried out by the three forestry companies has resulted in a gradual shift from domestic export companies specializing in pulp production to transnational companies active within a number of product areas. The new situation brings to the fore questions concerning the spatial distribution of production in the future. What role will the Swedish holdings play now that the companies have gone multinational?

The situation prior to the acquisitions of the 1980s was relatively clear cut. The majority of the facilities at that time were located in Sweden, with foreign holdings being primarily processing facilities and wholesale companies. This pattern could be understood in terms of the strategy of the time which was based on the effective utilization of Swedish wood fibre. This strategy was founded primarily on the characteristics of Swedish wood, and not on the needs of the consumer. This dominant role of raw materials led to a concentration on pulp production, which would later be integrated with bulk paper production. The production of both pulp and paper was situated in Sweden. In this setting it was only natural that the central R & D laboratories were established in connection to some of the domestic pulp factories. Activities in this period were concentrated in Sweden, with the rest of Europe serving primarily as an export market.

This situation changed dramatically in the 1980s. The old activities in Sweden naturally remained, but a large number of new acquisitions were based outside Sweden. Pulp and paper production were no longer only located in Sweden – the three companies now produce about the same amount of pulp and paper abroad as they do in Sweden. In addition to production facilities, SCA and STORA have also obtained R & D centres on the continent. They have also placed the main offices for two product divisions abroad, with STORA Feldmühle in Düsseldorf and SCA Packaging in Brussels.

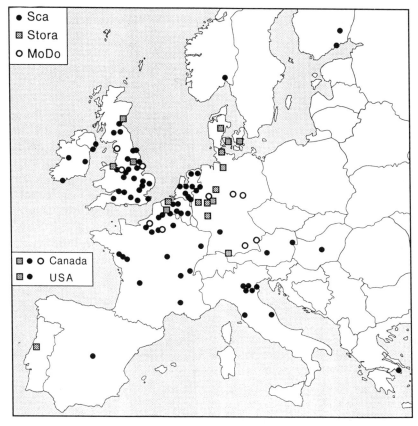

Figure 8.1   SCA, STORA and MoDo: geographical distribution

Today's geographic distribution (Figure 8.1) does not reflect any rational planning, but rather the structures of those companies that were purchased. The companies are now undergoing a long restructuring which will define their future geographic distribution. The end result of this restructuring process will be decided by many factors. The strategy choices of the companies and their ability to carry them out will play a large role, as will competition and managerial optimism. The rate of geographical restructuring varies between different functions. Management groups can be relocated quickly and with relatively few problems. The number of people affected by such a move is small, and their activities are not tied to heavy capital investments. One main argument for the relocating of management outside Sweden is that decisions should be made nearer the place of production, so that the larger a division's share of production that lies abroad, the greater the likelihood that the managerial staff will relocate. The above-mentioned foreign placement of two of SCA's and STORA's divisions' headquarters is an example of this, as more than half of their production capacity was positioned abroad.

The restructuring of the production structure, on the other hand, is a process which could take decades. It is therefore impossible to make any reliable predictions concerning its final shape, as a large number of unknown circumstances will affect the timetable and content of those investment and divestment decisions which will be made in the coming years. The best that can be ascertained now is the distinction of a possible trend in the restructuring pattern. Access to raw materials is still of great importance to Swedish pulp and paper production. As mentioned above, many of the companies' product choices have been steered by the price and characteristics of Swedish wood. During the past decade the competitive situation has been altered somewhat by the increased importance of recycled fibres as a raw material. Recycled fibre has become a sort of 'urban forest' which grows best in densely populated urban centres such as southeast England, Paris, Randstaat and the Ruhr area, with Scandinavia producing relatively little. It is therefore economically advantageous to locate production units in the densely populated areas outside Sweden. The bulk of the recycled fibre operations will be located on the continent, while Swedish facilities will be forced to concentrate on those products which demand virgin fibres.

The internationalization of SCA and STORA can be seen as an adjustment to a new environment. Through the purchase of Reedpack, SCA gained access to one of Europe's largest recycled-fibre collection facilities and a recycled-fibre-based paper mill. The acquisition of Italcarta allowed for the company's kraftliner board production in Sweden to be complemented by return-fibre-based testliner board production in Italy. At about the same time, the restructuring of the Swedish newsprint operations was begun, with one of the newsprint machines in Ortviken being replaced by an LWC machine. Newsprint is a product which is rapidly being dominated by recycled fibre production, a threat which SCA had chosen to meet by increasing the processing level of its Swedish newsprint, and expanding its recycled production abroad.

The pattern which seems to be appearing is that Swedish production is becoming of higher quality based on virgin fibres, while the companies are expanding recycled production on the continent and in Britain. Growth in production volume will occur outside Sweden, resulting in an increasing share of operations outside the country. The speed at which this will occur depends on both external and internal factors. As more qualities of paper are produced using recycled materials, the volume of Swedish production will be dependent upon the ability to develop new qualities which demand the use of virgin fibre. Future Swedish production is thus dependent upon both the rate at which recycled production expands and the innovative abilities of the Swedish companies. The financial position and profitability of the Swedish forestry companies influence their investment capacity, which in turn influences the rate at which Swedish production can be restructured. A weak financial position brings with it a risk that the restructuring will take the form of closures and layoffs.

A major question now is how these changes in management and production location will affect the localization of R & D activities. In a comparison with other Swedish multinational companies it is evident that external localization is an exception. Of 22 companies examined, only one – SKF with eight foreign research centres – had any substantial R & D operations outside Sweden (Forsgren, Holm and Johansson, 1991, p. 50). Against the background of this study it can be seen that internationalization of R & D activities begins late in the process. If this also holds true for Swedish forestry companies, then at least the foreign placement of MoDo's R & D operations is not of current interest, as they are presently located only in Sweden.

The situation here is different from SCA and STORA, since they gained foreign R & D centres through the purchases made in the 1980s. R & D restructuring does, however, take considerable time. At the time of STORA's purchase of Feldmühle, the company had not had time to integrate the activities of its two earlier purchases, Billerud and Papyrus. STORA Teknik, the group's collective research department, has laboratories in Falun and Säffle. The department serves primarily STORA Cell and STORA Billerud. STORA Papyrus has its own independent research section connected to its paper mill at Nymölla. When STORA took over Feldmühle the company had its own centralized research group, which was considerably smaller than STORA's. The company has yet to integrate that unit into STORA Teknik. The R & D activities at STORA's different units are historically determined and reflect production at the connected mills. The major disadvantage with the existence of many research groups working independently is that there can be overlap, but there are also benefits in that it may create a competitiveness which leads to increased innovation and can act as a lure to recruit qualified personnel.

The basic question is whether the companies will choose a centralized or decentralized R & D organization. Here, again, experience from other companies shows that if the company is to concentrate its R & D activity at a single location, then that is most likely to be located in Sweden (Sölvell, Zander and Porter, 1991, pp. 212–13). The forestry companies are still very dependent on Swedish competence for the development of products and production processes, and so are not yet at the point where they can detach themselves from their Swedish base (see Porter, 1990, pp. 613–15). Continued investment in R & D in Sweden can be seen as a prerequisite for successfully increasing competitiveness in the future. Concentration of R & D activities outside Sweden at this stage can be seen as incredibly risky.

The picture is somewhat different for those companies which choose to invest in more decentralized R & D. There are two major factors behind such a decision. The first is that the difficulties associated with R & D restructuring make it easier to continue building upon the structure that already exists. Those companies which began with several research groups will be tempted to leave the structure untouched. There are also strategic reasons to make such a choice. Earlier strategy was formed with raw-material-based production in mind, taking into account the special qualities of Swedish wood. The idea here was to take the raw materials from the Swedish forests and transform them into profitable products – products which were chosen based on the raw materials available. The management at the three companies has a different view today, with the customer taking priority over the raw materials. SCA is the company which has been most successful in transmitting this new view, with its annual report stating that the ultimate consumers' needs are met with expertise in the selecting of products which take advantage of the quality of the fibres. SCA is thus assumed to have an understanding of the consumers' needs, the products' needs and service in order to provide the best possible solutions (SCA, 1992, p. 4).

The reorientation of strategy towards a focus on consumer needs is leading to a gradual increase in the processing level of Swedish products, which can be expected to influence both the direction and the organization of R & D activities. The three companies' research divisions have been especially successful in the area of pulp production. Great advances have been made in improving manufacturing processes and control systems to achieve a higher and more even pulp quality. Increased environmental regulations led to increased research activity in this area as well during the 1980s, with successes here including environmentally friendly pulp-bleaching techniques. The Swedish successes in pulp research can be attributed to the fact that they have been branch specialists for a long time – especially MoDo and SCA. The technical competence within the paper area has been further increased through the trend towards increased refinement of products, but it has yet to reach the same level as in the pulp branch.

The broadening and deepening of the companies' competence brought about by a refinement of the product line occurred automatically to a certain extent through the experience of the purchased foreign companies. Both STORA and SCA obtained knowledge about the printing characteristics of paper through the acquisition of Feldmühle and Laakirchen. It was thus natural that these two companies concentrated their paper research in foreign units. One argument for this move is that the other country has a tradition with the product that does not exist in Sweden. A division of labour should therefore arise where research concerning pulp and environmental questions is placed in Sweden, while that regarding paper and recycled-fibre-based products should be located abroad. The companies' internationalization could thus serve to build up two home bases, something which may be necessary to secure markets, but which often simply undermines the old home base (Sölvell, Zander and Porter, 1991, p. 213).

There have been other arguments for a division of a forestry company's activities. Research at the companies' Swedish laboratories has a particularly academic characteristic, with high ambitions and a desire to develop new knowledge which may be of use to the company. Research in European companies is of a more practical nature, with the task being defined as using existing knowledge to solve practical problems (see Rehn, 1992, pp. 76–7). This difference in tradition opens up the possiblity for another type of division of labour. The academic research regarding pulp and paper can be carried out in Sweden, while engineering-type research is pursued in co-operation with customers in the rest of Europe. The first type of research is primarily internal, with customers being the other firms within the group. Pulp research is aimed at the group's paper mills, while paper research is aimed at the processing units. This type of distribution will ensure that competence within Swedish R & D is broadened.

R & D investments within the forestry industry become smaller as the products become more refined. This is partially the result of the fact that highly refined products tend to take on the characteristics of standard goods. Their quality is determined by products produced earlier in the line. If the companies are going to take seriously their goal of serving customers better, then they will have to develop solutions which are tailored to the individual customer's situation. The companies will then be forced to invest in new product development as never before. The development of new products requires combining competence regarding both wood fibres and recycled fibres with the customer's needs. Proximity to the customer and access to the required competence are necessary prerequisites for the success of such a development process.

A concentration of R & D activities in Sweden must therefore be combined with the establishment of a number of smaller development centres near the customers abroad. These centres will in turn serve as customers of the central research unit in Sweden. Their demands will serve as a guarantee that academic research in Sweden will be focused on relevant problems. There is, however, a considerable risk that conflicts will arise between the Swedish and foreign units. While the personnel in the foreign-based units will have no difficulty in seeing the company's activities as customer based, there is a risk that those in Sweden may still see them as raw material based.

Future division of labour

The conclusion is that the division of labour in the transnational Swedish forestry companies will probably be based on the individual characteristics of the regions. Sweden, with its deep tradition of academically orientated research into the characteristics of fibres, will remain the centre for research in that area. On the continent and in Britain, with their tradition of more engineering-based research and proximity to customers, a number of development centres will be established where the company, in co-operation with customers, can develop new products. The companies' prioritization of customer needs will ensure that growth within the R & D units will primarily occur outside Sweden. This will not, however, reduce the companies' dependence on Sweden, as it will play a major role in ensuring the companies' ability continuously to upgrade their competitiveness.

9

British Steel: the limits to internationalization

Ray Hudson

Introduction

Over the last three or four decades there has been a growing emphasis on internationalization in corporate activities, encompassing both an intensification of existing strategies and an active search for new ones. The extent of internationalization of flows of money capital, commodities and labour has expanded as both production and trade have become increasingly conducted within a global arena. Industries such as cars and consumer electronics have become exemplars of a new international division of labour in which different stages of the production process have been dispersed over a wide range of countries.

But not all companies, in all sectors, have either wished or been able to internationalize their activities to the same extent or in the same ways. Steel companies typically developed their operations historically in relation to national markets. Not least, this was because steel was seen as a key industry in relation to the production of armaments and the means of destruction. A powerful national steel industry was emblematically seen as a symbol of national economic and/or military virility – national industries as the guarantor of key national interests.

Whilst subsequently steel has ceased to be quite so strategically central an industry and steel companies have sought to internationalize both their supplies of raw materials and their markets, they have been much less heavily involved in this process than major companies in other key sectors. This is *a fortiori* the case in relation to the internationalization of production. An important reason for this in relation to steel companies in Europe is the considerable state involvement in the industry, either via the regulation of private companies or via public sector ownership and nationalization. Public ownership has imposed considerable political constraints on the spheres of operation of steel companies, especially as regards production. It has largely confined such activities to the national territory. Similarly, public sector steel companies are much more heavily constrained in the scope that they have for policies of product diversification, both upstream and downstream of basic steel and into other activities. It is against the background of these introductory remarks that the significance of differing forms of internationalization and the limits to these in the policies of the British Steel Corporation (BSC) will be assessed.

Setting the context: the legacy of private sector failure

Despite a growing general disillusionment with nationalization (see Crosland, 1956), in the specific case of steel, nationalization continued to exert its ideological fascination and to fulfil a 'symbolic role' (McEachern 1980) for both the Labour government and the wider labour movement in the 1960s (though support for it was not unanimous: see Wilson 1974). More pragmatically, a mechanism was needed to modernize the steel industry, for this was central to the Labour government's broader strategy for manufacturing set out in the National Plan (Department of Economic Affairs, 1965). Enhancing the efficiency of steel production would both help resist import penetration and increase exports. Moreover, steel was a key input for industries such as engineering, vehicles and consumer 'white goods'. Their international competitiveness was influenced by the price of steel. Reducing that price would require

Figure 9.1 BISF review of the British steel industry

major investment in modern production facilities but steel production was no longer profitable – the rate of profit in the steel industry had fallen dramatically from 17.3% in 1958 to 1.9% in 1967 (BSC, 1968).

Faced with collapsing profitability, the British Iron and Steel Federation (BISF) commissioned a review (BISF, 1966) of private sector plans for the industry. In summary, this advocated closing 65% of existing steelworks, writing off 9.0 million tonnes of existing capacity and adding 12.5 million tonnes of new capacity. This latter was to be concentrated at five coastal or near-coastal locations – Llanwern and Port Talbot in south Wales, Ravens-craig in Scotland, and Scunthorpe and Teesside in England (see Figure 9.1). Many of the major private steel companies had increasingly moved to coastal locations as domestic ores were exhausted and reliance on imports grew (see, for example, Hudson and Sadler, 1986), though production remained heavily focused on the national market. A further switch towards coastal locations would allow easy integration into world markets for both raw materials inputs and outputs of finished products.

The problem was how to fund this investment programme. On technical grounds its implementation was necessary to create a modern competitive steel industry but it constituted too great a financial risk to attract private capital from outside steel, while the steel companies lacked the resources to fund it themselves (Bryer, Brignell and Maunders, 1982). As with coal (Hudson, 1989) and the railways (Hudson, 1979) in the 1940s, nationalization offered a way out of this impasse, with generous compensation quelling opposition from the owners of the steel plants (Kelf Cohen, 1969), enabling them to switch their capital into more lucrative activities and locations. In short, the steel industry was seen to require a national and nationalized champion (HMSO, 1965).

In search of international competitiveness: nationalization, privatization and the restructuring of production within BSC

Planning for modernization and growth, 1967–76
What occurred in 1967 was nationalization *within* the steel industry, only encompassing the bulk-steel making interests of the 14 largest producers. Much of the more profitable special and engineering steels activities was thus left in the private sector. This political concession to the interests of private capital had significant implications for BSC's future.

Heavily constrained to bulk manufacture of ordinary steels, BSC began to implement its 'Heritage Strategy', the proposals contained in the BISF report. Compared to other countries, especially Japan, the overall scale of investment and the size of individual production complexes seemed inadequate, however (see Cockerill and Silbertson, 1973). A more radical approach, mimicking the Japanese, was necessary. The corporate response to this perceived need was formalized in the *Ten Year Development Strategy* (DTI, 1973).

This envisaged transforming BSC via a massive programme of fixed capital investment (£3,000 million over ten years, in 1972 prices), overall capacity expansion (from 27 to 33–5 million tonnes by the late 1970s and 36–8 million tonnes a year by the early 1980s), and marked increases in labour productivity (via closure of older technologically obsolete capacity and a reduction in employment from 230,000 to 180,000). Investment was to be further channelled towards the 'big five' integrated complexes to allow scale economies to be achieved in highly loaded, heavily automated, computer-controlled and technically efficient bulk iron and steel production and so to remould BSC into an internationally competitive and profitable producer. However, this presumed that the benefits of scale economies would automatically follow. There was no appreciation that, for these economies to be realized, *other* assumptions had to be met – not least those relating to growth in the international market – that were central to the proposals embodied in the *Strategy*.

Planning for cut-backs and closures in the context of collapsing markets, 1976–80
Initially, there were problems within the UK in implementing the *Development Strategy*, arising from the co-ordination of expansion in some locations, closures in others and political opposition to the latter. These were soon dwarfed, however, by those resulting from changes in domestic and international markets. Rather than expand as the *Strategy* had assumed, annual demand for BSC's output fell from around 25 million tonnes in the early 1970s to well under 20 million tonnes in 1974–5, and subsequently declined still further as both markets failed to expand in line with assumptions. Indeed, both national and international markets contracted sharply after 1974, whilst competition for shares of these markets intensified greatly, not least because BSC had not been alone in pursuing expansionist policies (see Hudson and Sadler, 1989).

This discrepancy between actual and projected output growth had severe effects on BSC's financial position, especially as it was undertaking considerable new fixed capital investment at a time when interest rates were rising sharply (Cockerill, 1980). In 1974–5, BSC needed to achieve 85% capacity utilization to break even. As demand fell, capacity utilization fell far below this, and from 1975–6 BSC began to accumulate a burgeoning deficit (Table 9.1). This coincided with growing political pressure, both domestic and international, for the Labour government to curb the growth of public expenditure (see Hudson and Williams, 1986). Consequently, BSC was forced to cut these growing losses. Expansion was replaced by savage retrenchment as BSC accepted a target capacity in the range 16–22 million tonnes per annum (DTI, 1978).

The financial constraints on BSC tightened in 1979 after the election of a Conservative government. It justified this via reference to EU policies following the declaration of a state of 'manifest crisis' in the steel industry in October 1980 (Sadler, 1985). Moreover, the deflationary effect of the government's economic policies precipitated a dramatic collapse in manufacturing output and a corresponding fall in steel demand in the UK (Townsend, 1983), a market on which BSC remained heavily reliant despite its efforts to increase its exports.

Table 9.1   BSC: key indicators, 1967–91

	Profit (loss) (£ million)	Crude steel output (m tonnes)	Capital expenditure net of grants (£ million)	UK employment at year end (000s)
1967–8	(22)	22.9	nd	254
1968–9	(23)	24.2	nd	254
1969–70[1]	12	12.3	nd	255
1970–1	(10)	24.7	nd	252
1971–2	(68)	20.4	nd	230
1972–3	3	24.2	154	227
1973–4	34	23.0	155	220
1974–5	70	20.8	273	228
1975–6	(268)	17.2	462	210
1976–7	(117)	19.7	494	208
1977–8	(513)	17.4	401	197
1978–9	(357)	17.3	267	186
1979–80[2]	(1,784)	14.1	261	166
1980–1	(1,020)	11.9	148	121
1981–2	(504)	14.1	164	104
1982–3	(869)	11.7	122	81
1983–4	(256)	13.4	164	71
1984–5	(383)	13.0	210	65
1985–6	38	14.0	220	54
1986–7	178	11.7	269	52
1987–8	410	14.7	253	52
1988–9[3]	461	15.4	307	52
1989–90	399	14.4	450	51
1990–1	19[4]	13.8	459	51

Notes:
1   Six-month trading period from October 1969 to March 1970.
2   Figures affected by strike action, January–March 1980.
3   The company was privatized in the course of the year.
4   First six months (April–September 1990) only. The comparable figure for 1989–90 was £307 million.

Source: British Steel, *Annual Reports*, 1967–91.

In these circumstances, the only way to stem haemorrhaging losses was substantial plant closure. The scale of retrenchment became clear as BSC unveiled its 1979 *Business Plan* and then further proposals in its *Corporate Plan* (BSC, 1980). The latter envisaged additional cuts in capacity to 14.4 million tonnes and in employment to below 80,000 (House of Commons Industry and Trade Committee, 1981). Furthermore, it was now clear that the major coastal complexes were no longer sacrosanct.

Planning for privatization, 1980–8: in search of new routes to international competitiveness and profits
From 1980, government policies increasingly aimed to return BSC to the private sector. The 1980 *Corporate Plan* and the Iron and Steel Act 1981 removed the statutory obligation on BSC to provide a full range of steel products and created opportunities for the privatization of profitable areas of its activities. The internal structure of BSC was radically reorganized. Regional divisions were replaced by discrete and decentralized product-based businesses. Each of these was a profit centre, facilitating privatization of profitable businesses. Furthermore, BSC was forced into a series of mergers with private-sector steel producers – the Phoenix mergers (ISTC, 1982) – thereby privatizing its more profitable special steels activities. Seven major Phoenix companies were created between 1981 and 1986 (Table 9.2; see also Hudson and Sadler, 1987a; 1987b), often at considerable public expenditure cost (Public Accounts Committee, 1985).

A crucial consequence of the Phoenix mergers was increasingly to confine BSC to bulk steel making at a time when its major international competitors were diversifying downstream into higher value-added steel products within engineering, into other more profitable sectors of manufacturing such as microelectronics or out of manufacturing and into various service activities. BSC was being pinned back even further to the bulk production of basic steel as its competitors in Germany and Japan were further diversifying out of it, intensifying

Table 9.2 The Phoenix companies

Company	Date of formation	Initial shareholdings
Allied Steel and Wire	1981	50% BSC, 50% GKN
Sheffield Forgemasters	1982	50% BSC, 50% Johnson Firth Brown
British Bright Bar	1983	40% BSC, 40% GKN, 20% Brynmill
Seamless Tubes	1984	75% BSC, 25% TI
Cold Drawn Tubes	1984	75% TI, 25% BSC
United Merchant Bar	1984	75% Caparo, 25% BSC
United Engineering Steels	1986	50% BSC, 50% GKN

Source: NEDO, 1986.

Table 9.3   Major capital investments by individual BSC works, 1983–9 (£ million)

Works	Facilities	Cost	Total
Port Talbot	Hot strip-mill modernization Hot strip-mill reheat furnace Blast furnace reline Second continuous casting plant	171 16 31 70	288
Teesside	Cokeovens rebuild Beam mill reheat furnace Blast furnace rebuild Ladle-arc furnace Beam mill modernization	44 17 50 13 69	193
Llanwern	Continuous casting plant Vacuum degassing facility Hot-dip galvanizing line	47 12 59	118
Shotton	Hot-dip galvanizing line Electrogalvanizing line	30 32	62
Scunthorpe	Sinter plant Ladle-arc furnace	45 15	60
Trostre	Continuous annealing line	48	48
Ravenscraig	Blast furnace coal-injection plant	15	15

Source: Compiled from British Steel, 1988.

pressures for it to become a profitable bulk steel producer as a necessary prelude to *its* own privatization. This posed great problems. Major capacity reductions to bring supply more in line with demand via complete closure of one or more of its five major integrated complexes were ruled out by political constraints (for example, see House of Commons Industry and Trade Committee, 1983). Under these circumstances, and those of the severe geographical and sectoral constraints imposed on its activities, BSC could only pursue the goals of international competitiveness and profitability via other routes. These involved a combination of partial capacity cuts, substantial job losses (reducing employment to just over 50,000) and a radical redefinition of working practices, allied to selective fixed capital investment (Table 9.3). Fresh capital investment was intended to increase competitiveness in two ways: first, by increasing output of products with growth prospects, such as zinc-coated and plastic-coated steels and, secondly, by raising labour productivity for existing products (for example, the proportion of continuously cast steel rose from 22% in 1980–1 to 70% in 1987–8). The climate of industrial relations, working practices and methods of wage determination were all radically redefined as part of the process of increasing labour productivity (see, for instance, Fevre, 1987; Boulding, 1988). Severe employment reductions were accompanied by deteriorating terms and conditions for those jobs that remained. Steel workers and their communities clearly bore a disproportionate share of the costs of restoring BSC to profitability in terms of lost jobs, in politically determined circumstances that denied it options of sectoral diversification and internationalization that were open to many of its main competitors (Table 9.1).

Back to the future: the private sector inheritance and the policies of BSC, 1988–92

By the second half of the 1980s, BSC had at last become a profitable steel producer. In 1988, therefore, after a capital reconstruction involving writing off £642 million of accumulated losses, it was privatized. A share issue valuing the company at £2,500 million was three times oversubscribed: 25% of the shares went to overseas investors (Sadler, 1990). As the ownership of BSC became in part international, many of the previous constraints on its activities

Table 9.4 Major capital investments by individual BSC works, 1990–1 (£ million)

Works	Facilities	Cost	Total
Comissioned in 1990–1			
Port Talbot	Second continuous casting plant	70	
	Two self-discharging bulk ore and coal carriers	64	
	Pickle line and cold mill integration	36	170
Teesside	Coil-plate mill replacement downcoiler	17	17
Skinningrove	Special-sections mill enhancement	21	21
Llanwern	Hot-dip galvanizing line	59	59
Scunthorpe	Blast furnace rebuild	42	
	Coke oven rebuild	15	57
Major schemes in progress, 30 March 1991			
Port Talbot	No. 4 blast furnace rebuild	66	
	Hot strip-mill shape and profile control (includes Llanwern)	47	113
Teesside	Lackenby beam mill, new stands	69	69
Hartlepool	20-inch pipe-mill enhancement	11	11
Llanwern	Second continuous casting plant	99	
	Continuous cold-rolling mill	37	
	BOS vessels replacement	13	149
Scunthorpe	BOS fume control	13	
	Coke ovens wet-charging system	10	23
Trostre	Wide electrolytic tinning line	40	40

Source: BSC, *Annual Report*, 1991.

– not least those on the scale and location of production – significantly weak-ened. This became immediately apparent in relation to the fate of the Rav-enscraig complex, which closed completely with the loss of the remaining 1,200 jobs in mid-1992.

In this way, BSC sought to counter a rapid deterioration in its financial position as profits again became losses and to underpin its position as an internationally competitive producer. Moreover, it was also eager to consoli-date this position through further changes in terms and conditions of work and remuneration. It introduced 'total quality performance' programmes, aimed at cutting costs by eliminating mistakes and incorporating workers' on-the-job learning so as to produce continuous gains in labour productivity, as a necess-ary condition for future plant survival. It also sought to restructure relations with its supplier companies whilst increasingly subcontracting activities such as catering, cleaning, and maintenance and repair. This involved reducing the number of suppliers by some 66% and seeking stable relationships with high-quality suppliers on a 'just-in-time' basis. Each of the remaining four major complexes is now involved in an interplant struggle for investment (Table 9.4), profits and survival as BSC seeks further to redefine its production configura-tion within the UK as part of its corporate pursuit of international competitive-ness and survival.

At the same time, BSC sought a greater degree of vertical integration in its activities within the UK to protect its market position there. In part, this has involved acquiring downstream processors of steel, often its own former customers such as Stelco Hardy, a manufacturer of stainless-steel tubes pur-chased in 1991. More significantly, it has extended its operations down-stream into distribution by purchasing steel stockists, both nationally and internationally, as state regulations which had previously prevented this were relaxed. Within Europe, it extended its purchases of such companies into Norway and Spain (Table 9.5). Within the UK, in 1990 it bought C. Walker and Sons, then the largest stockholder and its own biggest customer, for £330 million. This increased BSC's share of the stockholding market to over 33%. This strategically important shift in marketing strategy – one that BSC's competitors have also vigorously pursued – is also related to tech-nological changes in steel-consuming industries. Increasingly, stockholding companies secure increased profits by tailoring products to customers' speci-fications. The shift by motor vehicle manufacturers within the UK to just-in-time production strategies (Sadler, 1992) is also influencing these changes. By 1990–1, 45% of BSC's output was distributed through its own or other stockholders, whereas in 1967 only 25% was distributed in this way. The boundaries among final processing, stockholding and distribution have be-come more blurred as stockholding companies have installed processing plants (such as decoilers, cutters and profilers) and these latter activities are occupying an increasingly important position within the competitive strat-egies of the privatized BSC, as it seeks to protect its position in the national market from international competitors.

Table 9.5 British Steel stockholding companies: selected examples

Country	Company	Date of establish-ment	Comments
France	British Steel France SA	1975	Wholly owned subsidiary. Has three operating subsidiaries – UC2, Profilacier and HLI
Germany	British Steel-Walter Blume Handels	1976	British Steel took a 75% stake in 1976. In 1978 became a wholly owned subsidiary. Blume Handels Co. originally formed in 1948
	Fischer Profil	1987	Formed by sale of part of J. Fischer to British Steel. Wholly owned subsidiary. Fischer formed in 1938
The Netherlands	Feijen Group	1987	Acquired by BSC three operation companies. Established 1960
	Van der Vliet and DeJonge	1987	British Steel took a majority holding in 1987. Originally formed in 1917
Norway	Norsk Stål Distributions	1991	British Steel holds 24% of share capital, an associate company, comprising three wholly owned subsidiaries
Spain	Laminacion y Derivados SA	1988	British Steel bought 24% of share capital in 1988. Established 1941
Canada	British Steel Canada	1973	Formed by acquisition of H.M. Long Ltd. Has four operating companies
USA	British Steel USA	1969	Established by BSC. Six operating companies

Source: Compiled from BSC, 1991.

Internationalization and its limits within BSC

Clearly when BSC was a nationalized industry, a putative national champion, there were strong political limits on activities outside the UK. In particular, its production strategy was constrained to being wholly UK based. Privatization in principle removed such political limitations but significant economic ones remain. It is implausible, for example, to expect BSC to embark on major greenfield investment in new integrated production complexes outside the UK in a context of continuing global overcapacity in the 1990s. Nevertheless,

BSC's internationalization strategy has altered in significant ways since its formation in 1967 and these are further considered below in terms of raw material supplies, distributions and sales, and production.

Raw materials
From the outset, BSC's production strategy within the UK was premissed upon the use of imported iron ores in its major integrated complexes. There was nothing particularly new in this. Iron and steel companies had imported ores since the nineteenth century (see, for example, Hudson and Sadler, 1986). What was new was the increasing, and in the end total, reliance upon imported ores. This was partly a response to the exhaustion of domestic ores, partly a result of technical changes in production. The aim was to counter rising coal prices by reducing the amount of coke needed to produce iron through the use of richer imported ores. Furthermore, improvements in blast furnace technology and increases in blast furnace size and resultant scale economies would cut the costs of iron and in turn steel production and increase BSC's international competitiveness. As domestic production of iron ore fell – from over 17 million tons in 1960 to 4.3 million tonnes in 1978 and 50,000 tons by 1990 – BSC's imports of iron ore rose rapidly. Domestic production has declined to a point at which almost all the ore it smelted is imported. In 1990–1, BSC processed 17 million tonnes of iron ore, virtually all imported principally from Australia, Brazil and Canada.

Until 1979, however, there was a political constraint on BSC's permitted level of coking coal imports of around 1 million tonnes per annum. With the election of the Conservative government in that year, however, this limit was lifted. Moreover, it was removed at a time of increasing availability of cheap coking coal on the international market – to a considerable degree a consequence of major oil multinationals such as BP and Exxon diversifying into coal after the oil price rises of 1973–4. BSC was, therefore, able to move rapidly towards reliance upon imports. Although part of a long-term strategy to cut production costs, in the short term, in fact, it involved increased costs as a result of the necessity to rebuild coke ovens incorporating technologies appropriate to coking imported coals (see Hudson and Sadler, 1984). Almost all its coking coal is now bought on the international market. In 1990–1, for example, it imported 8 million tonnes of coal from Australia, Canada, Poland and the USA; it also bought a small amount, some 400,000 tonnes, from British Coal but 'at world market prices' (BSC, 1991). This is indicative of the changed relationship between two formerly nationalized companies. Once regulated through administrative decisions within the state it is now mediated through the pricing mechanisms of global commodity markets as BSC has chosen to become almost exclusively dependent on imports for supplies of its key raw materials. It is also a change that has wrought social and economic havoc in localities in which coking-coal collieries have closed because of these changes in BSC sourcing policies (see Beynon, Hudson and Sadler, 1991).

Distribution and sales

BSC's future as defined in the 1973 *Development Strategy* was predicated on its becoming an internationally competitive bulk producer of ordinary steels in an expanding market. It assumed 2.6% annual growth in UK domestic steel demand and of 4–5% growth in world steel trade (DTI, 1973). The central underlying assumption of strong growth in steel demand and BSC's ability to exploit this was, however, very quickly shown to be untenable. As the Chairman of BSC, Sir Charles Villiers, later remarked with studied understatement: 'I have to say that the 1973 Plan has been overtaken by events' (House of Commons Select Committee on Nationalized Industries, 1978, p. 517).

Nevertheless, BSC has made great efforts to increase export sales. In recent years, as part of its global marketing strategy, it has established or acquired sales offices, stockholders and joint-venture companies for distribution and, in some cases, processing in several other countries. It has, for example, established a worldwide network of over 130 sales agents and established (by 1991) sales offices in 17 countries. More significantly, in terms of market penetration and control, it has established stockholding and associated companies in the major markets of the capitalist world (Table 9.5).

Initially, it focused these efforts on North America but growing protectionism in the USA, a recurrent theme from the 1970s, forced it to look elsewhere. This intensified the pressures to expand export sales elsewhere in a climate of increasingly fierce intercorporate competition. Following the UK's entry to the EU, but especially in the period immediately before and after privatization, BSC sought to secure its position within the major markets of the EU, typically via acquisitions of, or mergers with, established stockholders and distributors. At the same time, EU entry opened the UK market to European producers and BSC's competitors sought to acquire stockholding outlets within the UK. For example, in 1990 Usinor-Sacilor took a 20% stake in ASD, the second-largest steel distributor within the UK. Therefore, British Steel's increasing vertical integration within the UK was a defensive move to protect its position within its national market whilst its strategy of internationalizing its distribution and stockholding activities is a key element of its offensive strategy to expand export markets. Both types of corporate strategy are part of a broader restructuring of the industry as companies search for competitive advantage.

British Steel's efforts to enhance its export markets have not been without success. It is the UK's eighth largest manufacturing exporter but still sold a majority – about 67% – of its output in the UK in 1991. It remains dangerously dependent on a fragile UK market and, for that reason, postprivatization, has sought increasingly to internationalize its markets not just through exports from the UK but through steel production in other countries.

Production

British Steel's profits first slumped dramatically, then became losses from the latter part of 1991, a direct reflection of the more generalized recession within the UK economy and of British Steel's continuing heavy reliance upon the UK market. Despite its efforts to internationalize its distribution and sales networks, it remained deeply dependent on the UK market. It is in this context that its postprivatization attempts further to internationalize its markets by increasingly internationalizing its productive activities through acquisitions, mergers and strategic alliances with steel producers in other countries must be understood. This, along with diversification out of steel, is the only route available to British Steel as it seeks to expand and consolidate its position. The latter approach is now under active and critical reconsideration by many German and Japanese companies that attempted it. Consequently, they are regrouping around their core activities because diversification has failed to yield expected profits. It is not surprising, therefore, that British Steel has sought to internationalize steel production, attempting to reinforce its world market position in product areas such as structural steels in which it already has a significant presence. One significant problem for BSC, however, is that it is internationally strong in relatively mature product areas and relatively weak in those with greater growth potential.

Furthermore, internationalization of production is proving a difficult and problematic strategy. In 1990 British Steel did successfully purchase the Troisdorf division of Klockner in Germany for £310 million, but this has been its sole major acquisition to date although it did conclude a much smaller joint venture with Svensk Stal of Sweden in 1992. Protracted discussions to buy Aristrain, a Spanish structural steel producer, came to nought while overtures to major steel makers elsewhere in Europe were rejected. British Steel therefore turned its attention to the USA but extended discussions with Bethlehem Steel about a joint venture to produce structural steels eventually collapsed in 1992 as the United Steelworkers Union rejected new working practices which British Steel was demanding. As Chairman Sir Robert Scholey put it: 'They [the USW] have got to understand that both us and Bethlehem are after world competitive costs. We are hopeful that we will get a sensible response from the USW – *then* we will unveil our plans' (*The Financial Times*, 2 July 1991). Such hopes, however, turned out to have been misplaced. As a result, British Steel's attempts to increase its penetration of non-UK markets via production abroad have – so far – amounted to very little. BSC's inability to internationalize its production activities more extensively contrasts with that of other UK private-sector steel makers. For example, in 1993 Caparo Industries embarked on a joint venture with the state government of Orissa, India, to establish an integrated plant with an annual capacity of 3 million tonnes. BSC's failure to achieve similar successes leaves it vulnerable to takeover because of its continuing heavy dependence on the fragile UK market. This was reinforced as BSC again slid into losses in 1992, reflecting the deepening depression in the UK economy and declining domestic demand for steel. Its exposed position is further emphasized by the fact that the price premium it currently enjoys in the UK market will almost certainly disappear as the UK becomes more integrated into European market structures in the 1990s.

Conclusion

Within the steel industry, there has historically been little internationalization of production. Companies have produced steel within countries for national markets, within the framework of national regulatory regimes. To some extent this pattern was altered within the European Coal and Steel Community from 1951 but, whilst regulation became to an increasing degree supranational, production remained organized on national bases with little crossnational collaboration. The one major attempt to forge a merger across international boundaries in the postwar period – between Hoesch and Hooghoven – ended in failure. In the 1980s, however, steel companies in Germany and Japan in particular increasingly and successfully sought to internationalize steel production, as a route to market penetration, via acquisitions, mergers and joint ventures whilst diversifying from steel into other manufacturing and service activities in search of profits.

Whilst it was a nationalized company, such options were denied to BSC. Internationalization was limited to raw material supplies and export markets. In order to compete with other steel producers, it could seek only to restructure production within the UK. Initially, it sought to do this by concentrating investment in its five major integrated complexes, seeking to achieve scale economies, enhance labour productivity and international competitiveness in this way. Once this strategy was overtaken by changes in international markets, it was left with no choice but to cut capacity and cut employment even more rapidly in an attempt to restore profitability. This was particularly so following the 1979 general election as the new Conservative government was intent on using the steel industry to demonstrate that trade union power and influence could be broken. Consequently, it tightened the financial constraints on BSC so that pressures to restructure *in situ* and introduce radically different terms and conditions of work and remuneration further intensified. By 1988, despite political constraints which prevented closure of any of its 'big five' complexes and the transfer of much of its more profitable special steels activities to the private sector via the Phoenix mergers, a combination of redefining working conditions and practices against a background of massive job loss within BSC, selective fixed capital investment and government write-off of accumulated debt made British Steel an eminently privatizable bulk-steel producer.

Once the political constraints of nationalization were removed, the newly privatized British Steel moved rapidly to close capacity and alter the geography of production within the UK and internationalize parts of its production. Diversification away from core steel activities was by now an increasingly unattractive strategic choice. By mid-1992 it had secured the total closure of Ravenscraig. Further closures, allied to heavy investment in its remaining UK complexes, will almost certainly follow in the 1990s. Its attempts to internationalize production via a mixture of acquisitions, mergers and joint ventures have been much more problematic, however. Internationalization has presented no easy 'spatial fix' for British Steel's problems. As a result, British Steel remains dangerously dependent on the fragile UK market. If it is to survive and prosper in the future, there is no doubt that British Steel must pursue its internationalization strategy with greater success than it has managed so far.

10

Conclusion

Jan-Evert Nilsson

The case studies show that the internationalization process can be understood as an interplay between four basic factors – corporate strategy, the corporations' internal assets, the competitive situation and the flow of opportunities with which the firm is confronted. The particular history and culture of the firm are extremely important. All firms are embedded initially in their home environment. The complex set of attributes of specific home environments plays an important part in influencing – though not determining – the behaviour of firms as they internationalize. A further critical variable is the role of the state. States invariably play an important regulatory role either individually of collectively (as in the case of the EU). Some states also intervene directly to support domestic firms. The importance of the different basic factors varies between firms and over time for a single firm. Sometimes the factors reinforce one another, while elsewhere they act as forces that counteract each other.

Arthur Andersen's (AA) internationalization seems almost to follow the textbook model of internationalization as a stepwise process governed by the firm's basic strategy (Chapter 5). AA's basic strategy was to follow their American clients when they internationalized their activities. Initially, international clients were offered services on the basis of transnational correspondent relationships. Such relationships were developed in countries representing important centres of client activity. This system offered only restricted opportunities for AA to control the services offered to its clients abroad. In the second phase of internationalization, AA started to develop local practices instead of correspondent relationships. Gradually the internationalization strategy became an integral part of a globalization strategy. The firm started to offer the same consultancy methods and products in all countries. During the last decade the speed of the internationalization process has accelerated as mergers and acquisitions have played an increasingly important part in the firm's internationalization strategy.

The importance of corporate strategy for the internationalization process is also very significant in the case of the formerly state-owned British Steel

Corporation (Chapter 9). As a nationalized industry there were strong political limits on its activities outside the UK. British Steel's production strategy was initially restricted to its UK base. Internationalization was restricted to export sales and to acquisitions of stockholders and distributors on important export markets. The privatization of British Steel in 1988 changed the situation. The corporate strategy was reformulated and internationalization was looked upon as a necessary condition for future success. So far its attempts to internationalize production via a mixture of acquisitions, mergers and joint ventures have been problematic.

In the British Steel case, the fact that it was a state-owned company constrained the firm's internationalization. The nature of its ownership – and the way in which the British govenrment prescribed its operations – was an important explanation for the lack of internationalization. However, the strategic situation for nationalized firms in other European countries was different. Thomson Consumer Electronics (TCE), which was nationalized in 1982, is an example of this (Chapter 6). In 1982 the corporation had just begun to internationalize. The French government sustained Thomson's investments in consumer electronics, and provided funds to help the company fight against the leading Japanese consumer electronics firms. State ownership made it possible for Thomson to become an important global contender by acquiring General Electrics' GE/RCA consumer electronics business. The acquisition doubled the size of TCE and the firm reached the second rank of world TV producers and the first rank of TV tube producers.

The French government also played a vital role in Alcatel's internationalization (Chapter 2). With the formation of Alcatel the company became the second-largest telecommunications equipment supplier in the world with a strong presence in a number of important European markets. The only viable strategy for the firm was to strengthen and expand its international position. The government backed Alcatel's strategy by allowing and supporting overseas acquisitions. Hence, the French government has supported internationalization in several industries, such support often being combined with French restrictions on foreign ownership of the leading French technology-based firms.

In these cases, therefore, the French and British governments exerted a strong influence on the firms' corporate strategy but in very different ways. However, the speed and pattern of the internationalization process was to a large degree shaped by the competitive situation and by the flow of strategic opportunities which presented themselves. For example, increasing price competition in the 1970s forced firms in consumer electronics to take advantage of scale economies, to increase manufacturing efficiency and relocate some manufacturing operations in low-wage countries in order to reduce costs. Thomson responded by relocating components and low-priced products manufacturing to east Asia. This process was deepened in the 1980s and 1990s.

The acquisitions made by the firms reflect such changes to a large degree. After the merger between CGE and Thomson's telecommunications activities,

Alcatel was number four globally in switching equipment sales. However, Alcatel was still a weak global contender, too dependent on the French market and reliant upon an outdated switch system. The acquisition of ITT's telecommunications group became the solution. Through the merger Alcatel got access to new markets and received a newly developed switch system – System 12. The acquisition was made possible because ITT was in economic difficulties involving the late delivery of the System 12 and increasing R & D costs. From ITT's perspective the sale of the telecommunications group turned a low-profit asset into much-needed cash. In this way circumstances created an opportunity for a merger.

In many cases the basic driving force behind internationalization is the competitive situation. It finds different expressions in different markets. In some industries internationalization is a reaction to the imperative of reducing manufacturing costs. The relocation of production units in the consumer electronics industry is an example of this. In other industries internationalization reflects firms' efforts to secure a foothold in foreign markets. Hence, much of Tootal's expansion of overseas production was geared to supplying regional markets (Chapter 7). SCA's (the Swedish pulp and paper producer) acquisition of corrugates board factories was an important step to secure the firm's position on different foreign markets (Chapter 8). The German machine producer Gildemeister AG is another example (Chapter 3). The firm established sales agents and production units in its most important market. In industries characterized by fast technological changes, this is an important driving force behind internationalization. In TCE a strategy of technological agreements was central to the internationalization process. A joint venture with the American RCA was created in order to get access to colour-tube technology. Some years later a licensing agreement and a joint venture with the Japanese company JVC was established in order to gain access to VLR technology.

Internal assets, such as financial resources and former experience of foreign activities, also influence the internationalization process. Access to financial assets makes it possible for a firm to make the best use of an acquisition opportunity. Unexpected events may create such opportunities. When SCA made a bid for the German forestry company Feldmühle, that opened a unique possibility for STORA to merge with Feldmühle. STORA's financial situation made it possible for the firm to make use of the opportunity.

The internationalization process of the two German machine-tool producers – Gildemeister and Maho – is the history of firms which late and slowly acquired international experiences. Pressures for internationalization were weak owing to the fact that their chosen strategies were based on local competence and owing to a large and important domestic market. For decades the firms exported without any particular foreign organization. Only when the competitive situation on the German market was changed did internationalization appear as an attractive alternative. Gildemeister started to establish a foreign distribution network in the 1970s. However, the firm remained for the most part an exporter to European countries and to the USSR. Maho started its investments in an international distribution network of its own ten years later. The objective was to strengthen the firm's position in Europe and to establish a foothold in the USA and southeast Asia. The early internationalization experiences of the two pharmaceuticals firms which came together in 1989 to form SmithKline Beecham were also very different from one another (Chapter 4). Embedded in different national contexts – the USA and the UK, respectively – it was ultimately a combination of the stringent regulatory pressures in the pharmaceuticals industry, the huge R & D costs involved in developing new drugs and the need to develop larger geographical markets which stimulated the merger.

It is not only that different driving forces are important in the internationalization process in different firms. The importance of different forces also varies over time in a single firm. Some of the cases illustrate this. The basic motive for internationalization in the Swedish forest industry in the 1960s was to expand the raw material base. Companies in regions with timber surpluses were acquired. In the 1970s a new motive became central. Now the primary objective of internationalization was to secure access to markets. The firms' interest moved from regions with timber surpluses to regions with a large demand for paper. The basic motive changed a third time in the second half of the 1980s when the imperative for the Swedish pulp and paper industry became one of preventing American competitors from acquiring European forest companies.

TCE shows a similar internationalization pattern. In the 1970s internationalization was an important element in the strategy to acquire technological know-how. Joint ventures with American and Japanese companies were established in order to access important technologies. In the 1980s the basic driving forces behind the internationalization were the desire to reach a sales volume required to obtain heavy R & D expenses and the realization of scale economies. Weak European competitors were targeted as acquisition candidates. At the same time, production was relocated to low-wage countries in east and southeast Asia.

The forces behind the pattern of internationalization change over time. Hence, internationalization should not be looked upon as one single process, but as a chain of separate but linked processes. The end of one chain represents the point of departure for the next. Internationalization can be described as a 'sedimentation process', where different phases are stratified upon each other. In each company internationalization becomes a process with many unique elements. To understand the internationalization process at the corporate level, the firm's specific history and changes in the competitive and regulatory environment must be understood. The importance of firm-specific factors contributes to unexpected outcomes of internationalization as the case studies in this book demonstrate. In their different ways they make the case for a more nuanced understanding of the internationalization process, one which is sensitive to the contingent and variable ways in which this process is manifest in different corporate settings.

References and bibliography

Abelshauser, W. (1983) *Wirtschaftsgeschichte der Bundesrepublik Deutschland, 1945–1980* (*Economic History of the Federal Republic of Germany, 1945 to 1980*), Suhrkamp, Frankfurt.

Alcatel (1987–92) *Annual Report*, Acatel NV, Amsterdam.

Amin, A., Charles, D.R. and Howells, J. (1992) Corporate restructuring and cohesion in the single market, *Regional Studies*, Vol. 26, pp. 319–32.

Arthur Andersen Worldwide Organization (1991) *Annual Report*, Arthur Andersen Worldwide Organization, Chigico, Ill.

Arthur Andersen Worldwide Organization (1992) *Annual Report*, Arthur Andersen Worldwide Organization, Chicago, Ill.

Babel, W. (1986) Mikroelektronik im Werkzeugmaschinenbau (Microelectronics in the machine tool sector), in G. Neipp and W. Pfeiffer (eds) *Strategien der industriellen Fertigungswirtschaft (Strategies of Industrial Production)*, Erich Schmidt, Berlin, pp. 59–70.

Babel, W. (1989) Mikroelektronik im Werkzeugmaschinenbau (Microelectronics in the machine tool sector), in Bundesverband der Deutschen Industrie (ed.) *Industrieforschung. Mikroelektronik-Anwendung (Research for Manufacturing: The Application of Microelectronics)*, BDI, Köln, pp. 59–71.

Baber, M. (1993) Active ingredient manufacture – time to reconsider? *Scrip Magazine*, Vol. 17, pp. 35–9.

Banyard, R. (1987) Profile of Tootal: international manufacturing and distribution, *Textile Outlook International*, Vol. 40, pp. 20–32.

Bartlett, C.A. and Ghoshal, S. (1989) *Managing Across Borders: The Transnational Solution*, Hutchinson, London.

Bertram, H. (1993) Werkzeugmaschinenbau in Deutschland und die globale Konkurrenz (The machine tool industry in Germany and global competition), *Geographische Rundschau*, Vol. 45, pp. 486–92.

Bertram, H. and Schamp, E.W. (1991) Flexible production and linkages in the German machine tool industry, in M. de Smidt and E. Wever (eds) *Complexes, Formations and Networks, Netherlands Geographical Studies* 132, Netherlands Geographical Studies, Utrecht, pp. 69–80.

Beynon, H., Hudson, R. and Sadler, D. (1991) *A Tale of Two Industries: The Contraction of Coal and Steel in the North East of England*, Open University Press, Milton Keynes.

Bloom, M. (1993) L'industrie européenne de l'électronique grand public, in S. Sachwald (ed.) *L'Europe et la globalisation, acquisitions et accords dans l'industrie*, IFRI, Paris, pp. 219–58.

Boddewynn, J.J. (1979) Foreign direct investment: magnitude and factors, *Journal of International Business Studies*, Vol. 10, pp. 21–7.

Boulding, P. (1988) Reindustrialisation strategies in steel closure areas in the UK, doctoral dissertation, University of Durham.

Boulding, P., Hudson, R. and Sadler, D. (1988) Consett and Corby: what kind of new era? *Public Administration Quarterly*, Vol. 12, pp. 235–55.

Briggs, P.S. (1990) *The SmithKline Beecham Merger*, PJB Publications, Richmond.

British Iron and Steel Federation (1966) *The Steel Industry: The Stage One Report of the Development Coordinating Committee*, BISF, London.

British Steel Corporation (1967–91) *Annual Reports and Accounts*, British Steel Corporation, London.

British Steel Corporation (1979) *Business Proposal*, British Steel Corporation, London.

British Steel Corporation (1980) *Corporate Plan*, British Steel Corporation, London.

British Steel Corporation (1988) *Prospectus: BSC plc Offer for Sale*, British Steel Corporation, London.

British Steel Corporation (1991) *Distribution*, British Steel Corporation, London.

Bryer, R.A., Brignell, T.J. and Maunders, R.A. (1982) *Accounting for British Steel*, Gower, Aldershot.

Buckley, P.J. (1988) Organisation forms and multinational companies, in S. Thompson and M. Wright (eds) *International Organisation, Efficiency and Profit*, Phillip Allan, Oxford, pp. 127–44.

Byrne, F. (1993) Pharmaceutical manufacturing – a competitive advantage? *Scrip Magazine*, Vol. 17, pp. 31–3.

BZQ (Barclays de Zoete Wedd Research) (1988) *Tootal*, BZW, London.

Carr, Kitcat and Aitken (1989) *The Textile Sector*, Carr, Kitcat and Aitken, London.

Carr, Kitcat and Aitken (1991) *The Textile Sector*, Carr, Kitcat and Aitken, London.

Cawson, A., Morgan, K., Webber, D., Holmes, P. and Stevens, A. (1990) *Hostile Brothers: Competition and Closure in the European Electronics Industry*, Clarendon Press, Oxford.

Charles, D.R. (1991) Procurement in European telecommunications, *Utilities Policy*, Vol. 1, pp. 134–43.

Charles, D.R., Monk, P. and Sciberras, E. (1989) *Technology and Competition in the International Telecommunications Industry*, Pinter Publishers, London.

Clairmonte, F.F. and Cavanagh, J.H. (1981) *The World in their Web*, Zed Press, London.

Cockerill, A. (1980) Steel and the state in Great Britain, *Annals of Public and Cooperative Economy*, Vol. 5, pp. 439–57.

Cockerill, A. and Silbertson, A. (1973) *The Steel Industry: International Comparisons of Industrial Structure and Performance*, Cambridge University Press, Cambridge.

Collins, T.M. and Doorley, T.L. (1992) *Les alliances stratégiques*, Interéditions, Paris.

Commission of the European Communities (1992) *The European Telecommunications Industry: The State of Play, Issues at Stake and Proposals for Action*, SEC (92) 1049, CEC, Brussels.

Contractor, F. and Lorange, P. (1987) *Co-operative Strategies in International Business*, Lexington Books, Lexington, Mass.

Crosland, A.R. (1956) *The Future of Socialism*, Jonathan Cape, London.

DAFSA (1986) *Thomson*, Collection des Analyses de Groupes, Paris.

Dawkins, W. and Wyles, J. (1990) Logical link-up of European giants, *The Financial Times*, 5 October.

Department of Economic Affairs (1965) *The National Plan*, Cmnd 2764, HMSO, London.

Department of Trade and Industry (1973) *British Steel Corporation: Ten Year Development Strategy*, Cmnd 5226, HMSO, London.

Department of Trade and Industry (1978) *British Steel Corporation: The Road to Viability*, Cmnd 5710, HMSO, London.

De Smidt, M. (1990) Philips: a global electronics firm restructures its home base, in M. de Smidt and E. Wever (eds) *The Corporate Firm in a Changing World Economy*, Routledge, London, pp. 55–76.

De Smidt, M., Helsloot, M., Komdeur, E. and van de Wiel, L. (1991) Corporate strategies and geographical redistribution of operations: the case of Akzo, mimeo, University of Utrecht.

De Smidt, M. and Meijerink, G. (1990) The internationalization of a Dutch corporation: the case of Akzo, *Tijdschrift voor Economische en Sociale Geografie*, Vol. lxxxi, pp. 225–32.

Dicken, P. (1992) *Global Shift: The Internationalization of Economic Activity* (2nd edn), Paul Chapman, London.

Dicken, P. and Thrift, N. (1992) The organization of production and the production of organization: why business enterprises matter in the study of geographical industrialization, *Transactions, Institute of British Geographers*, Vol. 17, pp. 279–91.

Dodsworth, T. (1987) The CGE-ITT deal: it looks like a turning point, *The Financial Times*, 7 January.

Dore, R. (1986) *Flexible Rigidities: Industrial Policy and Structural Adjustment in the Japanese Economy, 1970–1980*, Athlone Press, London.

Doz, Y.L. (1978) Managing manufacturing rationalization within multinational companies, *Columbia Journal of World Business*, Vol. 13, pp. 82–94.

DS (1991) *Svensk massa – och pappersindustri i förändring (The Swedish Pulp and Paper Industry in Transition)*, Ministry of Industry, Stockholm.

Dunning, J.H. (1977) Trade, location of economic activity and the MNE: a search for an eclectic approach, in B. Ohlin, P.O. Hesselborn and P.M. Wijkman (eds) *The International Allocation of Economic Activity*, Macmillan, London, pp. 395–431.

Dupuy, C., Milelli, C. and Savary, J. (1991) *Stratégies des multinationales*, La Documentation Française, Paris.

Elson, D. (1989) The cutting edge: multinationals in the EEC textiles and clothing industry, in D. Elson and R. Pearson (eds) *Women's Employment and Multinationals in Europe*, Macmillan, Basingstoke, pp. 80–110.

Elson, D. (1990) Marketing factors affecting the globalization of textiles, *Textiles Outlook International*, March, pp. 51–61.

Eurostaf (1991) *Thomson face aux défis de la décennie 1990*, Collection Analyses de Groupes, Paris.

Eurostaf-DAFSA (1988) *L'électronique grand public en Europe*, Collection Analyses de Secteurs, Paris.

Extel Financial (1991) *Weekly Financial News Summary*, United Newspapers Group, London.

Fevre, R. (1987) Subcontracting in steel, *Work, Employment and Society*, Vol. 1, pp. 509–27.

The Financial Times (1986) World telecommunications survey, 1 December, special supplement.

Fischer, M. (1993) Auf die Nerven (On the nerves), *Wirtschaftswoche*, Vol. 47, pp. 160–3.

Fleming, S. (1983) The long struggle to survive: Gildemeister, one of Europe's leading lathe manufacturers, thinks it has ground for optimism, *The Financial Times*, 13 April.

Forsgren, M. (1989) *Managing the Internationalisation Process: The Swedish case*, Routledge, London.

Forsgren, M. (1990) Managing the international multi-centre firm: case studies from Sweden, *European Management Journal*, Vol. 8, pp. 261–7.

Forsgren, M., Holm, U. and Johansson, J. (1991) Internationalisering av andra graden (Internationalization of the second degree), in R. Andersson, E. Ekstedt, R. Henning and A. Malmberg (eds) *Internationalisering, Företagen och det Lokala Samhället* (*Internationalization, the Company and the Local Community*), SNS Förlag, Stockholm, pp. 44–61.

Foss, N.J. (1993) Theories of the firm: contractual and competence perspectives, *Journal of Evolutionary Economics*, Vol. 3, pp. 127–44.

Fourier, J.M. (1978) Développement d'une entreprise à vocation internationale, *Revue humanisme et entreprise*, Vol. 8, pp. 10–22.

Fröbel, F., Heinrichs, J. and Kreye, O. (1980) *The New International Division of Labour*, Cambridge University Press, Cambridge.

Fuchs, M. and Schamp, E. (1990) Standard Elektrik Lorenz, introducing CAD into a telecommunications firm: its impact on labour, in M. de Smidt and E. Wever (eds) *The Corporate Firm in a Changing World Economy*, Routledge, London, pp. 77–99.

Gallouj, F. (1992) L'Innovation dans de conseil, doctoral dissertation, University of Lille I.

Garbe, C. (1992) Strategien zur Internationalisierung sind nun gefragt (Strategies for internationalization are now called for), *Handelsblatt*, 13 February.

Gårdlund, T. (1986) *MoDo 1940–1985*, MoDo Örnsköldsvik.

Garnett, N. (1986) Maho – how to profit from detail, *The Financial Times*, 21 November.

Gatt (1990) *International Trade, 1989–1990*, Gatt, Geneva.

Ghoshal, S. and Bartlett, C.A. (1990) The multinational corporation as an inter-organizational network, *Academy of Management Review*, Vol. 15, pp. 603–25.

Ghoshal, S. and Nohria, N. (1993) Horses for courses: organizational forms for multinational corporations, *Sloan Management Review*, Winter, pp. 23–35.

Gildemeister AG (1987–92) *Annual Reports*, Gildemeister AG, Bielefeld.

Gowdy J.M. (1992) Higher selection processes in evolutionary economic change, *Journal of Evolutionary Economics*, Vol. 2, pp. 1–16.

Grabher, G. (1994) *Lob der Verschwendung. Redundanz in der Regionalentwicklung: Ein Sozioökonomisches Plädoyer* (Praise of Wastefulness. Redundancy in regional development: a socio-economic plea) Sigma, Berlin.

Greiner, L.E. and Metzger, R.O. (1983) *Consulting to Management*, Prentice-Hall, Englewood Cliffs, NJ.

Hagedoorn, J. (1990) Partnering and reorganization of research and production, in J. Gidlund and G. Törnqvist (eds) *European Networks*, Centre for Regional Science, Umeå, pp. 73–94.

Hakanson, L. (1990) International decentralisation of R & D – the organisational challenges, in C.A. Bartlett, Y.L. Doz and G. Hedlund (eds) *Managing the Global Firm*, Routledge, London, pp. 256–78.

Håkansson, H. (1987) *Industrial Technological Development: A Network Approach*, Croom Helm, London.

Häusler, J. (1992) Adapting to an uncertain environment: R & D in the West German machinery industry, in H. Ernste and V. Meier (eds) *Regional Development and Contemporary Industrial Response: Extending Flexible Specialisation*, Belhaven, London, pp. 97–112.

Henry Cooke Lumsden (1991) *Textile Industry Bulletin*, Henry Cooke Lumsden, London.

Hills, J. (1986) *Deregulating telecoms: Competition and Control in the United States, Japan and Britain*, Pinter, London.

Hindle, T. (1990) Management consultancy: an American monopoly, *Eurobusiness*, October, pp. 30–3.

HMSO (1965) *The Future of the Steel Industry*, Cmnd 2641, HMSO, London.

House of Commons Industry and Trade Committee (1981) *The Effects of BSC's Corporate Plan, House of Commons Paper* 336, HMSO, London.

House of Commons Industry and Trade Committee (1983) *The British Steel Corporation's Prospects, House of Commons Paper* 212, HMSO, London.

House of Commons Select Committee on Nationalized Industries (1978) *Session 1977/8, The British Steel Corporation (Second Report), House of Commons Paper* 1271, HMSO, London.

Howells, J. (1990) The globalization of research and development: a new era of change? *Science and Public Policy*, Vol. 17, pp. 273–85.

Howells, J. (1992) Pharmaceuticals and Europe 1992: the dynamics of industrial change, *Environment and Planning A*, Vol. 24, pp. 33–48.

Howells, J. (1995) Going global: the use of ICT networks in research and development, *Research Policy*, Vol. 24, pp. 169–84.

Howells, J. and Wood, M. (1993) *The Globalisation of Production and Technology*, Belhaven, London.

Hudson, R. (1979) State policies and changing transport networks: the case of post-war Britain, in A.D. Burnett and P.J. Taylor (eds) *Political Studies from Spatial Perspectives*, Wiley, London, pp. 467–88.

Hudson, R. (1989). *Wrecking a Region: State Policies, Party Politics and Regional Change in North East England*, Pion, London.

Hudson, R. and Sadler, D. (1984) *British Steel Builds the New Teesside?* Cleveland County Council, Middlesbrough.

Hudson, R. and Sadler, D. (1986) *The Development of Middlesbrough's Iron and Steel Industry, Middlesbrough Locality Study Working Paper* 2, Department of Geography, University of Durham, Durham.

Hudson, R. and Sadler, D. (1987a) *The Uncertain Future of Special Steels*, Sheffield City Council, Sheffield.

Hudson, R. and Sadler, D. (1987b) Manufactured in the UK? Special steels, motor vehicles and the politics of industrial decline, *Capital and Class*, Vol. 32, pp. 55–82.

Hudson, R. and Sadler, D. (1989) *The International Steel Industry: Restructuring, State Policies and Localities*, Routledge, London.

Hudson, R. and Williams, A. (1986) *The United Kingdom*, Paul Chapman, London.

Idate (1991) Les 100 qui font les télécom, *Télécom magazine*, No. 10, November/December, pp. 36–74 (supplement in 01 Informatique No. 1187, 22 November).

Ietto-Gillies, G. (1992) *International Production: Trends, Theories, Effects*, Polity Press, Cambridge.

Input Corporation (1990) *Professional Services Challenges: Western Europe 1989–1994*, Input Corporation, London.

Iron and Steel Trades Confederation (1982) *Phoenix Two: The Threat to Engineering Steels*, ISTC, London.

Iwabuchi, A. (1992) *Andersen Consulting: The 21st Century Strategy of a Worldwide Organization*, Diamond Inc., Tokyo.

Johansson, B. and Westin, L. (1987) Technical change, location and trade, *Papers of the Regional Science Association*, Vol. 62, pp. 13–25.

Johansson, J. and Mattson, L.-G. (1988) Internationalization in industrial systems, in N. Hood and J.E. Vahlne (eds) *Strategies in Global Competition*, Croom Helm, New York, pp. 287–314.

Käckenhoff, U. (1978) Werkzeugmaschinen-Hersteller vor gravierenden Entscheidungen (Machine tool producer facing serious decisions), *Handelsblatt*, 19 December, p. 17.

Keil, J. (1972) Werkzeugmaschinenfabrik Gildemeister and Comp.Akt.Ges., in J. Keil *Die westdeutsche Wirtschaft und ihre führenden Männer, Land Nordrhein-Westfalen, Teil I (The West German Economy and its Leading Men, Northrhine-Westphalia, Part I)*, Julius Keil GmbH, Oberursel, pp. 436–41.

Kelf Cohen, R. (1969) *Twenty Years of Nationalisation*, Macmillan, London.

Kocka, J. (1975) *Unternehmer in der deutschen Industrialisierung (Entrepreneurs in German Industrialization)*, Vandenhoeck and Ruprecht, Göttingen.

Kubr, M. (1986) *Management Consulting: A Guide to the Profession* (2nd edn), International Labor Office, Geneva.

Lazell, H.G. (1975) *From Pills to Penicillin: The Beecham Story*, Heinemann, London.

Lera, E. (1987) The Spanish telecommunications sector in search of its future, *Telecommunications Policy*, Vol. 11, pp. 347–56.

Liebenau, J. (1984) Industrial R & D pharmaceutical firms in the early twentieth century, *Business History*, Vol. 26, pp. 329–46.

Lloyd, P. and Shutt, J. (1985) Recession and restructuring in the north west region, 1974–82: the implications of recent events, in D. Massey and R. Meegan (eds) *Politics and Method: Contrasting Studies in Industrial Geography*, Cambridge University Press, Cambridge, pp. 13–60.

Locksley, G. (1987) Ringing the changes: new structures of telecommunications manufacturing in Europe, paper presented to Communications Policy Research Conference, 6–8 July, Windsor Great Park, London.

Lönnstedt, L. and Randers, J. (eds) (1979) Wood resources dynamics in the Scandinavian forestry sector, *Studia Forestalia Suecica*, Vol. 152.

Maho (1970) *Fünfzig Jahre MAHO Werkzeugmaschinenbau Babel and Co. (Fifty Years of Maho Machine-Tool Production at Babel and Co.)*, MAHO, Pfronten.

Maho AG (1988–92) *Annual Reports*, Maho AG, Pfronten.

Maurice, M. and Sorge, A. (1990) *Industrielle Entwicklung und Innovationsfähigkeit der Werkzeugmaschinenhersteller in Frankreich und der Bundesrepublic Deutschland (Industrial Development and Innovation Capacity of Machine Tool Producers in France and the Federal Republic of Germany)*, WZB Discussion Papers FS I 90–11, WZB, Berlin.

McCormick, J. and Stone, N. (1990 From national champion to global competitor: an interview with Thomson's Alain Gomez, *Harvard Business Review*, May–June, pp. 127–35.

McEachern, D. (1980) *A Class Against Itself*, Cambridge University Press, Cambridge.

Mintzberg, H. (1988) The structuring of organizations, in T. Quinn, H. Mintzberg and R.M. James (eds) *The Strategy Process: Concepts, Contexts and Cases*, Prentice-Hall, Englewood Cliffs, NJ, pp. 277–304.

Mitter, S. (1985) Industrial restructuring and manufacturing homework: immigrant women in the UK clothing industry, *Capital and Class*, Vol. 27, pp. 37–80.

Monopolies and Mergers Commission (MMC) (1986) *The General Electric Company PLC and the Plessey Company PLC: A Report and the Proposed Merger*, Cmnd 9867, HMSO, London.

Moulaert, F. and Martinelli, F. (1992) Le conseil en informatique: conseils en systemes et systemes de conseil, in J. Gadrey, C. Gallouj, F. Gallouj, F. Martinelli, F. Moulaert and P. Tordoir (eds) *Manager le conseil*, Ediscience International, Paris, pp. 79–101.

Moulaert, F., Martinelli, F. and Djellal, F. (1990) *The Role of Information Technology Consultancy in the Transfer of Information Technology to Production and Service Organizations*, NOTA, The Hague.

Moulaert, F. and Tödtling, F. (eds) (1995) The geography of advanced producer services in Europe, *Progress in Planning*, forthcoming.

National Economic Development Office (1986) *Steel: The World Market and the UK Steel Industry*, NEDO, London.

Nilsson, J.E. (1986) *Norway's Industrial Future*, Royal Norwegian Council for Scientific and Industrial Research, Oslo.

North West Industry Research Unit (1984) *Greater Manchester County – Industrial Restructuring in Textiles and Clothing: The Impact of Recent Change*, NWIRU, University of Manchester.

OECD (1976) *Technical Co-operation Agreements between Firms: Some Initial Data and Analysis*, OECD, Paris.

OECD (1991) *Telecommunications Equipment: Changing Markets and Trade Structures*, ICCP Report 24, OECD, Paris.

OECD (1992) *Telecommunications Type Approval: Policies and Procedures for Market Access*, ICCP Report 27, OECD, Paris.

Ohmae, K. (1985) *Triad Power: The Coming Shape of Global Competition*, Free Press, New York.

Oman, C. (1989) *New Forms of Investment in Developing Country Industries: Mining, Petroleum, Automobiles, Textiles, Food*, OECD, Paris.

OSI (1988) *Cent acteurs dans la compétition mondiale*, Observatoire des Stratégies Industrielles, Economica, Paris.

OSI (1990) *Marché unique, marché multiple – stratégies européennes des acteurs industriels*, Observatoire des Stratégies Industrielles, Economica, Paris.

Payne, M. (1992) Profile of Coats Viyella plc, *Textile Outlook International*, Vol. 40, pp. 53–74.

Penrose, E.T. (1980) *The Theory of the Growth of the Firm* (2nd edn), Blackwell, Oxford.

Piore, M.J. and Sabel, C.F. (1984) *The Second Industrial Divide*, Basic Books, New York.

Polastro, E. and Mellor, N. (1992) Primary production – asset or liability? *Scrip Magazine*, Vol. 7, pp. 39–42.

Porter, M. (1990) *The Competitive Advantage of Nations*, Macmillan, London.

Pouillot, D. and Dartois, O. (1991) La globalisation dans les telecommunications (Dossier Prospectif No. 2, Globalisation de l'Economie et de la Technologie, Vol. 10) *FAST Occasional Publication* No. 282, CEC, Brussels.

Public Accounts Committee (1985) *Control of Monitoring of Investment by British Steel Corporation in Private Sector Companies – The Phoenix Operations, House of Commons Paper* 307, HMSO, London.

Quatrepoint, J.M. (1984) Un échec exemplaire: l'affaire Grundig, *Revue d'économie industrielle*, Vol. 27, pp. 31–41.

Randow, G.V. (1992) Maschinenguru mit Sinn für Geschichte (Machine guru with a sense of history), *Die Zeit*, Vol. 47, p. 46.

Rassam, C. and Oates, D. (1991) *Management Consultancy: The Inside Story*, Mercury, London.

Rehn, M. (1992) Transnationella skogsföretag (Multinational forestry companies), *Institutionen för skogsekonomi Rapport* 99, Swedish University of Agricultural Science, Umeå.

Reis Arndt, E. (1987) A quarter of a century of pharmaceutical research: new drug entities, 1961–1985, *Drugs Made in Germany*, Vol. 30, pp. 105–12.

Rippetau, J. (1986) The ITT-CGE deal: a hole in the system's heart, *The Financial Times*, 28 July.

Roses (1990) *L'industrie de la Pologne*, Etude pour le Ministère de l'Industrie, Paris.

Rydberg, S. (1990) *Papper i perspektiv. Svensk skogindustri under 100 år (Paper in Perspective: The Swedish Forestry Industry during the Past 100 Years)*, Gidlunds, Stockholm.

Sadler, D. (1985) Region, class and the restructuring of the EEC steel industry during the recession, doctoral dissertation, University of Durham.

Sadler, D. (1990) Privatizing British Steel: the politics of production and place, *Area*, Vol. 22, pp. 47–55.

Sadler, D. (1992) *Strategic Change in the West European Automotive Components Industry, Discussion Paper 8, Change in the Automobile Industry: An International Comparison*, Department of Geography, University of Durham, Durham.

Sally, R. (1993) Alcatel's relations with the French state: the political economy of a multinational enterprise, *Communications and Strategies*, Vol. 9, pp. 67–95.

Sauviat, C. (1991) Les mutations du marché de l'expertise et du conseil, *Problemes économiques*, Vol. 2238, pp. 4–14.

Sauviat, C. (1992) *Le conseil: un marché reseau*, IRES, Paris.

Savary, J. (1984) *French Multinationals*, Frances Pinter, London.

Savary, J. (1991) Des stratégies multinationales aux stratégies globales, in J.P. Gilly (ed.) *L'Europe industrielle: horizon 93, 1 – Les groupes et l'intégration européenne*, La Documentation Française, Paris, pp. 79–108.

Savary, J. (1992a) Cross investments between France and Italy and the new European strategies of industrial groups, in J. Cantwell (ed.) *Multinational Investment in Modern Europe: Strategic Interaction in the Integrated Community*, Edward Elgar, Cheltenham, pp. 150–91.

Savary, J. (1992b) The international strategies of the French firms and eastern Europe: the case of Poland, *MOCT-MOST Economic Journal on Eastern Europe and the Soviet Union*, Vol. 3, pp. 69–99.

SCA (1979) *SCA 50 år: studier kring ett storföretag och dess föregångare (SCA 50 Years: Studies of a Large Company and its Predecessors)*, SCA, Sundsvall.

SCA (1992) *SCA Årsredovisning (SCA Annual Report)*, SCA, Sundsvall.

Schonberger, R.J. (1982) *Japanese Manufacturing Techniques*, Free Press, New York.

Scrip (1990) SmithKline Beecham's 'rationalized' R & D portfolio, *Scrip*, Vol. 1505, pp. 8–10.

Scrip (1993) Output of NCEs constant over 20 years, *Scrip*, Vol. 1792, p. 22.

Sölvell, Ö., Zander, I. and Porter, M. (1991) *Advantage Sweden*, Norstedts, Stockholm.

Soulage, B. (1981) Stratégies industrielles et sociales des groupes français, doctoral dissertation, University of Grenoble.

Soulal, M.J. (1977) Research and development in Beecham Pharmaceuticals, in Engineering, Technology and Society *Proceedings of Section X of the British Association for the Advancement of Sciences, Lancaster 1976*, University of Aston, Birmingham, pp. 50–4.

Spur, G. (1991) *Vom Wandel der industriellen Welt durch Werkzeugmaschinen: eine kulturgeschichtliche Betrachtung der Fertigungstechnik (Changes in the Industrial World by Machine Tools: A Cultural Historic Examination of Production Techniques)*, Hanser, München.

Steedman, H. and Wagner, K. (1989) Productivity, machinery and skills: clothing manufacture in Britain and Germany, *National Institute Economic Review*, Vol. 128, pp. 40–57.

Storper, M. and Walker, R. (1989) *The Capitalist Imperative: Territory, Technology and Industrial Growth*, Blackwell, Oxford.

Swann, J.P. (1988) *Academic Scientists and the Pharmaceutical Industry*, Johns Hopkins University Press, Baltimore, Md.

Syedian, H. (1989) SmithKline Beecham's early trials, *Management Today*, November, pp. 99–104.

Taylor, M. and Thrift, N. (eds) (1982) *The Geography of Multinationals: Studies in the Spatial Development and Economic Consequences of Multinational Corporations*, Croom Helm, London.

Thomas, L.G. (1988) Multifirm strategies in the US pharmaceutical industry, in D.C. Mowery (ed.) *International Collaborative Ventures in US Manufacturing*, Ballinger, Cambridge, Mass., pp. 147–81.

Tootal (1976–91) *Annual Reports*, Tootal, Manchester.

Tootal Group (1988) *Tootal Group: Winning Leadership in World Markets*, Tootal, Manchester.

Tootal Group (1991a) *Protect Your Investment . . . Keep Tootal Independent*, Tootal, Manchester.

Tootal Group (1991b) *The Declining Value of Coats . . . Reject Coats' Final Offer*, Tootal, Manchester.

Tordoir, P. (1992) Le conseil en management: structure de secteur, concurrence et strategies, in J. Gadrey, C. Gallouj, F. Gallouj, F. Martinelli, F. Moulaert and P. Tordoir (eds) *Manager le conseil*, Ediscience International, Paris, pp. 29–43.

Townsend, A. (1983) *The Impact of Recession on Industry Employment and the Regions*, Croom Helm, London.

VDMA (Verein Deutscher Maschinen-und Anlagbau) *Statistisches Handbuch für den Maschinenbau* (Statistical Handbook for Mechanical Engineering) VDMA, Frankfurt, different volumes.

Vernon, R. (1966) International investment and international trade in the product cycle, *Quarterly Journal of Economics*, Vol. 80, pp. 190–207.

Walker, R. (1989) A requiem for corporate geography: new directions in industrial organization, the production of place and uneven development *Geografiska Annaler*, Vol. 71B, pp. 43–57.

Welch, L.S. and Luostarinen, R. (1988) Internationalization: evolution of a concept, *Journal of General Management*, Vol. 14, pp. 34–55.

Wilkes, D. (1992) Capitalizing on R & D, *Scrip Magazine*, Vol. 2, pp. 28–31.

Wilson, H. (1974) *The Labour Government, 1964–70*, Penguin Books, Harmondsworth.

Index

AA *see* Arthur Anderson
AC (Anderson Consulting) *see* Arthur
  Anderson
acquisitions 25–7, 32, 161, 162
  see also Thomson Consumer
    Electronics, acquisitions
Akso 7
Alcatel 12, 14, 18, 87, 162, 163
  acquisitions 25–7, 32
    cables 25–6; satellites 26–7;
    subscriber equipment
    distribution 27
  divestment 28–9
  history of 20–5
  merger with ITT 22–3
  R & D 33–4
    expenditure 35
  structure:
    organizational 29–31; sales 32;
    spatial 31–4
Arthur Anderson 12, 161
  activities 75–6
  globalization strategy 82–7
    flexibility 85–7; human resources
    policy 83–4; 'one-firm
    concept' 82–3; service
    provision 84–5
  history of 74–5
  market change 87–8
  overseas regional organization
    81–2
    Asia-Pacific 81–2; Europe/middle
    east/Africa/India 81
Asea 9
AT&T 18, 21, 22, 24, 36, 87

Beecham 63–4
BSC *see* British Steel Corporation
British Steel Corporation 12, 161–2
  distribution and sales 157
  future strategy 159–60
  planning 148–53
    cut-backs and closures 149–51;
    modernization and growth 148–9;
    privatization 151–3
  private sector policies 153–4
  raw materials 156
business services *see* Arthur Anderson

Cap Gemini Sogeti 87, 88
CGE 20, 21, 25, 90
chemicals companies 7
  see also SmithKline Beecham
Coats Viyella 109, 111, 114, 116,
  125–8
competition:
  global 99
  international 9, 17
  partnerships with the 10
competitive:
  advantage 8
  situation 161
corporate strategy 128–9, 161
Courtaulds 110, 111
custom-based companies:
  internationalization 8–10
  production 3, 4–5, 11

Decker AG 40, 47–8, 51, 56, 58, 60
distribution 27, 50–2, 60
  and sales 157

economies:
  influences on transnational
    companies vi
  of scale 131
electronics industry 13
  global competition 99
  see also Thomson Consumer
    Electronics
Ericsson 20, 21, 33

Feldmühle 138, 139, 163
forestry companies (Swedish) 132, 164
  future division of labour 145
  geography of 140–5
  market position 138
  markets abroad 134–40
  R & D 142–5
  raw materials 132–4
  see also MoDo; SCA; STORA
Fujitsu 19, 35

GEC 18, 90, 101, 103
Gildemeister AG 12, 40, 163
  domestic sales and production
    networks 55
  expansion into eastern Europe 56
  growth of 41–4
    capital and finance 49–50;
      distribution 50–1, 52; labour
      52–4; technological
      trajectories 45–6;
      47–8
  history of 39, 40, 41
  sector collapse 56–9
  spatial pattern of plants 42, 53
global brands 8
global integration 121–4
global refocusing 71
global shifts 111–12

Hahn & Kolb 44, 47
'hollowing out' 119–21
home-base protection 38–9, 59–60, 144
  domestic large-scale enterprise 41–7
  internationalization in Europe 47–56
  growth:
    global euphoria and crash 56–9
    slow phase 39–41

IBM 87, 88
internai assets 161
internationalization:
  conceptual framework for analysis
    2–6

limits 155–8
process 6–11, 162
  custom based 8–10
  labour intensive 7–8
  R & D based 10–11
  resource intensive 6–7
theories of 1–2
ITT 18, 20, 22–3, 28–9

JVC 96, 107, 163

labour:
  spatial division of 2
  see also Gildemeister AG; Maho AG
labour-intensive companies:
  internationalization process 7–8
  production 3, 4, 11
low-cost countries 7–8, 105
low-cost production 101–2

machine-tool companies 38–9; *see also*
  Gildemeister AG; Maho growth 39–41
    of German production and
      exports 44–5
  Europe:
    expansion into eastern 56
    market collapse 56–7
  restructuring 60
Maho AG 12, 40, 163–4
  growth of 41, 44
    capital and finance 49–50;
      distribution 50, 51–2, 52;
      labour 52–3, 54–6;
      technological trajectories 45, 47,
      48–9
  history of 39–41
  sector collapse 56–8
  spatial pattern of plants 42
mass production 3
mergers 61–8, 116–17, 124–8, 151–3,
  161
models of growth 47
MoDo 12
  geographical distribution 141
  market position 139–40
  markets abroad 137
  R & D 143
  raw materials 133–4
  structural change 130–2
  see also forestry companies

nationalization 21, 91–2
  of British steel companies 148–53, 162
NEC 19, 35

Northern Telecom 22, 26, 33, 35

'one firm concept' 82–7
opportunities flow 161, 162
out-sourcing 2, 60

Philips 19, 100, 107
production:
  colour television 95
  custom based 3, 4–5
  integration 110
  labour intensive 3, 4
  R & D based 3, 6–7
  resource intensive 3–4
  see also British Steel Corporation;
    low-cost production; pulp and paper
    industry
pulp and paper industry 6, 130
  integration economies 134
  production 140
  raw materials 132–4, 142
  restructuring 142
  Swedish firms 130–2, 164
  see also MoDo; SCA; STORA

RCA 90, 93, 96, 101, 103, 107, 163
R & D:
  in Alcatel 33–4, 35
  flexible organization 86–7
  investment in 3
  in SmithKline Beecham 64–8
  see also forestry companies;
    production
R & D-based companies:
  internationalization 10–11
  production 3, 6–7, 11
repositioning:
  Smith-Kline Beecham 67, 68, 70
resource-intensive companies:
  internationalization process 6–7
  pharmaceuticals 64–5
  production 64–5
restructuring 130–2
  corporate:
    Courtaulds 110; SmithKline
      Beecham 67–8; Tootal 129
  of pulp and paper production 142
Rockwell 26, 32, 35

SCA (Svenska Cellulosa
  Aktiebolaget) 12, 163
  market position 138–9, 140
  markets abroad 135–6
  R & D 144

raw materials 132–4
structural change 130–2
see also forestry companies
SEL 22, 25, 31
SGS 92, 100
Siemens 19, 21, 22, 32
SmithKline and French 61–3
SmithKline Beckman 61–3
SmithKline Beecham 11–12, 164
  future development 71–2
  global expansion 68–70
  history:
    merger 64–8; premerger 61–4
state involvement:
  in steel industry 146–7
  in Thomson Consumer
    Electronics 98–9
state-regulated service sector:
  liberalization process 16–17
    effects of 17–18
STC 19, 23, 26, 32, 33
steel industry 6
  BISF review 147–8
  historical development 146
  see also British Steel Corporation
STORA 12, 163
  market position 138–40
  markets abroad 135–6
  R & D 143, 144
  raw materials 132–4
  spatial distribution 140–5
  structural change 130–2
  see also forestry companies
strategic alliances 1
strategic reorganization 115–16
structure:
  global 123
  organizational 29–31

TCE *see* Thomson Consumer Electronics
telecommunications industry
  economies of scale 17–18
  globalization trends 14–20
  largest suppliers of equipment 17–18
  spatial restructuring 36
  see also Alcatel
textile industry
  global shifts and restructuring 111–12
  internationalization in 109–10
  in Japan 112
  see also Tootal
Thomson Consumer Electronics 12,
  20–1, 162, 164
  acquisitions 93, 96–7, 101

CGE and 21
future expansion 105–7
'growth eras':
  domestic leader 92–4; European
    expansion 94–9;
    globalization 99, 104, 105–7
history of 90–2
nationalization of 21, 91–2
present position 104–5
transnational companies:
  categories of 2
  economic influence on vi
  organization change 11
  significance of 1

Traub AG 40, 58
Tootal 12, 163
  company development 114–16
  corporate strategy 128–9
  global structure 123
  history of 109–10, 112–14
  internationalization 116
    corporate exposure 124–8;
      corporate consolidation 116–17;
      global expansion 117–19; global
      integration 121–4; 'hollowing
      out' 119–21

unique products 3